Eric Eve is Fellow and Tutor in Theolᵒ
He has published a number of articles and other short pieces on various aspects of the Gospels and Jesus (usually related either to miracles or to the Synoptic Problem) and is also the author of *The Jewish Context of Jesus' Miracles* (2002), *The Healer from Nazareth* (2009) and *Behind the Gospels* (2013).

WRITING THE GOSPELS

Composition and memory

ERIC EVE

First published in Great Britain in 2016

Society for Promoting Christian Knowledge
36 Causton Street
London SW1P 4ST
www.spck.org.uk

British Library Cataloguing-in-Publication Data
A catalogue record for this book is available from the British Library

ISBN 978–0–281–07340–5
eBook ISBN 978–0–281–07341–2

Typeset by Graphicraft Limited, Hong Kong
First printed in Great Britain by Ashford Colour Press
Subsequently digitally printed in Great Britain

eBook by Graphicraft Limited, Hong Kong

For the Principal and Fellows of
Harris Manchester College, Oxford

Contents

Contents

Acknowledgements

The writing of this book has been greatly helped by the congenial atmosphere for research and writing provided by Harris Manchester College, and in particular the generosity of its President, Robert Conway, in donating to a book fund for its Fellows. I should also like to thank Philip Law, who commissioned this book for SPCK, Mollie Barker, my conscientious copy-editor, and Rima Devereaux, who saw the book through to production.

Abbreviations

‖	Synoptic or other parallel text
?‖	Questionably parallel text
1 Apol.	Justin Martyr, *First Apology*
2DH	Two Document Hypothesis
2GH	Two Gospel Hypothesis
Ag. Ap.	Josephus, *Against Apion*
AJP	*American Journal of Philology*
AJS	*American Journal of Sociology*
Ant.	Josephus, *Jewish Antiquities*
ASR	*American Sociological Review*
BETL	Bibliotheca ephemeridum theologicarum lovaniensium
BPC	Biblical Performance Criticism
BTB	*Biblical Theology Bulletin*
CQ	*Classical Quarterly*
CSEL	Corpus scriptorum ecclesiasticorum latinorum
EC	*Early Christianity*
ETL	*Ephemerides theologicae lovanienses*
FH	Farrer Hypothesis
Hist. eccl.	Eusebius, *Ecclesiastical History*
HTS	*Hervormde Teologiese Studies*
Inst.	Quintilian, *Institutio oratoria* (The Orator's Education)
JBL	*Journal of Biblical Literature*
JHS	*Journal of Hellenic Studies*
JSHJ	*Journal for the Study of the Historical Jesus*
JSNT	*Journal for the Study of the New Testament*
JSNTSup	Journal for the Study of the New Testament: Supplement Series
JSOTSup	Journal for the Study of the Old Testament: Supplement Series
J.W.	Josephus, *Jewish War*
LNTS	Library of New Testament Studies
LXX	Septuagint
NIGTC	New International Greek Testament Commentary
NovT	*Novum Testamentum*
n.s.	New series
NTS	*New Testament Studies*
quom. hist.	Lucian, *quomodo historia conscribenda sit* (How to Write History)
SBL	Society of Biblical Literature
SF	*Social Forces*
SNTSMS	Society for New Testament Studies Monograph Series

Introduction

We do not really know who wrote the four Gospels contained in the New Testament; traditionally they are attributed to the four Evangelists Matthew, Mark, Luke and John. The content of the Gospels suggests that the Evangelists were Christians writing primarily for other Christians, while both the content and the style suggest that they did not enjoy elite status, although they must have had some education. It seems likely that the Gospels were written in the latter part of the first century, or (in the case of Luke and John) perhaps very early in the second. Beyond that we have little more to go on than ancient tradition (which may not always be entirely reliable) and the informed guesswork of modern scholars.

We also know rather less than we might like about *how* the Gospels were written. A naive view may picture Matthew or Luke sitting at his desk in the privacy of his study, pen in hand, with copies of Mark and other sources lying open in front of him, vying for space on a desktop cluttered with notes transcribed from oral tradition. But such a view is a projection of modern authorial methods back into the very different conditions of antiquity. So far as we know, first-century writers did not use desks; they relied on memory of sources far more than a modern author would; and they often preferred to dictate to a scribe rather than wield a pen for themselves. Most of the assumptions we take for granted about how authors work are based on the way texts are produced and employed in a print culture.[1] This is hardly news to specialists working in the field. It was recognized at least a century ago and has been addressed in an ever-growing number of more recent publications.[2] But the implications have yet to be fully felt in the study of the Gospels. For example, most nineteenth- and twentieth-century scholarship on the Synoptic Problem (the issue of the literary relationship between the three Synoptic Gospels, Matthew, Mark and Luke) proceeded almost entirely as if the Evangelists had been working with

---

[1] For a detailed discussion of the profound changes the advent of the printing press enabled, see Elizabeth Eisenstein, *The Printing Press as an Agent of Change: Communications and Cultural Transformations in Early-Modern Europe* (Cambridge: Cambridge University Press, 1980).

[2] See William Sanday, 'The Conditions under Which the Gospels Were Written, in Their Bearing upon Some Difficulties of the Synoptic Problem' in William Sanday (ed.), *Oxford Studies in the Synoptic Problem* (Oxford: Clarendon Press, 1911), 3–26; more recent examples include F. Gerald Downing, *Doing Things with Words in the First Christian Century* (JSNTSup, 200; Sheffield: Sheffield Academic Press, 2000); R. A. Derrenbacker, *Ancient Compositional Practices and the Synoptic Problem* (BETL, 186; Leuven: Peeters-Leuven, 2005); Werner H. Kelber, *Imprints, Voiceprints and Footprints of Memory: Collected Essays of Werner Kelber* (Resources for Biblical Study, 74; Atlanta: SBL, 2013); and many others that will be cited in the course of this book.

printed texts (an unconscious assumption that the use of printed synopses will have done little to discourage).

While there is increasing recognition that something needs to change, it is harder to agree on what model of composition should replace our print-centric one. Our appreciation of the way texts work has been thoroughly conditioned by our total immersion in a print culture from the time we first learned to read and write, throughout our formal education and, for those of us who work with texts for a living, throughout our professional lives. Our notions about the way texts work have become as natural and transparent to us as our native language. Merely knowing that written texts in a manuscript culture functioned differently from the way in which printed or electronic texts function today neither removes the distorting spectacles of our ingrained modern assumptions nor tells us precisely what to put in their place. As Werner Kelber has pointed out, it is actually easier for modern people to understand a purely oral culture, in which writing plays no part at all, than to comprehend the oral–scribal culture of the first century.[3] Our common-sense notions of contemporary speech and writing keep getting in the way, while trying to compensate for them can result in over-correction, leading to an exaggerated caricature of first-century media culture.

A central difficulty is arriving at a satisfactory account of how speech and writing both interacted with and differed from each other in antiquity. That speech and writing are fundamentally different modes of communication has been both maintained and disputed.[4] This has led to quite different views on whether taking written form is fundamental or merely incidental to the composition of texts such as the Gospels.[5] Related to this is whether the Gospels should be seen as literary compositions or as oral-traditional texts, and so whether to model their genesis on the basis of the working methods of elite Graeco-Roman authors or those of oral storytellers.[6] It may be that neither model is fully appropriate, and that different models should be applied to different Gospels. Luke, for example, looks more consciously literary than Mark.

The first step is to recognize that there is a problem. Once we start trying to rid ourselves of anachronistic assumptions that are likely to (but may not necessarily

---

[3] Kelber, *Imprints*, 50–1, citing Eisenstein, *Printing Press*, 9.

[4] Compare, for example, Walter J. Ong, *Orality and Literacy: The Technologizing of the Word* (New Accents; London and New York: Routledge, 2002) and Ruth Finnegan, *Literacy and Orality* (Oxford: Basil Blackwell, 1988).

[5] Compare, for example, Werner H. Kelber, *The Oral and the Written Gospel: The Hermeneutics of Speaking and Writing in the Synoptic Tradition, Mark, Paul and Q* (Voices in Performance and Text; Bloomington and Indianapolis: Indiana University Press, 1997); Richard A. Horsley and Jonathan A. Draper, *Whoever Hears You Hears Me: Prophets, Performance and Tradition in Q* (Harrisburg, PA: Trinity Press International, 1999); Richard A. Horsley, *Text and Tradition in Performance and Writing* (BPC, 9; ed. D. Rhoads; Eugene, OR: Cascade, 2013).

[6] For the Gospels as oral-traditional literature see the discussion of the Oral Composition Hypothesis in Chapter 4.

in every case) lead us astray, it is far from obvious what to put in their place. The Evangelists tell us nothing about how they went about their task, and few ancient sources have very much to say about the working methods of authors and scribes, and about the composition of texts, since these were things that would largely have been taken for granted by those involved. We can discern something about the working methods of a few elite authors from the occasional remarks they make and by making deductions from the texts they produced. We know something about oral storytelling and oral poetry as it can be observed in various societies today, enough to know that 'oral composition' is far from being a uniform phenomenon to which one model can be applied in all times and in all places. We know little about the education and working methods of the non-elite persons who composed the Gospels, just as we are ignorant of their precise social and geographical locations.

This does not, however, make it a hopeless task to enquire how the Gospels were written. Provided we proceed with due caution, we can extrapolate from what little we do know. The Gospels do provide a few clues, or at least checks on our speculation. There are several fields of knowledge on which we can draw in trying to narrow down the possibilities. And if certainty is unattainable, nevertheless some models of the Evangelists' working models should emerge as more plausible than others, so that we can arrive at a general understanding of how they are likely to have worked even if the details are inevitably left fuzzy.

In an earlier book I concluded that memory may be a more helpful category than oral tradition in discussing how material about Jesus was transmitted.[7] The present book will argue that memory also played a major role in the composition of the Gospels. Much of this book will be taken up with establishing that claim and exploring its implications. It will be argued that our working default assumption should be that the Evangelists relied primarily on their memories of their material. That is not to deny that the Evangelists consulted written sources, but rather to assert that, at least in the act of composition, their primary use of sources (written or oral) would often have been via memory rather than eye contact or ear contact, or at least that we should assume this to be the case in the absence of clear evidence to the contrary.

Chapter 1 will set the scene with a general discussion of reading and writing in the first century. Chapter 2 will ask *why* the Gospels were written, a question to which the answer may not be immediately obvious given that copies of the Gospels could hardly be disseminated by print and relatively few people would have been able to read them. Chapter 3 will look at the various kinds of raw material (or 'sources') that may have been available to the Evangelists, and will argue that the use of them in composition will frequently have involved memory in one way or

---

[7] Eric Eve, *Behind the Gospels: Understanding the Oral Tradition* (London: SPCK, 2013), 185.

another. Chapter 4 will then explore various models of composition, that is, the ways in which the Evangelists may have gone about writing their works. Chapter 5 will examine the role of memory in composition, first of all arguing that most pre-print authors relied heavily on their memories (and were well trained to do so) and then exploring the implications of that from the point of view of individual psychology. Chapter 6 will go on to discuss how collective memory might bear on the composition of the Gospels. Chapter 7 will explore the implications of the use of memory for the Synoptic Problem (although not with the intention of trying to arrive at any particular solution, since this can hardly be achieved in the course of a single chapter). The final chapter will then draw together the threads of the previous seven and spell out some of the implications, not least of trying to locate the Gospel writers as neither elite authors nor oral-traditional storytellers.

1

Reading and writing in
New Testament times

It is not easy for us to form an adequate picture of the media realities of the first-century Mediterranean world. The obvious danger is that we naively view matters through our own cultural assumptions, and so unconsciously suppose that ancient manuscripts were employed in much the same way as modern printed texts. The opposite danger is that we over-correct for this, either 'exoticizing' ancient reading and writing practices or exaggerating the role of oral communication to the point where writing is left with scarcely any practical function at all.[1] While exaggerations may have some value as correctives to our usual habits of thought, the danger is that they simply mislead us into a different set of oversimplifications. Graeco-Roman antiquity was certainly not modern print culture, but neither was it a purely oral one. Reading, writing, speech and memory interacted in a number of complex ways which could vary from place to place and from one social situation to another. The uses of literacy among the Roman elite cannot simply be assumed to be identical with those among Judaean scribes, let alone with that of the kinds of people who made up the primitive Church and worked with its texts, although it is the literary practices of the (political and intellectual) elites that are best known to us.

As a first step it will be helpful to sketch what is known about reading and writing in antiquity in general. The picture that emerges will be far from complete, and far from neat and simple. It may seem at times as if confident generalizations are being made only to be undermined by conflicting points of view. The aim is to provide a reasonably nuanced overview of reading and writing in antiquity to frame the discussion that follows.

Orality and literacy

The first seeming paradox is that the first-century Roman Empire was a society which made considerable use of writing, but in which oral communication

---

[1] On the dangers of over-correction, see Larry W. Hurtado, 'Oral Fixation and New Testament Studies? "Orality", "Performance" and Reading Texts in Early Christianity', *NTS* 60 (2014), 321–40; and Holt N. Parker, 'Books and Reading Latin Poetry' in W. A. Johnson and H. N. Parker (eds), *Ancient Literacies: The Culture of Reading in Greece and Rome* (New York: Oxford University Press, 2009), 186–229 (191).

remained hugely important.[2] Of course when stated at that level of abstraction, it is far from obvious how that differs so very much from today, since a great deal of our everyday communication is oral, whether in conversation with family, friends or colleagues, or at formal meetings, or conducting our routine affairs with shops, banks and other institutions where, although transactions may necessitate some exchange of paper or digital data, our wishes are often conveyed by word of mouth. Even if we exclude the use of electronically mediated orality (or what Walter Ong calls 'secondary orality') such as speaking to people on the telephone or listening to the news on the radio, most of us conduct a substantial proportion of our everyday lives by face-to-face word of mouth without committing anything to writing or consulting any texts. The difference between antiquity and the present, therefore, is one of degree rather than one of polar opposition, but it hardly gets to the root of the issue simply to say that ancient people spoke more and read less than we do and leave it at that.

It is generally recognized that far fewer people could read and write back then. To be sure, there is no fully reliable method of arriving at ancient literacy rates, since no one collected statistics on literacy at the time. The very notion of literacy is in any case problematic, since it is not a case of people being either literate or illiterate. There are (and were) degrees of literacy. The ability to read did not necessarily imply the ability to write, and the ability to read or write a simple document such as a short personal letter or contract did not necessarily imply the ability to read or write a sophisticated piece of literature.[3] To be counted as fully literate in Graeco-Roman society was not merely to possess the ability to recognize (and perhaps inscribe) the letters of the Greek or Roman alphabet, but to possess a thorough knowledge of one's literary tradition.

Thus, in discussing ancient literacy, we are inevitably discussing a somewhat fuzzy notion. The number of people who possessed the basic scribal skills needed to conduct their routine business affairs, scribble a graffito or sign their name on a document was probably far in excess of those capable of producing the great literary works of antiquity. While only a minority of people in the first-century Roman Empire were literate, some ability to read and write extended well beyond the elites, and writing penetrated well down the social spectrum (although the

---

[2] Pieter J. J. Botha, *Orality and Literacy in Early Christianity* (BPC, 5; ed. H. E. Hearon and P. Ruge-Jones; Eugene, OR: Cascade, 2012), 21–6; William V. Harris, *Ancient Literacy* (Cambridge, MA and London: Harvard University Press, 1989), 29–36, 326–7.

[3] Rosalind Thomas, *Literacy and Orality in Ancient Greece* (Key Themes in Ancient History; ed. P. A. Cartledge and P. D. A. Garnsey; Cambridge: Cambridge University Press, 1992), 8–12; Harry Y. Gamble, *Books and Readers in the Early Church: A History of Early Christian Texts* (New Haven and London: Yale University Press, 1995), 3–4.

evidence for this penetration seems to be more plentiful in Roman than in Palestinian circles).[4]

That said, recent estimates of ancient literacy rates tend to vary between about 3 and 10 per cent, the former figure having been suggested for Palestine and the latter for the empire as a whole, perhaps rising to as much as 15 or even 30 per cent among urban males. Estimates are based on factors such as the lack of any large-scale provision of the primary education needed to support mass literacy and the absence of any mass-produced texts (i.e. printing), without which mass literacy would have little point since relatively few people would be able to gain direct access to reading materials.[5]

An additional point is that even those who could read and write generally preferred to conduct much of the everyday business of their lives by word of mouth. There could be a number of reasons for this, some technological, some more sociological. Among the technological reasons would be that ancient manuscripts were not particularly well suited for ready reference (a point to which we shall return below). There would thus be less point in committing material to writing if it was felt to be easier to rely on one's memory (as people in antiquity did to a far greater extent than we do today) than to hunt down a written record. Another technical point is that it would be rather more laborious to inscribe something on papyrus with a reed pen than it is for us to write on paper with a ballpoint or fountain pen (let alone to type notes on a computer or tablet). But such technical factors may be less significant than sociological ones, such as the ways in which people in Graeco-Roman antiquity chose to use or were accustomed to use writing and the kinds of value placed on writing. For example, the mere ability to write (in the sense of inscribing words on a writing surface as opposed to the ability to compose a sophisticated literary work) carried little social prestige unless accompanied by a substantial cultural education; many would have seen it as just a manual craft. A complementary factor was the high prestige accorded to oral competence; to be a successful, respected member of the elite required one to be able to speak well in public, whereas, while the ability to write well could certainly enhance one's prestige in certain elite literary subcultures, one was not compelled to indulge in such literary pursuits.

---

[4] Hurtado, 'Oral Fixation', 330–4; Catherine Hezser, *Jewish Literacy in Roman Palestine* (Texts and Studies in Ancient Judaism, 81; Tübingen: Mohr Siebeck, 2001), 488–502; for a more optimistic estimate of Jewish literacy extending well down the social scale see Alan Millard, *Reading and Writing in the Time of Jesus* (The Biblical Seminar, 69; Sheffield: Sheffield Academic Press, 2000), 84–131, 154–84.

[5] Harris, *Ancient Literacy*, 10–24, 173, 281–4; Chris Keith, *Jesus' Literacy: Scribal Culture and the Teacher from Galilee* (LNTS, 413; ed. M. Goodacre; New York, London: T. & T. Clark, 2011), 81–5; Richard A. Horsley and Jonathan A. Draper, *Whoever Hears You Hears Me: Prophets, Performance and Tradition in Q* (Harrisburg, PA: Trinity Press International, 1999), 125–7; Gamble, *Books and Readers*, 4–5.

That said, writing in antiquity was plentiful. It appeared on public monuments, coins, 'published' scrolls, private notebooks, letters, business documents and ostraca (pottery fragments used as writing surfaces). A large number of texts, both literary and documentary, survive from antiquity, and there must have been many more that were produced but did not survive. At least some records (such as debt records and basic accounts) were kept, and there was clearly a thriving literary culture among the elite (as mentioned above and discussed further below). Moreover, knowledge of (or at least some acquaintance with) the contents of written texts need not have been restricted to those who could read them, since manuscripts were often read aloud to an audience. Yet despite the existence of many middlebrow texts apparently aimed at middle-ranking people with some education, there was no popular written literature aimed at a mass market in the modern sense, since no such market existed.[6]

It is not immediately apparent where the Gospels might fit into this picture. They are clearly not literary productions aimed at the elite. Writings such as the Gospels and the Jewish Scriptures may have been somewhat atypical in the way they were used. The relatively low literacy rates and the absence of any means of mass production make it most unlikely that the majority of Jews or Christians could read such texts for themselves (let alone possess copies of such texts for private reading), but many Jews and Christians were presumably made familiar with the content of their sacred texts through hearing them read.[7] The extent to which synagogues existed in rural first-century Galilee or to which they might have been able to afford a complete set of scriptural scrolls if they did may be debatable, but it is rather more likely that Scripture was read in the synagogue worship of the large towns and cities of the diaspora where Christianity first took significant root, and all four canonical Gospels appear to presuppose a considerable knowledge of Scripture (or of the Israelite traditions contained in Scripture) on the part of their target audiences.

Reading

Reading an ancient manuscript would certainly have been different from reading a modern printed book. Although a skilled scribe writing in a formal book-hand could produce an aesthetically pleasing text with a very neat appearance, Greek (and Latin) manuscripts of the first century lacked virtually all the visual aids to reading that we take for granted. At least as a first approximation, it may be said that in bookrolls intended for elite consumption there were no spaces between words, and no page numbers or headings; punctuation was sparse and there was

---

[6] Harris, *Ancient Literacy*, 25–8, 226–8, 231–3; Hurtado, 'Oral Fixation', 333.
[7] Gamble, *Books and Readers*, 4–10.

no distinction between upper- and lower-case letters, and thus little to guide the reader through the text apart from a continuous stream of letters, *scriptio continua*, typically written in narrow columns (although the columns often sloped, which may have been intended as an aid to the eye).[8]

It would seem that manuscripts written in this way, particularly if written on scrolls, would not readily lend themselves to reference purposes, such as looking up a particular passage in order to check it. Even if one knew roughly where in the work the desired passage occurred, so that one could wind the scroll to approximately the right place, it would take some effort to locate the passage one was looking for among the mass of words written in continuous capitals with no visual cues. The problem would only be slightly alleviated in a codex (the page format of the modern book); turning the pages would be easier than winding or unwinding a scroll, but there was still an absence of any visual cues to guide one to a particular passage. Perhaps someone who knew the text well could home in on a particular passage by recognizing passages that came before or after it, but someone who knew the text well enough to search it in that way would hardly need to look up a passage in the first place. This is not to say that no one ever looked up anything in a written text, but rather to point out that it would have been sufficiently inconvenient that most people would be unlikely to attempt it without some compelling reason and would otherwise have been much more inclined to rely on their memory of the text. That said, there are a few ancient anecdotes that indicate that people could and sometimes did look up particular passages in bookrolls.[9]

It used to be suggested that ancient manuscripts were never used for private reading (in the sense of silent, solitary, visual perusal) but were always employed as scripts for oral performance. That ancient literary manuscripts were often read aloud is not in doubt. In an article that has proved highly influential in New Testament scholarship Paul Achtemeier argued that this was always the case, but this overstates the matter.[10] It seems likely that some written material, especially that of a more technical sort, was intended for private consumption and that readers of a more scholarly disposition read such material for themselves, silently or otherwise. There also seem to have been at least some literary compositions, such as picture-poems, that were designed for private, silent reading rather than being read aloud to an audience.[11] While there was thus far more reading aloud of texts to audiences than is the case today, it was not to the total exclusion of private reading.

---

[8] Gamble, *Books and Readers*, 47–8; William A. Johnson, *Readers and Reading Culture in the High Roman Empire: A Study of Elite Communities* (New York: Oxford University Press, 2010), 17–25.
[9] Johnson, *Readers and Reading*, 89 n. 40, 95, 110–11, 201.
[10] Paul J. Achtemeier, 'Omne verbum sonat: The New Testament and the Oral Environment of Late Western Antiquity', *JBL* 109 (1990), 3–37.
[11] Harris, *Ancient Literacy*, 126–7; Hurtado, 'Oral Fixation', 326–7; Johnson, *Readers and Reading*, 2–9, 91–2, 114–17.

A reason often advanced for the comparative rarity of private, silent reading in antiquity is the alleged difficulty of silently construing a manuscript written in *scriptio continua*.[12] Whether this would have seemed so difficult to people at the time who would have been used to manuscripts written in this format is less clear.[13] To help present-day readers judge for themselves, here is some (English) text presented in a format resembling that of an ancient scroll, that is, all capital letters in a relatively narrow column:

NOWAREOURBROWSBOUND
WITHVICTORIOUSWREATHS
OURBRUISEDARMSHUNGUPF
ORMONUMENTSOURSTERNA
LARUMSCHANGEDTOMERRY
MEETINGSOURDREADFULM
ARCHESTODELIGHTFULMEA
SURESGRIMVISAGDWARHAT
HSMOOTHEDHISWRINKLEDF
RONTANDNOWINSTEADOFM
OUNTINGBARBEDSTEEDSTO
FRIGHTTHESOULSOFFEARFU
LADVERSARIESHECAPERSNI
MBLYINALADYSCHAMBERT
OTHELASCIVIOUSPLEASING
OFALUTE

When I try this extract on my students, most of them remark that it is hard to read, but most of them nevertheless manage to read it aloud. Many also find it far easier to read a second time, once the sense had been made out. Familiarity with the contents of a text in this format thus appears to be an important factor in the ease of reading it. Readers familiar with Shakespeare's *Richard III* may like to test this for themselves on the (perhaps more familiar) beginning of the Duke of Gloucester's opening soliloquy from which the previous extract was taken:

NOWISTHEWINTEROFOURDI
SCONTENTMADEGLORIOUSS
UMMERBYTHISSUNOFYORK
ANDALLTHECLOUDSTHATL
OURDUPONOURHOUSEINTH
EDEEPBOSOMOFTHEOCEAN
BURIED

---

[12] Gamble, *Books and Reading*, 203.
[13] Hurtado, 'Oral Fixation', 327–8; Gamble, *Books and Reading*, 203–4.

While this extremely limited experiment with modern readers proves little or nothing about ancient ones, it does perhaps suggest that we should not be too quick to assume that ancient readers used to seeing text in this format would have found it as hard to read as we might imagine. To be sure, psychological tests do suggest that the lack of space between words slows readers down, a factor that may be rather more important for silent reading than for reading aloud for others to hear.[14] That said, these tests were not conducted on ancient readers who had been trained to acquire facility with texts written in this format (although Quintilian regards it as a skill that requires considerable practice, *Inst.* 1.1.33–34).[15] Moreover, in contrast to manuscripts intended for use by the literary elites, many early Christian manuscripts did have some aids for the reader such as rudimentary punctuation and spacing.[16] The columnar format described above was a feature of elite objects intended for a particular kind of elite use.[17]

The alleged difficulty of reading texts in this format is one reason sometimes given for the ancient preference for reading aloud rather than silently. In the article previously mentioned, Paul Achtemeier argued that all ancient reading was reading aloud, citing Augustine's surprise at finding Bishop Ambrose reading silently as the exception that proves the rule.[18] This position has since been challenged on a number of grounds, not least that it was not the fact but the occasion of Ambrose's private reading that Augustine found odd, and that elsewhere Augustine suggests that he read silently himself. The occasional passage in other ancient literature, such as a scene in a play which depends on a character silently reading a letter, implies that the practice of silent reading can hardly have been unknown. Indeed, it seems to have been quite common and often expected by the authors of literary texts.[19] Moreover, while it has been argued that even private reading in antiquity was not true silent reading, since the ancients subvocalized the text, it has also been argued that the ability to read aloud presupposes the cognitive ability to make sense of the text silently.[20]

Arguing from the format of manuscripts and speculating about the cognitive capabilities of people who lived two millennia ago can only get us so far. A more productive approach is to enquire not what people in antiquity were able to do with texts but what they chose to do with them. William Johnson has pointed

---

[14] Jocelyn Penny Small, *Wax Tablets of the Mind: Cognitive Studies of Memory and Literacy in Classical Antiquity* (Abingdon: Routledge, 1997), 19–20.

[15] Hurtado, 'Oral Fixation', 327–30.

[16] Hurtado, 'Oral Fixation', 336–7.

[17] Johnson, *Readers and Reading*, 21–2; Rex Winsbury, *The Roman Book: Books, Publishing and Performance in Classical Rome* (London: Bristol Classical Press, 2009), 35–6, 164–5.

[18] Achtemeier, 'Omne verbum sonat'.

[19] Parker, 'Books and Reading', 191–8, 200, 215–24.

[20] A. K. Gavrilov, 'Techniques of Reading in Classical Antiquity', *CQ* 47 n.s. (1997), 56–73; Frank D. Gilliard, 'More Silent Reading in Antiquity: Non Omne Verbum Sonabat', *JBL* 112 (1993), 689–94.

out that reading is a socially embedded activity whose meaning is to some extent socially determined. Johnson goes on to examine the practice of reading among the Graeco-Roman elites, and finds that in this particular context the preference was indeed for works of literature to be read aloud to an audience as a form of highbrow entertainment. A host might get a slave to read to his dinner guests, for example, following which there might be a discussion of what had just been heard. Participating in this kind of literary activity was seen as a badge of belonging to the elite who could appreciate it, a sort of ancient equivalent of going to the opera.[21]

Members of the elite seem often to have preferred to have texts read to them on other occasions as well. Thus, for example, Pliny the Elder had a slave read to him in the bath or when travelling or at other convenient times as a means of conducting his researches. To be sure, we cannot assume that every ancient writer preferred to work in this manner, but it is clear that our modern practice of silently perusing texts in private was far from the only ancient practice. It would be an exaggeration to say that the ancients' approach to written texts was wholly oral–aural, since, for example, Quintilian advises would-be orators to learn texts from the wax tablet on which they have inscribed them, on the principle that the familiar *visual* appearance of the text will aid memorization (*Inst.* 11.2.32–33), a supposition he could hardly have made if his contemporaries had little or no visual apprehension of a written text. He also advises students on the comparative advantages of perusing a text for private study and hearing it read aloud, implying that the former was sometimes to be preferred (*Inst.* 10.1.16–19).

Nonetheless, it does seem that writing (at least of literary texts) was generally oriented towards oral performance, and there may be a number of reasons why this should be so.[22] The high residual orality in Graeco-Roman culture was surely one. Another that has been suggested is that handling a long scroll would have been quite physically laborious, and that being able to read from it in possibly less than optimal lighting conditions probably required a degree of visual acuity that not everyone would have possessed in an age of rudimentary eye care. Reading may thus well have been seen as a task better delegated to a slave, at least for some purposes on some occasions. But none of this should be pressed too far, since elite persons clearly did often read for themselves, and handling a scroll with reasonable ease is a skill many people would have acquired.[23] Once again we have to maintain a balance between recognizing that the ancient use of texts differed from our own and falling into the trap of overstating that difference.

---

[21] William A. Johnson, 'Toward a Sociology of Reading in Classical Antiquity', *AJP* 121 (2000), 593–627.
[22] Thomas, *Literacy and Orality*, 3–4; Gamble, *Books and Readers*, 204–5.
[23] Hurtado, 'Oral Fixation', 329–30.

Quintilian's advice calls attention to another aspect of the use of ancient texts that is different from the way writing is typically used today, and that is that texts were often employed as aids to memorization rather than the substitutes for memory they have since become. To be sure, modern people usually hope to remember some of what they read, but they seldom make a conscious effort to commit a text to memory (except for certain very specific purposes such as learning lines to be performed on stage). In antiquity people were much more likely to memorize texts, or at least texts that were sufficiently important for them to know.

How far this picture of reading drawn from elite practices can be applied to the primitive Church is unclear. We have little direct evidence for how the first-century Church used texts, apart from the apparent expectation that some of Paul's letters would be read aloud to his recipients and exchanged with other congregations, to the extent that Colossians 4.16 (in a probably pseudonymous letter) can be used as evidence of that. We do have some evidence for the second century, such as Justin Martyr's notice (*1 Apol.* 67) that in meetings for worship the Prophets and the 'memoirs of the apostles' (the Gospels) were read for as long as time permitted (however long that may have been), but what Justin says about the second century cannot simply be assumed to hold for the first, not least since in the first century the relative importance of written texts and oral tradition would have been somewhat different from what it had become by Justin's time.[24]

That said, we can make several judgements of probability given what else we know. First, given the likely social mix of the primitive Church, it is to be expected that the majority of its members were unable to read or write, although there is some evidence to suggest that literacy extended further down the social scale than is often allowed for.[25] Any text that aimed to reach more than the literate few would thus have to be read aloud (or performed from memory), and it is overwhelmingly likely that this was so in the case of the Gospels. Presumably, then, the Gospels were read aloud or performed aloud in meetings for either worship or instruction. It is perhaps conceivable that they were also performed publicly for missionary purposes, although it is less clear how the primitive Church would have gone about attracting an audience. This does not of course preclude the possibility that some people such as literate church leaders may have studied one or more Gospels privately for their own edification or to prepare themselves for preaching, teaching and debate.

Second, we also know that the primitive Church had firm roots in Judaism, a religion that had a strong orientation towards sacred texts. The Gospels clearly presuppose some knowledge of those sacred texts, or at the very least of their

---

[24] Gamble, *Books and Readers*, 205–7.
[25] Hurtado, 'Oral Fixation', 330–4.

existence and general contents, so it seems plausible that the reading aloud or performance of Jewish Scriptures (or at the very least the rehearsal and exposition of traditions akin to them) formed part of primitive Christian worship and instruction (although strictly speaking there is no clear evidence for this; it does not, for example, feature in Paul's account of what might happen in the context of primitive Christian worship in 1 Corinthians 14). While the Gospels were presumably not immediately received as Scripture, it seems likely they would have been received as authoritative statements of tradition (otherwise their survival and promulgation become hard to explain). The speedy adoption of the codex-form (on which see below) for the Gospels and other early Christian texts may argue against their being seen as analogous to Jewish sacred texts, which were written on scrolls, except that the Church seems to have used codices for their copies of the Jewish Scriptures as well.

Writing

People of my vintage have witnessed remarkable changes in the process of writing over our lifetimes. Writing used to be something most of us did by hand with pen, ink and paper (or maybe a ballpoint pen and paper). If it was a text we expected to revise, then we might write it on alternate lines to allow space for revisions and corrections to be marked (rather as Quintilian advises students to leave blank spaces in their drafts for subsequent additions, *Inst.* 10.3.31–33). If a fair copy was required we (or someone else on our behalf) might bash it out on a manual typewriter. But the original creative work would usually be done with pen in hand. With the advent of word processing it became easier to correct one's work, to move text around, correct mistakes, and accommodate second, third or umpteenth thoughts. Over the years many of us have gradually abandoned the pen as the primary tool of composition and now prefer to compose even first rough drafts with the aid of keyboard and screen. The same technology is then used to revise the text, and a final electronic version can often be submitted direct to a publisher, a possibility undreamt of four decades ago. The fact that the mechanics of writing have changed so much in living memory should alert us to the fact that they would also have been very different in antiquity.

The first point to bear in mind is that, especially when talking about antiquity, the word 'writing' can refer to two different activities: the act of composing a text and the act of physically inscribing it on a writing surface. While these could sometimes be performed by the same person, the preferred method of composition was usually by dictation; we know, for example, that Paul often dictated his letters (see Romans 16.22; Galatians 6.11), and this also seems to have been the gener-ally preferred practice of the literary elite, at least at a preliminary stage in the process.[26] Whether it also applies to the authors of the Gospels we have no direct means of knowing, and in any case they may have differed among themselves.

Writing in the sense of composition is something that will be addressed in more detail in Chapter 4, so for now we shall focus more on the physical aspects. The preferred medium for writing a literary text was the scroll, which was generally made of a number of papyrus sheets stuck together to form a continuous roll about 3.5 metres long, although this could be cut down if a shorter scroll was required, or (more usually, it seems) glued to another scroll to produce a longer one; the average length of a bookroll was 7–10 metres (anything much longer than that would have been too cumbersome to handle). An alternative material was parchment (made of animal skins), although this was not so common in the first century as it later became. The text was typically written in narrow columns about 6–9 centimetres wide and 15–24 centimetres high, running transverse to the direction of scrolling, so that rolling and unrolling the scroll would reveal successive columns.[27]

The surviving evidence suggests that writing desks or tables were not used in the first century (or indeed, for several centuries thereafter). Instead, scribes would sit either on the ground or on a low stool with the scroll draped over their upper leg, and would write on that portion of the scroll supported by their leg or lap.[28] To those of us used to writing on a desk, this method of working may seem almost perverse, but it may in fact have been more practicable. A long scroll placed on a flat surface such as a desk or table would tend to roll up (the writing surface was usually the inside of the scroll), making it awkward to work with. Even if the scribe used a collection of weights to try to hold the scroll in place and stop it curling up over the column he or she was currently working on, it could prove a somewhat cumbersome method. On the other hand, if the scribe was seated with the scroll draped over his or her leg, the weight of the rolled-up portions would tend to make them hang down either side of the scribe's lap rather than rolling over the portion currently being worked on. The upper leg would then provide a reasonably firm surface to rest the scroll on that more or less matched the typical width and height of a column written on the scroll, while the writing surface would be at a convenient distance from the eyes and optimally positioned for the hands.[29]

To be sure, not all writing was done on scrolls. Although the scroll was the predominant form for literary works, the codex had come into use as a notebook,

---

[26] For the warning that dictating initial notes or a rough draft should not be confused with composition in performance, see Hurtado, 'Oral Fixation', 335.
[27] Gamble, *Books and Readers*, 44–8.
[28] Botha, *Orality and Literacy*, 62–5.
[29] Cf. Winsbury, *Roman Book*, 37, who suggests that the columnar format may have been due to scribal posture.

either as a papyrus or parchment codex (the format of a modern book) or as two or more wooden tablets (often waxed) tied together. A wax tablet was particularly suited for notes and rough drafts, since a text could be inscribed with a stylus and subsequently erased by smoothing over the wax. While there may have been some precedents for handbooks and the like, the Christian Church appears to have pioneered the use of the codex for its literature (perhaps because it regarded its Gospels, Epistles and other writings not so much as 'literature' as texts for practical use), although it is not clear how early this started (since no Christian manuscripts from the first century survive).[30] There is, however, nothing to suggest that scribes adopted a different posture when writing in a codex. It seems that the writing habits learned from inscribing scrolls were applied to other formats as well. It is probably no coincidence, though, that writing desks only started to be used after the codex had displaced the scroll as the predominant format, but this was not until several centuries after the composition of the Gospels.

In any case, it is often assumed that the Gospels were originally distributed on scrolls. This is first because this would have been regarded as the normal format for such works at the time, and the Church may have not been that quick to innovate, and second because the Gospels are all of roughly the right length to fit conveniently on a scroll; in particular the typical capacity of a scroll would explain the need to split Luke–Acts into two separate volumes. This falls far short of proof, however. We cannot even be sure that all four Gospels were originally distributed in the same format (or that a consistent format was always used when copying them), and given the means readily available to create scrolls of various lengths it may be perilous to place too much weight on the capacity of a 'typical' scroll.

Once a written composition was considered complete (typically when a fair copy had been made of a corrected first, second or subsequent draft), it was then ready for distribution; one can speak of this as 'publication' only if one avoids most of the modern connotations of the word. Although there is some evidence for a book trade (which presumably involved some commercial book-copying), this does not seem to have been the main means by which literary works were distributed, and there seems to have been no generally available means for the mass production of texts (such as dictation to a number of scribes in a scriptorium).[31] In antiquity, 'publishing' a work meant making it available to be copied or giving one or more public performances of it. At least in Roman society the semi-public *recitatio* (reading aloud) of a new book to an invited audience may have been the most important part.[32] Otherwise the most an author could do to

---

[30] Gamble, *Books and Readers*, 49–66, 80–1; Millard, *Reading and Writing*, 61–83.
[31] Winsbury, *Roman Book*, 53–66.
[32] Winsbury, *Roman Book*, 95–110.

promote circulation would be to have a few copies made to pass on to friends in the hope that they in turn would lend them to others to copy, so that the book would gradually spread through a social network.

Thus 'publication' meant placing a work in the public domain. Once a work was released, the author had no further control over it, and in particular no means of preventing the plagiarism or corruption of his or her text as it continued to be copied (apart, that is, from relying on the social disapproval that would probably deter most people from attempting to pass someone else's work off as their own and the desire many people would have had for reasonably accurate copies of works they wished to acquire).[33] The contents of a literary work might subsequently spread to a far wider audience than those who could read it for themselves or attend a formal *recitatio*, since the predominantly oral environment of the first-century Roman world promoted a shared culture across all classes through the theatre, street debates, domestic entertainments and numerous other such occasions.[34]

We have no direct information on how the Gospels were originally distributed, but it is most unlikely that commercial booksellers played any role in their circulation; far more likely is a process similar to the informal spread of literature through networks of friends.[35] In the case of the Gospels the network probably consisted of churches to whom the Gospels would have been useful rather than of friends who wanted to be edified or entertained, although Richard Last has warned against seeing the Evangelists as narrowly confined to Christian social circles, arguing that they would also have mixed with fellow literates engaged in similar writing projects.[36] Again, we should allow for some variation between the Gospels. In particular, Luke 1.3 suggests that Theophilus may have been a patron Luke hoped would help promote the distribution of his work.[37]

Uses of writing

If the mechanics of writing (and promulgating) texts were rather different from those familiar to us today, so are at least some of the uses to which written texts might be put. We have already seen that many literary works were written to be read out as a form of erudite entertainment for the upper classes. Even technical manuals on subjects such as agriculture and architecture were sometimes used

---

[33] Winsbury, *Roman Book*, 87–91; Gamble, *Books and Readers*, 83–93; Harris, *Ancient Literacy*, 224–5.

[34] Winsbury, *Roman Book*, 169–73; F. Gerald Downing, *Doing Things with Words in the First Christian Century* (JSNTSup, 200; Sheffield: Sheffield Academic Press, 2000; repr. T. & T. Clark, 2004), 21–40.

[35] Gamble, *Books and Readers*, 93–4.

[36] Richard Last, 'The Social Relationships of Gospel Writers: New Insights from Inscriptions Commending Greek Historiographers', *JSNT* 37 (2015), 223–52.

[37] Gamble, *Books and Readers*, 101–2.

in this way. Monumental inscriptions (which probably only a minority of people could actually read) seem to have been intended more as symbols of power and prestige rather than to convey information. Magical texts were often thought to be powerful simply as a result of being written down, hence their use in amulets and the like. For example, Numbers 5.11–31 describes a procedure in which a woman suspected of adultery is made to drink water into which has been washed the words of a written curse; if the woman is guilty, the curse she has drunk will then supposedly cause painful swelling.[38]

Writing was also employed for more workaday purposes in documentary texts such as accounts, contracts and letters, although even then such uses may not always have been exactly the same as they are today. In the absence of any postal service a letter could only be conveyed by the hand of a trusted carrier, who therefore might also act as messenger to explain and expand on the contents of the letter (as could well have been the case for Paul's Epistles). Although official government archives were kept, it is not clear how often they were consulted; they may have existed more for symbolic than for practical purposes.[39]

The Scriptures of Israel seem to have been something of a special case since, as has been already mentioned, Judaism (later followed by Christianity) was distinctive among the ancient religions of the Roman Empire in the role it gave to sacred texts. In synagogue worship the reader was required to read from the text (rather than recite from memory), while, if the text required translation from Hebrew into the vernacular (Aramaic), this had to be done without the aid of any written text, thus marking a clear distinction between the written word of God and its human interpretation. Scriptural scrolls thus had a symbolic value going well beyond their practical usefulness for supplying the wording of texts that many educated Israelites may well have known by heart.

The physical characteristics of many early Christian manuscripts suggest that many of them were intended to be read aloud to a group. This is suggested by the aids to such reading they contain, such as large letters, the presence of at least some rudimentary punctuation and the signalling of sense units by spacing, all indications, perhaps, that they were intended for reading aloud by non-elite persons who had not been trained to a high level of facility with literary *scriptio continua* texts. Moreover, early Christian writings often describe texts being read aloud to groups (rather than, say, being performed from memory, which seems not to be envisaged).[40] It may be that Christian practice was influenced by the reading of Scriptures in the synagogue in this regard, or it may simply have been a pragmatic concession to the abilities of the typical Christian *lector*.

---

[38] Thomas, *Literacy and Orality*, 19–20.

[39] See Harris, *Ancient Literacy*, 26–7 for a list of the various purposes of writing in antiquity.

[40] Hurtado, 'Oral Fixation', 336–9.

Overall, attitudes to writing seem to have been ambivalent. On the one hand, aspects of its practical usefulness for preserving texts across time or distributing them across space were clearly recognized. On the other hand there seems to have been a certain wariness about writing even among the most literate. Plato's worries about the threat writing posed to memory and the inability of dumb manuscripts to respond to questioning are perhaps the most famous examples of this (Plato, *Phaedrus* 275d–e), but he was not alone.[41] When Papias (according to Eusebius, *Hist. eccl.* 3.39.3–4) wrote that he felt he could learn more from the 'living and abiding voice' of oral history than from books, he was expressing a cultural commonplace. The ancient ideal of education was not book-learning but face-to-face interaction with a teacher, whom one could both question and imitate (and Plato's doubts about the value of writing should be understood in this context).[42] The ancient ideal of historical research was as far as possible to rely on the testimony of eyewitnesses who could be cross-examined (so, e.g., Lucian, *quom. hist.* 47); written documents might also be employed, but very much as a secondary resource to supply information that was not available at first hand.[43] And yet, ironically, we know of Papias's preference for orality over writing only because he chose to write about it, and the very historians who preferred oral testimony to written records were writing history to preserve it for posterity.

If the attitudes towards writing held by literate elites appear somewhat paradoxical, those held by everyone else may have been even more curious. On the one hand, the uses to which writing was put were probably understood well enough in the main, but the existence of magical uses of writing also suggests that there may have been some quite odd notions about it (or at least, notions that we would regard as quite odd). Again, while on the one hand writing may have appeared useful even to those who could not read or write themselves (for example, when they listened to a text being read aloud, or got someone to write a letter or contract on their behalf), it may also have been seen as an instrument of oppression, both politically (since writing was used by the imperial administration) and economically (for example, because wealthy creditors held written debt records that poorer, illiterate people had no means of checking for themselves). It is significant that one of the first acts of the Jewish Revolt in 66 CE was the burning of debt records (Josephus, *J.W.* 2.427).

It seems, then, that ordinary people regarded writing with a mix of pragmatic understanding, suspicious resentment, superstition and awe that it is hard if not virtually impossible for us to fully grasp today, while even the literate elites simultaneously valued and disparaged it. On the one hand it was an instrument

---

[41] Botha, *Orality and Literacy*, 28–31.

[42] Gamble, *Books and Readers*, 30–2; Botha, *Orality and Literacy*, 31–3.

[43] Samuel Byrskog, *Story as History – History as Story: The Gospel Tradition in the Context of Ancient Oral History* (Leiden and Boston: Brill, 2002), 48–65, 93–9.

of prestige functioning as a display of elite culture or a repository of valued traditions; on the other it was less valued than oral, rhetorical competence and was regarded as an inferior means of both gaining and imparting information when compared with face-to-face oral communication. In some ways, then, attitudes to writing in antiquity were analogous to present-day attitudes to information technology, which has been greeted with a similar mix of enthusiasm and suspicion.

Who wrote?

It may be helpful to conclude with a brief discussion of who actually wrote things, both in the sense of composition and that of inscribing on a surface. Roughly speaking, we may identify five (probably overlapping) groups. First, at the very top of the social scale, were members of the ruling elite who composed literary texts as part of their contribution to high culture, carried out correspondence with friends, and may from time to time have issued edicts and other documents in furtherance of their governing or financial interests. Such people mostly dictated their texts to others, but on occasion some preferred to handwrite for themselves. Second would have been senior members of the retainer class, such as high-ranking military officers and administrators working in the service of the elite, at least some of whose business would have been conducted in writing. Here one might also include certain professionals such as doctors, engineers and architects. Third would have been the slaves, sometimes highly literate slaves, who acted as secretaries (and even administrators) to the wealthy elites (and maybe some better-off retainers), and who would have provided assistance both with their business correspondence (in the widest sense of the term) and with their literary endeavours. Fourth would have come a number of small merchants, shopkeepers and relatively prosperous artisans who may have had at least some rudimentary writing skills, at least to the extent of being able to keep basic accounts and lists, signing their own name and perhaps writing a few basic sentences (although the precise extent of literacy skills further down the social scale is hard to determine). Fifth were professional scribes.[44]

People designated 'scribes' would have overlapped with at least two of the groups (the second and third) mentioned above, and the whole discussion of scribes is bedevilled by the broadness of the term (much as 'clerk' or 'secretary' in English can indicate positions ranging from very senior to very junior, not all principally involving writing). The issue of who and what exactly scribes were is complicated by the fact that the underlying Greek word *grammateus* appears

---

[44] Millard, *Reading and Writing*, 168–84; Winsbury, *Roman Book*, 79–85.

to have been used in two different senses. In ordinary secular Greek it meant a secretary, clerk or notary, someone who earned his or her living as a professional writer, but it was also the word used in the LXX to translate the Hebrew *sopher*, which designated a number of administrative functions related to reading and writing but could also be associated with expertise in wisdom, knowledge of the Jewish law, instruction, the interpretation of dreams and the writing of books.[45] The scribes who appear in the Gospels would seem to have been of the latter sort, although scribes in the sense of professional clerks and copyists were also employed in Jewish Palestine, as is evidenced by the fact that most surviving letters and documents of the period from that area were produced by such professional scribes.[46]

Anthony Saldarini sees scribes as belonging to the retainer class, that is, as working for and being economically supported by the wealthy ruling class. Richard Horsley largely agrees, while proposing some modifications to Gerhard Lenski's model of an agrarian society from which this notion of retainer is drawn, since Horsley sees the Judaean priests as being rulers rather than retainers. Christine Schams criticizes Saldarini for ignoring data that does not fit Lenski's model and for assuming that all literate activity was scribal, while Catherine Hezser suggests that while many scribes would have been based in Jerusalem working for the Temple and the government (and would thus have been retainers in Saldarini's and Horsley's sense), there may also have been lower-status scribes who worked for private individuals.[47]

The differences here may be more apparent than real given the fuzziness of the term 'scribe', and so we can take all these suggestions as supplying parts of the picture. That is, in Jewish (and to some extent wider) usage, the term 'scribe' could denote anyone from a high-status professional intellectual serving the wealthy ruling class and perhaps even drawn from its ranks, through a large range of retainers who worked for the ruling class in a number of clerical, administrative and intellectual roles, an indeterminate number of secretaries and clerks who may have worked for individuals wealthy enough to employ them, or as jobbing clerks who hired out their services as professional writers of letters, contracts and other documents for relatively ordinary people, down to lowly village scribes who were minor administrative officials, sometimes possessing only rudimentary literacy. The one thing all these people had in common was that, with the

---

[45] Christine Schams, *Jewish Scribes in the Second-Temple Period* (JSOTSup, 291; ed. D. A. Clines and P. R. Davies; Sheffield: Sheffield Academic Press, 1998), 25–6, 284–6.

[46] Hezser, *Jewish Literacy*, 288, 327.

[47] Anthony J. Saldarini, *Pharisees, Scribes and Sadducees in Palestinian Society* (Grand Rapids/Cambridge/Livonia, MI: Eerdmans/Dove, 2001), 155, 249–54; Richard A. Horsley, *Scribes, Visionaries and the Politics of Second Temple Judea* (Louisville, KY and London: Westminster John Knox Press, 2007), 54–70; Schams, *Jewish Scribes*, 34; Hezser, *Jewish Literacy*, 118–19.

exception of village scribes, they were far more likely to be found in an urban than a rural environment.

It is perhaps conceivable that a non-literate storyteller could have dictated a Gospel to a scribe (we shall return to this possibility in Chapter 4), but at least one literate person must have been involved at some stage in the production of the written text of each Gospel. The people who wrote the Gospels were hardly part of the intellectual and political elite, but clearly possessed more than the rudimentary writing competence that was limited to the production of basic legal documents and the keeping of simple accounts or lists. This almost certainly means they must have been either scribes (though probably in the more modest sense of the word), or literate slaves allowed some liberty to contribute their skills to the Christian communities to which they belonged, or literate professionals such as physicians or engineers trying their hand at a narrative text, or, just possibly (especially in the case of Mark), gifted artisans, shopkeepers or small merchants attempting literary composition.

It has often been suggested, partly from the content of his Gospel, and partly on the strength of the saying at Matthew 13.52, that Matthew may have been a former scribe converted to Christianity. This is disputed by Schams on the grounds that the interpretation of Matthew 13.52 is uncertain and that the kind of expertise in scriptural exegesis Matthew exhibits was not necessarily the province of scribes,[48] but given the wide range of meaning 'scribe' can have and the limited number of other options, that Matthew was a scribe in some sense of the word arguably remains a reasonable guess. The same probably applies to the other Evangelists, although Luke could have been some other kind of literate professional (on which see Chapter 2) and it has been argued that Mark was an oral storyteller (on which see Chapter 4). The fact that the Gospels are highly critical of the Jewish leadership and generally take the side of the poor against the rich does not automatically rule out their having been produced in scribal retainer circles, since such features appear in other texts that may have been produced by scribal retainers.[49]

On the other hand, despite William Arnal's argument that the hypothetical source-document 'Q' was the literary product of village scribes, it seems far more likely that the Gospels would have been written in an urban setting, since it is far from clear either what purpose a written Gospel would serve in a rural setting or that village scribes possessed the literary competence to write extended narrative texts (as opposed to basic documents).[50] The most likely conclusion, then, is

---

[48] Schams, *Jewish Scribes*, 178, 194–6.
[49] So Horsley, *Scribes*, 67–9, 145–6.
[50] William E. Arnal, *Jesus and the Village Scribes: Galilean Conflicts and the Setting of Q* (Minneapolis: Fortress Press, 2001); cf. Schams, *Jewish Scribes*, 292; Saldarini, *Pharisees*, 263; Hezser, *Jewish Literacy*, 500; Josephus, *J.W.* 1.479.

that the Evangelists were low- to middle-ranking scribes or literate professionals, artisans or small traders located in an urban environment. Given the fuzziness of the term 'scribe' this conclusion may well appear indefinite, but hopefully a little more definition will emerge from the discussion that follows. The next step towards understanding the writing of the Gospels is to ask *why* they were written.

2

Why write a Gospel?

The reason Paul wrote letters seems obvious: it was a means of communicating with his churches at a distance when he could not be present in person. The reasons for writing a Gospel are not so immediately apparent, however, especially given that relatively few people could read and that the Church had presumably got on perfectly well telling its stories of Jesus by word of mouth. It might seem obvious to us that people would want to put an account of their founding figure in writing, but people in the first century did not share our cultural assumptions, so we need to be a little cautious about rushing to conclusions about the reasons people may have had for writing things down.

The question of genre

Genre is usually some indication of purpose, so although it may not take us as far as we might like, in asking why the Gospels were written a brief discussion of their genre could be a good place to start. For present purposes, 'genre' may be defined as a set of conventions governing audience expectation. Presumably no one would go to the effort of writing a Gospel without a reasonably clear idea of how he wished the target audience to receive it. We may assume, therefore, that the Evangelists would have chosen (or adapted) a genre they deemed suitable for their purpose, so that if we can determine the former we may learn something about the latter.[2] We need not assume that the Gospels all belonged to precisely the same genre (especially as Luke has a second volume), but there is insufficient space (and little need) here for a detailed discussion of the genre of each individual Gospel.

The classical position (taken, for example, by the form critics) was that the Gospels were *sui generis*, that is, that they did not conform to any pre-existing genre, but this seems unlikely, since if the Gospels conformed to no recognizable genre, audiences would not have known what to make of them. Saying that, however, does not mean that the Evangelists could not have innovated at all, or that the Gospels had to exactly follow the prescriptions of some already existing

---

[1] Cf. Richard Bauckham, 'For Whom Were Gospels Written?' in Richard Bauckham (ed.), *The Gospels for All Christians: Rethinking the Gospel Audiences* (Edinburgh: T. & T. Clark, 1998), 9–48 (27–9).

[2] See, e.g., Christopher Bryan, *A Preface to Mark: Notes on the Gospel in Its Literary and Cultural Settings* (Oxford: Oxford University Press, 1993), 9–15.

genre. The conventions that govern audience expectations could be quite loose, and could certainly be adapted to specific purposes or borrow from other genres, and we need to keep these possibilities in mind.

The most persuasive suggestion has been that the Gospels were ancient *bioi* or lives.[3] A *bios* is a genre of 'biographical' writing that needs to be distinguished carefully from that of a modern biography. Unlike a modern biography, an ancient *bios* showed no interest in tracing the development of its subject or exploring his or her motivations or even necessarily giving a connected chronological account of the subject's life. A *bios* might well say something about its subject's birth, origins and parentage, since to an ancient audience this would provide valuable background about the subject's status and reputation. It might well outline the course of the subject's life, but would principally be interested in presenting him or her as an example to be emulated or avoided, and to that end it might tend to use a series of anecdotes depicting its subject in speech or action to typify the virtues or vices he or she exemplified.

As Richard Burridge has argued, this characterization of *bioi* fits the Gospels quite well. All four Gospels contain a number of anecdotes showing Jesus in action or expounding his teaching. While John gives some impression of a connected account, the other three Gospels are quite episodic, with only a very loose sense of chronology. In common with other *bioi* the Gospels show no interest in Jesus' inner development or in analysing his motivations, but simply present him as a figure to be admired and emulated while exemplifying the kinds of thing he stood for. Matthew and Luke also follow the *bios* convention of beginning with an account of Jesus' origins and parentage, and concluding with the events after his death, as also recommended in progymnastic topic lists. (While, strictly speaking, these lists are intended as guidance on composing *encomia*, passages praising or perhaps excoriating a person or thing, as a preliminary exercise in speech writing, since they would have been used in the education of writers as well as orators, they may be regarded as relevant to the *bios* genre as well.)[4]

Yet despite this apparent fit, there are problems with straightforwardly classifying the Gospels as *bioi*. Even if one qualifies the appellation *bios* with the epithet *encomiastic*, it is hard if not impossible to find any other examples of *bioi* whose subjects play such a central role in a religion, with the sole possible exception of

---

[3] A case made particularly by Richard A. Burridge, *What Are the Gospels? A Comparison with Graeco-Roman Biography* (paperback edn; SNTSMS, 70; Cambridge: Cambridge University Press, 1995). For earlier versions of this thesis see, e.g., David E. Aune, *The New Testament in Its Literary Environment* (Cambridge: James Clarke, 1988), 22–67; and Bryan, *Preface to Mark*, 22–64.

[4] Michael W. Martin, 'Progymnastic Topic Lists: A Compositional Template for Luke and Other Bioi?', *NTS* 54 (2008), 18–41. For the relevant *progymnasmata* see George A. Kennedy, *Progymnasmata: Greek Textbooks of Prose Composition and Rhetoric* (Atlanta: SBL, 2003), esp. 50–5, 81–4, 108–15, 154–62.

Philo's *Life of Moses*. But the *Life of Moses* reads rather differently from the Gospels (in part due, no doubt, to the very different social location of its author and intended audience), and there is no indication that it ever played the kind of role the Gospels came to play.

Moreover, *bios* is not the only genre that has been proposed for the Gospels. Mary Ann Tolbert, for example, has argued that Mark more closely resembles the ancient romance (a kind of prose fiction). While few have followed her, F. Gerald Downing suggests that Mark may have borrowed his intercalation ('sandwich') technique from popular storytelling techniques exemplified in romances.[5] This in turn suggests two things: first that genres are far from being rigid categories so that the Gospels may well blend elements of different genres even if one seems to predominate, and second, that at least one secondary aim of Mark (and quite probably of the other Evangelists as well) was to entertain;[6] a Gospel that failed to keep its audience's attention would hardly be able to achieve any other goal.

Again, despite the obvious affinity in form and content between Luke and the other three canonical Gospels, taken together Luke–Acts may come closer to history than to *bios*.[7] To the extent that both ancient and modern writers recognize that the boundaries between history and biography can be quite blurred, the other Gospels may also contain some elements of (ancient) historiography, even if that is not their primary genre.

Another potential issue is whether the Gospels should be classified according to a Graeco-Roman genre at all, first because, especially in the case of Mark, some scholars claim that the background should be seen as oral-traditional rather than literary (a point to which we shall return in Chapter 4) and, second, because their background is so obviously Jewish. Opinions may differ on just how familiar any of the Evangelists were with Graeco-Roman literature, but it is clear that they were all steeped in the Jewish Scriptures (or, at the very least, in many of the traditions they contained). It would thus seem perverse not to consider what the Gospels may have owed to biblical exemplars, even though these are generally taken as being more remote in genre from the Gospels than the Graeco-Roman models discussed above.[8]

A number of suggestions have been made that take this Jewish background into account, but not all of them are satisfactory. Howard Clark Kee, for example, has suggested that Mark should be read as apocalyptic, but apart from the

---

[5] Mary Ann Tolbert, *Sowing the Gospel: Mark's World in Literary-Historical Perspective* (Minneapolis: Fortress Press, 1989); F. Gerald Downing, *Doing Things with Words in the First Christian Century* (JSNTSup, 200; Sheffield: Sheffield Academic Press, 2000), 118–32.

[6] See, e.g., Downing, *Doing Things with Words*, 125–32 (on Mark), 209–12 (on Luke).

[7] See, e.g., Aune, *Literary Environment*, 77–157; Downing, *Doing Things with Words*, 206–7.

[8] See, e.g., Aune, *Literary Environment*, 36–43; Bryan, *Preface to Mark*, 23–5.

uncertainties surrounding the precise meaning of this term, Mark is quite distinct generically from such clearly recognizable apocalypses as Revelation. At the most, one can say it contains some apocalyptic elements. Another suggestion that has been canvassed is that the Gospels are midrash,[9] but if this is intended as a description of their genre it would seem to be a category mistake.[10] The Gospels are plainly not of the same genre as the later Jewish texts that are classified as such, which broadly follow some part of a biblical narrative and expand on it. Proponents of the Gospels as midrash generally appeal to their employment of midrashic method, but method is not the same thing as genre, and using 'midrash' in too broad a sense undermines its usefulness as a description of genre.

The midrashic proposal does, however, have the merit of highlighting the intimate connection each of the Gospels has with Scripture, which is one major factor that distinguishes the Gospels from Graeco-Roman *bioi* in at least two respects. The first is the influence of the style of biblical narrative on the composition of the Gospels. This is perhaps most apparent in the opening chapter of Luke, which not only adopts a Greek style similar to that of the LXX, but also contains strong reminiscences of the opening of 1 Samuel. But all the Evangelists seem indebted at least to some extent to the biblical accounts of salient figures such as Moses, Elijah, Elisha and David.[11]

It may be objected that the biblical accounts of these figures form part of a wider story not focused on these figures alone, but this is a second point of contact between the Gospels and the Jewish Scriptures. None of them is as self-contained as a typical Graeco-Roman *bios*. Rather, each of them presents itself as an especially climactic part of a larger story of God's dealings with his people. Each of the Gospels opens with some kind of link back to the story of God and Israel (or God and humanity), and each in a different way looks forward to the culmination of that story.[12] Moreover (as will be made clearer below and in Chapter 6), each is concerned with community identity – or the identity of the people of God – in ways that go far beyond the role of a typical *bios*.

Thus, while the Gospels do display considerable affinity with ancient *bioi*, they also display some affinity with the Jewish Scriptures, whose story they are in some

---

[9] So M. D. Goulder, *Midrash and Lection in Matthew* (London: SPCK, 1974); Marie Noonan Sabin, *Reopening the Word: Reading Mark as Theology in the Context of Early Judaism* (Oxford and New York: Oxford University Press, 2002).

[10] Philip. S. Alexander, 'Midrash and the Gospels' in Christopher M. Tuckett (ed.), *Synoptic Studies: The Ampleforth Conferences of 1982 and 1983* (JSNTSup, 7; Sheffield: JSOT Press, 1984), 1–18; R. A. Derrenbacker, *Ancient Compositional Practices and the Synoptic Problem* (BETL, 186; Leuven: Peeters-Leuven, 2005), 177–85.

[11] On the Jewish character of the Gospel *bioi* and a discussion of possible Old Testament (OT) precedents, see Aune, *Literary Environment*, 22, 36–43.

[12] On which see Morna D. Hooker, 'Beginnings and Endings' in Markus Bockmuehl and Donald A. Hagner (eds), *The Written Gospel* (Cambridge: Cambridge University Press, 2005), 184–202.

sense intended to complete (or fulfil, as Matthew would have it). We might thus tentatively assign the Gospels to the hybrid genre of *biblically oriented bioi*, or *biblical bioi* for short, meaning that the audience expectations would be guided both by the *bios* form and by their knowledge of Scripture (or of the traditions it contained), and that part of the purpose of the Gospels would be to show how Jesus fitted into and fulfilled the story of God's dealings with humanity narrated in Israelite Scripture and tradition. Particularly in the case of Mark, the influence of the Graeco-Roman *bios* might be relatively slight compared with scriptural models together with popular storytelling, or it might be seen as a deliberately countercultural *bios* centred on a very different kind of subject from the famous 'kings, generals and other prominent figures' typically treated in Graeco-Roman *bioi*.[13]

Reasons for writing

Discussion of the genre of the Gospels may provide some clues about their purpose, but it does not answer the question why they should have been written at all. Even in a situation where only a minority of people could read, writing would have had some reasonably obvious functions. Writing something down would help to preserve the text in a more stable form than would be possible by oral transmission, not least for an extended prose narrative like the Gospels. It would also enable essentially the same text to be sent to other places, so that a version of the Jesus story that was found useful or persuasive could be shared with other churches. But while these advantages of writing may have been a factor, they do not by themselves explain why the *Gospels* should have been written, since in principle they could apply to almost any potential writing. It should also be borne in mind that writing in a scribal culture was not nearly so effective in preserving and propagating a text as print has proved to be post-Gutenberg.[14]

A more debatable suggestion is that writing allowed the creation of a new kind of story that would not have been possible orally, since it enabled the Gospel authors (and particularly Mark) to fix the elements of the story in a particular relation to each other that created a new meaning potentially at odds with the previous oral tradition. On this understanding, Gospel authors could put their particular interpretation on the Jesus material unconstrained by the immediacy of oral performance in front of an audience. This is essentially

---

[13] Richard A. Horsley, *Hearing the Whole Story: The Politics of Plot in Mark's Gospel* (Louisville, KY: Westminster John Knox Press, 2001), 21–4, esp. 22.

[14] This is one of the core emphases running throughout Elizabeth Eisenstein, *The Printing Press as an Agent of Change: Communications and Cultural Transformations in Early-Modern Europe* (Cambridge: Cambridge University Press, 1980).

the position of (the early) Werner Kelber, building on the work of Erhardt Güttgemanns.[15]

At least two objections might be raised, however. The first is that Kelber presupposed the form-critical assumption that prior to the composition of the Gospels the Jesus tradition circulated almost entirely in isolated units, so that putting the Gospels in writing created the first connected accounts of Jesus' ministry. But connected accounts of Jesus' ministry could have been composed and circulated orally before ever being written down. After all, it might be argued, the story told in the Gospel of Mark is not really more complex than that told in some oral epics, so that although Mark is not in verse, it is far from inconceivable that the gist of something of that length could be transmitted orally even if one would not expect the exact wording to be preserved. But then 'gist' is one thing, and the precise arrangement of pericopae in Mark's structure that gives rise to the particular meaning Mark creates in his narrative is another, and opinions differ on whether the latter could be adequately preserved through oral storytelling.[16]

The second, related, objection is that, contrary to what Güttgemanns and the early Kelber suppose, it is impossible to maintain the existence of any hard boundary between oral and written storytelling in general, just as there is no hard boundary between oral and written poetry.[17] Yet the lack of a *hard* boundary means only that some material may defy easy classification into 'oral' or 'written'; it does not abolish all distinctions. Some kinds of material could only originate (and be perpetuated) in writing (such as the present book). Arranging material in a particular way creates a particular kind of meaning, and, far from being a more or less random collection of Jesus material, each of the Gospels is clearly arranged to present a particular point of view. While it may be possible to *create* such arrangements orally (although there surely must be limits to what can be achieved without the aid of writing), it would be much harder to *preserve* them by oral transmission alone, so that one purpose of writing might be to fix a particular configuration of the Jesus tradition that interprets it in a particular

---

[15] Werner H. Kelber, *The Oral and the Written Gospel: The Hermeneutics of Speaking and Writing in the Synoptic Tradition, Mark, Paul and Q* (Voices in Performance and Text; Bloomington and Indianapolis: Indiana University Press, 1997), 90–131; Erhardt Güttgemanns, *Candid Questions Concerning Form Criticism: A Methodological Sketch of the Fundamental Problematics of Form and Redaction Criticism* (Pittsburgh Theological Monograph Series, 26; ed. D. Y. Hadidian; tr. William. G. Doty; Pittsburgh, PA: Pickwick Press, 1979), 96–125, 196–9, 277–90; for a more detailed discussion see also Eric Eve, *Behind the Gospels: Understanding the Oral Tradition* (London: SPCK, 2013), 47–65.

[16] For a discussion of how ancient memory techniques could have been employed to fix Mark's order in oral performance, see Whitney Shiner, 'Memory Technology and the Composition of Mark' in R. A. Horsley, J. A. Draper and J. M. Foley (eds), *Performing the Gospel: Orality, Memory and Mark* (Minneapolis: Fortress Press, 2006), 147–65.

[17] See Ruth Finnegan, *Oral Poetry: Its Nature, Significance and Social Context* (Bloomington and Indianapolis: Indiana University Press, 1992), 126–33, 258–9.

way, and this is something that someone might reasonably suppose it was important to do.

Another possible reason for writing a Gospel might be to lend it additional weight. How far this would have been the case is admittedly unclear. While we tend to give more weight to something we see in print than to something we merely hear, we cannot simply assume that the first-century Church would have preferred manuscript to speech in the same way. The Roman world of the first century was becoming familiar with a book culture in which some prestige could attach to authoring a work that was well received, but this was more applicable to the circles of the literary elite than to the social level of the early Church, and the Gospels were plainly not written in order to gain prestige in elite circles. On the other hand, as we have already noted, the primitive Church would have been familiar with the authority accorded the written Scriptures in Judaism, so the Church may have been ready to accord authority to written texts it perceived as 'biblical *bioi*', accounts of its founder clearly related to the biblical narrative. Even if this was not the case, the comparative rarity of writing could have lent weight to something that was written down, especially in an environment where writing was often associated with authority and learning.

It is less likely, however, that the Gospel writings were intended as purely symbolic, on analogy with Torah scrolls which were more objects to be venerated than texts to be read.[18] The early Church's rapid adoption of the codex in preference to the scroll suggests a pragmatic rather than a symbolic orientation towards its texts. A Gospel manuscript as a physical, visible, tangible object may nevertheless have had *some* symbolic cultural significance for the early Christian Church.

A different kind of reason that might be offered for writing the Gospels is to preserve the tradition at a time when the eyewitnesses were dying out. A frequent criticism of this explanation is that the Gospels do not simply preserve tradition (at the very least they interpret it) and that their purpose does not seem to be primarily historical.[19] The suggestion nevertheless gains some support from Jan Assmann's distinction between communicative memory and cultural memory and his notion of a *Traditionsbruch* (rupture in tradition). By 'communicative memory' Assmann means the memory of persons and events passed on by word of mouth at first or second hand, a process that can last no more than a hundred years at most. After that, if memory of these persons or events is to be preserved at all, it can only be so in the form of 'cultural memory'. In societies with writing, cultural memory inevitably includes committing material to writing. Without writing, a society can have no collective memory save of the recent past that lies within living memory and the primary, mythical past.

---

[18] Catherine Hezser, *Jewish Literacy in Roman Palestine* (Texts and Studies in Ancient Judaism, 81; Tübingen: Mohr Siebeck, 2001), 497–8.

[19] See in particular Werner H. Kelber, *Imprints, Voiceprints and Footprints of Memory: Collected Essays of Werner Kelber* (Resources for Biblical Study, 74; Atlanta: SBL, 2013), 13–14, 40.

Why write a Gospel?

This does not mean, however, that a society will typically wait for a hundred years before committing anything to writing. According to Assmann, there is normally a *Traditionsbruch* after about 40 years, which often precipitates the production of written texts. This is typically brought about by some kind of crisis that ruptures oral tradition and threatens group identity. The crisis could just be the passing of the generation to whom the originating events are part of living memory, but it could also be something more catastrophic such as, in the case of primitive Christianity, the crucifixion, the Neronian persecution, or the destruction of Jerusalem and the Temple.[20] If the usual datings for the crucifixion (around 30 CE) and the writing of Mark's Gospel (around 70 CE) are correct, then they would correlate well with Assmann's period of 40 years.

Assmann further proposes that texts that come to have primary significance for cultural memory tend to have either a *formative* or a *normative* function (or both of these functions).[21] The formative function is to provide a myth of origins answering such questions as what the community exists for and how it came to be, while the normative function is to provide guidance for the present by describing, illustrating and encouraging appropriate behaviour. Both functions are crucial to community identity, which is also a central concern of collective memory, a topic to which we shall return in Chapter 6.

While Assmann's observations are illuminating, they do not answer the question why anyone in particular would write a Gospel unless one subscribes to an implausible model of sociological determinism. The fact that a *Traditionsbruch* typically occurs after 40 years is not itself an explanation for why Mark (or his amanuensis) picked up his pen sometime around 70 CE, or indeed, why anyone should have done so, let alone which particular crisis the writer would have been responding to. While holding that Assmann's concept of a *Traditionsbruch* may form part of the explanation of why Mark wrote, Chris Keith has accordingly proposed that Assmann's notion of the *zerdehnte Situation* (expanded situation) also needs to be factored into the account.[22] 'Expanded situation' refers to the repeated communication of cultural texts (that is, texts with normative and

---

[20] Jan Assmann, *Cultural Memory and Early Civilization: Writing, Remembrance, and Political Imagination* (tr. David Henry Wilson; Cambridge: Cambridge University Press, 2011), 34–41. Cf. Werner H. Kelber, 'The Works of Memory: Christian Origins as MnemoHistory – A Response' in Alan Kirk and Tom Thatcher (eds), *Memory, Tradition, and Text: Uses of the Past in Early Christianity* (SBL Semeia Studies, 52; ed. G. A. Yee; Leiden; Boston: Brill, 2005), 221–48 (244); reprinted in Werner H. Kelber, *Imprints, Voiceprints and Footprints of Memory: Collected Essays of Werner Kelber* (Resources for Biblical Study, 74; Atlanta: SBL, 2013), 265–96 (290).

[21] Jan Assmann, *Religion and Cultural Memory* (tr. Rodney Livingstone; Stanford, CA: Stanford University Press, 2006), 38, 104.

[22] Chris Keith, 'Prolegomena on the Textualization of Mark's Gospel: Manuscript Culture, the Extended Situation, and the Emergence of the Written Gospel' in Tom Thatcher (ed.), *Memory and Identity in Ancient Judaism and Early Christianity: A Conversation with Barry Schwartz* (Semeia Studies, 78; ed. G. O. West; Atlanta: SBL, 2014), 161–86 (170–8).

formative significance) across time and space. A purely oral culture can institutionalize this by means of oral tradition, typically in the form of rituals and festivals that require the presence of memory specialists as performers of the tradition and the co-presence of an audience at the same time and place. Committing cultural texts to writing frees the communication of cultural messages from the cycle of rituals and the need for co-presence, making cultural texts more generally accessible; one still needs someone capable of reading, but, providing a competent reader is available, performances of the tradition are no longer tied to particular times and places. A written text is thus likely to prove more effective at stabilizing group identity and communicating its formative and normative messages over time (and space).[23]

At first sight this may seem to be simply repeating our initial suggestion that writing something down helped to preserve it in a relatively fixed form and to transmit it to other places. That, however, was primarily a thesis about *storage* while Assmann's notion of the expanded situation is primarily about *communication*, although the two are clearly linked.

In sum, then, the principal reasons for first committing a Gospel to writing are likely to have included the desire to fix a particular interpretation of the Jesus tradition in a form that was less susceptible to change, to disseminate this interpretation among a number of churches and to give added authority to this interpretation through the symbolic weight accorded to writing. Writing's ability to address the expanded situation more flexibly (in the sense of not being tied to specific occasions) than oral tradition will also have made it more effective in solidifying group identity in the wake of a rupture in tradition caused, say, by the passing of living witnesses to the originating events coupled with some catastrophic event such as the destruction of Jerusalem. Whereas we cannot entirely rule out an evangelistic aim, the primary purposes of the Gospels are likely to have been formative and normative, roles well suited to the genre of the Gospels as biblical *bioi* and their clear relation to the sacred Scriptures of Israel. A subsidiary aim, which cannot be developed further here, may have been to counter elements of the surrounding Graeco-Roman culture (and in particular, Roman imperial ideology), which may have been more effectively achieved through the use of written texts for the kinds of reason adumbrated above.[24] To put this in terms that will be taken up in Chapter 6, the principal reason for writing a Gospel will have been to solidify collective memory and communal identity.

---

[23] Assmann, *Religion*, 103–14.

[24] On the possible countering of imperial claims in Mark, see, e.g., Downing, *Doing Things with Words*, 133–51; and Eric Eve, 'Spit in Your Eye: The Blind Man of Bethsaida and the Blind Man of Alexandria', *NTS* 54 (2008), 1–17.

Writing as response to other writing

So far we have considered why a Gospel may have been written in the first place, but once at least one written Gospel existed, it is likely to have been a significant factor in provoking the writing of other Gospels. On the assumption of Markan priority we may suppose that Matthew became at least generally familiar with Mark. He may then have wished to promote an interpretation of the Jesus tradition that he believed to be more suitable for sustaining the identity of his own community (or that of the Church as a whole),[25] in part by addressing some of the shortcomings he perceived in Mark. To achieve this he would probably have felt it necessary to write another text in order to compete on equal terms. Even supposing Matthew were able to come up with a compelling oral performance that both incorporated and reinterpreted Mark, it would be almost impossible to perpetuate that performance in competition with a written text, and if the reasons for writing Mark had been to lend it the authority of a written text, to fix a particular narrative rendering of the tradition and to address an expanded situation, then Matthew's version would also need to be written in order to compete with it.

In fact, Matthew probably aimed at not just competing with Mark but replacing it, as, for example, David Sim has argued.[26] This is suggested by the fact that Matthew incorporates most of the content of Mark, in a way that could easily have rendered Mark's Gospel redundant (as it very nearly became), while arguably retaining a great deal of whatever authority and prestige Mark's Gospel may previously have attained through its incorporation into his own text. Matthew does not merely expand Mark through the use of material he obtained from other sources (such as the hypothetical Q), as if his sole aim had been to supplement Mark's narrative with teaching material he happened to come across elsewhere. By rearranging some of Mark's material and mixing it with his own, Matthew produces a substantially different account with substantially different emphases, even while following the broad outline of Mark's narrative.

For example, Matthew's text lays much greater stress on adherence to the Mosaic law as reinterpreted by Jesus' teaching, on the content of that teaching and on the threat of eschatological sanctions for failing to obey that teaching. While the disciples in Matthew are by no means infallible, compared with the Markan disciples they are more obviously models for following Jesus. Conversely, the polemic against the Jewish authorities is greatly sharpened. By adding birth and

---

[25] Throughout this book the term 'community' will be used in a loose sense to denote the group or groups of believers with which an Evangelist identified and/or was in contact.

[26] David C. Sim, 'Matthew's Use of Mark: Did Matthew Intend to Supplement or to Replace His Primary Source?', *NTS* 57 (2011), 176–92.

infancy narratives Matthew sets out his theological stall from the start much more clearly than Mark (as well as conforming his account more closely to the expectations of the *bios* genre). In particular Matthew firmly places his account in the context of the story of God's dealings with Israel and presents Jesus as both new Moses and true Israel who is son of God both by virtue of his obedience to his heavenly Father and of the authority the Father grants him. By adding a final resurrection appearance Matthew not only rounds off the oddly open-ended Markan account but makes the call to ongoing mission and obedience far more explicit. Matthew's written Gospel thus responds to Mark's by absorbing it and reconfiguring it to Matthew's own ends.

Luke's Gospel is a more explicit response to previous texts, since he mentions the existence of 'many' previous narratives in his opening verse (Luke 1.1). While he does not go on to offer any explicit criticism of these previous attempts, the fact that 'it seemed good' for him 'to write an orderly account' is surely an implicit criticism, since if Luke thought that one or more of the previous accounts was completely satisfactory, he would have seen no reason to write another one of his own. This remains the case even on the assumption that Luke planned a two-volume work from the beginning, since if Luke had been completely satisfied with Mark (say) he would not have needed to rewrite it just so he could follow it with Acts.

Luke's response to Mark is in some respects different from Matthew's, and in others remarkably similar. While, like Matthew, he seems content more or less to follow the Markan outline, he uses rather less of Mark than does Matthew and keeps his other material more distinct from his Markan source. His emphases are very different from Matthew's, famously showing particular care for the poor and for women in his Gospel, and interest in the Gentile mission in Acts. Perhaps as part of his concern to give an 'orderly account' he largely delays any hint of a Gentile mission until Acts, which may in part explain his suppression of the material in Mark 6.45—8.26. Like Matthew, on the other hand, he starts with birth and infancy narratives that clearly situates his own account as a continuation of the story of God's dealings with Israel, although unlike Matthew he seems to take 1 Samuel rather than Genesis–Exodus as the jumping-off point for his biblical linkage, and unlike Matthew he adopts a Septuagintal style to reinforce that link.

This is not the place to discuss whether the differences (and occasional similarities) between the Matthean and Lukan infancy narratives suggest Luke's independence of Matthew or his aggressive rewriting of Matthew, although if it is the latter it would suggest that Luke's use of Matthew was rather different from his use of Mark. The main point to note here is that Luke's response to Mark was rather different from Matthew's response to Mark. Matthew almost totally absorbs Mark; Luke uses Mark more selectively. Matthew seems to have been trying to replace Mark; and it could well be that Luke was too;[27] but if Luke knew Matthew, then it may have been Matthew's Gospel he was more concerned to displace.[28]

Whether or not John was responding to Mark (or any of the other Gospels) as a written text is harder to decide. The fact that John clearly did not use Mark in the way that Matthew and Luke did does not in itself show that John was not responding to Mark as a written text, whether with the intention of displacing Mark or of supplementing it. Sim argues that John was trying to displace Mark on the basis that he used its contents so sparingly and replaced them with many of his own traditions, but this argument is in some tension with Sim's appeal to Matthew's and Luke's inclusion of a great deal of Markan material as an argument for their wish to displace Mark. If both the inclusion and the exclusion of a sizeable proportion of a source can be used as evidence for a desire to displace that source, then it is hard to see what might count as evidence against. Thus while Sim makes a strong case in relation to Matthew and Luke, it may be more plausible to see John as writing to supplement Mark, as Richard Bauckham has argued.[29]

The fact that John produced a work in the broadly similar genre of biblical *bios* would seem to be an argument in favour of John's familiarity with at least one other work in this genre.[30] The question whether John was in some sense responding to one or more of the Synoptic Gospels is independent of whether he used a substantial body of distinctively Johannine tradition; the main issue here is whether John's knowledge of one or more written Gospels may have formed part of his motivation to write, again so that his version could compete on equal terms with the others.

Other canonical Gospels may not have been the only written texts our Evangelists were responding to.[31] That several non-canonical gospels also existed is attested both by surviving fragments and by patristic references. It is also suggested by Luke's mention of 'many' predecessors, unless this is simply a rhetorical flourish (or a conventional way of indicating the importance of his chosen topic). Thus, for example, Mark may not have been the only gospel Matthew was responding

---

[27] So also Sim, 'Matthew's Use', 188–90.

[28] John C. Poirier, 'Delbert Burkett's Defence of Q' in John C. Poirier and Jeffrey Peterson (eds), *Marcan Priority without Q: Explorations in the Farrer Hypothesis* (LNTS, 455; London: Bloomsbury T. & T. Clark, 2015), 191–225 (208–9); Eric Franklin, *Luke: Interpreter of Paul, Critic of Matthew* (JSNTSup, 92; Sheffield: JSOT Press, 1994), 169–73.

[29] Sim, 'Matthew's Use', 191–2; Richard Bauckham, 'John for Readers of Mark' in Richard Bauckham (ed.), *The Gospels for All Christians: Rethinking the Gospel Audiences* (Edinburgh: T. & T. Clark, 1998), 147–71.

[30] So Udo Schnelle, *The History and Theology of the New Testament Writings* (tr. M. Eugene Boring; London: SCM Press, 1998), 496–502.

[31] A point made forcefully by Francis Watson, *Gospel Writing: A Canonical Perspective* (Grand Rapids, MI and Cambridge: Eerdmans, 2013), 271–85.

to or hoping to displace, even though it was the one that most influenced his own composition.

Explicit reasons

Two of the Gospels, Luke and John, explicitly state why they were written. Our discussion of why the Gospels were written should therefore take a brief look at these statements.

According to John 20.30–31, Jesus did many other signs that were not recorded in John's Gospel, 'but these are written that you may believe that Jesus is the Christ, the Son of God, and that believing you may have life in his name'. Textual variants in the second of these verses make it unclear whether the word translated 'believe' was originally *pistuēte* (present subjunctive, meaning 'continue to believe') or *pistusēte* (aorist subjunctive, meaning 'come to believe'). The former would suggest that the primary motive for writing the Gospel was to confirm and strengthen the existing faith of its target audience, while the latter would suggest a more evangelistic motive. Either way, the motive for writing is said to be to promote life-giving faith in Jesus as Messiah and Son of God (rather, than, say providing historical information about him or supplying a convenient summary of his teaching). Yet even if this statement of intent can be taken at face value, it still does not explain why John chose to write a Gospel rather than, say, to promote life-giving faith through oral proclamation or organizing a missionary campaign.

The question why John chose to *write* a Gospel is discussed at some length in a monograph by Tom Thatcher.[32] Thatcher takes the statement at John 20.30–31 to mean that John's reasons for writing were rhetorical as opposed to archival, in other words that rather than writing simply to preserve traditions about Jesus, John intended to use the prestige of a written book to promote his own view of how Jesus should be interpreted.[33] According to Thatcher, John would have seen no reason to write an account of Jesus' life and teaching simply to preserve the traditions about him, since John subscribed to a 'charismatic' view of memory, namely that it was the Holy Spirit that acted as guarantor of the way Jesus was remembered in the community (John 14.26). This, however, left him vulnerable to the claims of the 'Antichrists' (identified from the Johannine Epistles, which Thatcher believes predated the Gospel), who could claim the authority of the Spirit for their new (and in John's view, heretical) teaching. Given his own belief in Spirit-inspired memory, he could not directly attack his opponents' seemingly similar appeal to such memory.

---

[32] Tom Thatcher, *Why John WROTE a Gospel: Jesus – Memory – History* (Louisville, KY: Westminster John Knox Press, 2006).

[33] Thatcher, *Why John WROTE*, 37–49.

John's solution was to write what Thatcher several times refers to as a 'history book', meaning a supposedly 'objective' account of what Jesus had said and done. Such a solution would have conferred a number of advantages from John's perspective. It would have fixed a particular version of the tradition in a medium that was far less flexible than community memory. Moreover, by foregrounding the words and deeds of Jesus it narrates, it would have effectively silenced the rest (Thatcher reads John 20.30 and 21.25 as declaring the remainder of the Jesus tradition irrelevant). Furthermore a 'history book' would have the advantage of appearing to give a specific, objective account (thereby hiding the historian's agenda) while at the same time being hard to challenge since few people could actually read it. John may also have intended the production of his Gospel to form a watershed, dividing a past in which the oral tradition might be debated and reshaped from a future in which the interpretation of his text would become the main focus of debate.[34] Finally, as intimated above, John could have been relying on the symbolic value accorded a written text (especially if he was writing for a community familiar with the weight given to the Jewish Scriptures). The very fact that the Gospel existed would allow people to appeal to its authority in a way analogous to that in which many modern people appeal to the American Constitution or the Magna Carta without actually being all that familiar with their contents.

One may want to question several of the details of this thesis. One difficulty is that the (unspecified) beliefs of the 'Antichrists' are nowhere in evidence in John's narrative. John's Gospel seems primarily concerned to assert its view of Jesus in the face of opposition from 'the Jews'; John's principal opponents as reflected in his Gospel appear to be unbelieving Jews and an unbelieving world, not heretics in his own community, which would make his Gospel an odd response to whatever the Antichrists were proclaiming. One may also wonder how John's Gospel could counter the threat of the Antichrists' 'heretical' teaching if hardly anyone knew what it said, even given the modern parallels just cited. After all, John chose to write a narrative giving a very particular account of Jesus, not some random scribble which could just as well have been a washing bill; presumably the content of what John wrote *mattered* to John, or he would not have taken such care in presenting such a distinctive portrait of Jesus. Moreover, the fact that not many people could read the text for themselves did not mean that they could not have become broadly familiar with its contents through hearing it read, since this was a common way of disseminating written culture throughout the Roman Empire.

Yet despite such reservations, much of Thatcher's proposal remains valuable. His discussion of memory will be left until Chapter 6. Whatever reservations one

---

[34] Thatcher, *Why John WROTE*, 145–55.

may have about the term 'history book' to describe John, the fact remains that by committing his Gospel to writing, John would have put it in a form that was as fixed as he could possibly make it, and far more fixed than oral tradition could achieve. Even if one rejects the idea that John was responding to the Antichrists or that the Johannine Epistles preceded the Gospel, Thatcher could still be right about the basic mechanism that precipitated the writing of the Gospel. One might hypothesize, perhaps, that the crisis John's community faced was the temptation to lapse back into Judaism, or at least to abandon many of John's higher claims for Jesus in response to pressure from a more traditional segment of the Jewish community; potential lapsers within the Johannine community could still be appealing to the guidance of the Spirit ('charismatic memory') for their views, and John would then still be faced with the same type of problem Thatcher describes, even if the precise details of the precipitating crisis would be different.

Again, while Thatcher appears to be trying to have it both ways by suggesting that the point of putting the Gospel in writing was to fix its contents while leaving people vague about what those contents were so they were not in a position to challenge them (which might seem self-defeating), one could see how that might work in a situation in which a few literate people in positions of leadership were well acquainted with the contents of the Gospel while the remainder were largely dependent on this literate minority to learn about its contents. A text known mainly through oral performance rather than close literary study can leave a strong overall impression on people who do not know its contents in detail. For example, Shakespeare's *Richard III* has succeeded in propagating an image of its eponymous anti-hero as a hunchbacked, scheming tyrant who usurps the throne and murders his nephews, but few people whose image of Richard has been shaped by Shakespeare's play could quote much more from it than 'A horse, a horse, my kingdom for a horse' and perhaps 'Now is the winter of our discontent made glorious summer by this sun of York', let alone give an adequate summary of its plot. A text can thus have a widespread effect on people who are not that familiar with its actual contents.

Many of Thatcher's suggestions echo those made earlier in this chapter, namely that reasons for writing a Gospel could include making a particular view of Jesus more permanent and capitalizing on the authority given to a written text, especially in a community used to the authority of written Scriptures. John 5.39 may be apposite here: Jesus tells his Jewish interlocutors that they search the Scriptures in the belief that there they will discover eternal life, whereas, according to John 20.31, the gaining of life is precisely the purpose of his own writing.

The statement in Luke's preface is more complex, and has given rise to more discussion than can possibly be covered here, a discussion complicated by widely varying scholarly assessments of Luke's literary and rhetorical abilities. At first sight, it looks as if Luke's intentions are both more historical and more literary than those of the other Gospel writers, both on account of the relative formality of the prose in Luke 1.1–4 and because of the content of Luke–Acts. Considered as a two-volume work, Luke–Acts reads no longer so much as a biblical *bios* as a cross between biblical and Hellenistic history, although views differ on which is the dominant influence. By delaying any material relating to the Gentile mission until Acts and by presenting the earthly Jesus somewhat as a miracle-working prophet, Luke reverses the trend found in Mark and even more strongly in Matthew to overlay the earthly Jesus with the risen Lord, thus making the Lukan Jesus look more like a figure of the past, an impression strengthened by the continuation of the story in Acts. Moreover, the undertaking in Luke 1.1–4 to write an orderly account based on eyewitness tradition (as well, perhaps, as previous written narratives), in order to present the dedicatee with a truthful version of what he has previously been informed about, might seem to suggest both an historical motive and an historical method – that is, an ancient historical method with a preference for autopsy (eyewitness accounts).[35]

Loveday Alexander has, however, argued that Luke's prologue has more in common with the prologues of ancient technical or 'scientific' writing than those of ancient histories, and that when it is examined closely it turns out to be both conventional and uninformative; it says virtually nothing about what subject matter Luke is going to tackle, but simply that he is writing an orderly account to confirm what Theophilus already knows.[36] But these contentions have been disputed. Samuel Byrskog takes Alexander to task for concentrating on the word *autopsis* and its cognates (denoting eyewitness testimony), which she claims is more characteristic of technical writers than historians and so links Luke more with the former than the latter. Byrskog observes that the idea is clearly present in the writings of historians even when they do not use the word.[37]

Richard Bauckham further points to the usage of Polybius and Josephus as relevant parallels to Luke's use of *autoptai* (eyewitnesses) at Luke 1.2, and claims that from its context the word in Luke 'carries the historiographic meaning of people who witnessed firsthand the events of Luke's gospel story'.[38] Bauckham further refers to David Aune's suggestion that since the majority of ancient Greek histories have been lost, and since the Greek histories that do survive were written by persons of higher social status than Luke, Luke's preface may more

---

[35] See Samuel Byrskog, *Story as History – History as Story: The Gospel Tradition in the Context of Ancient Oral History* (Leiden and Boston: Brill, 2002), 228–34.

[36] Loveday Alexander, *The Preface to Luke's Gospel: Literary Convention and Social Context in Luke 1.1–4 and Acts 1.1* (paperback 2005 edn; SNTSMS, 78; ed. Margaret E. Thrall; Cambridge: Cambridge University Press, 1993), esp. 200–1.

[37] Byrskog, *Story as History*, 48–9.

[38] Richard Bauckham, *Jesus and the Eyewitnesses: The Gospels as Eyewitness Testimony* (Grand Rapids and Cambridge: Eerdmans, 2006), 119.

closely resemble those of the hundreds of mediocre histories that have perished than the few elite ones that have survived.[39]

John Moles has argued that the language of Luke's preface most closely resembles that of the Greek decree and thereby evokes Greek classical historiography.[40] Moles recognizes the presence of some 'scientific' language in the preface, but suggests that it was not so unusual for historians to employ such language. The use of decree-like language (which might more typically be found on an inscription) would further serve to emphasize the monumental, durable and available character of the work (in other words, both its symbolic weight as a written text and its ability to function in an expanded situation). The decree form also suggests, in Moles' view, that Luke is presenting Christianity as a philosophical *politeia* in contrast to the Roman political and Greek philosophical *politeiai*, so that the switch to a more 'Jewish' (or biblical) mode of narration following the more classical preface is a way of emphasizing the importance of the (seemingly parochial but in fact universally significant) Jewish–Christian world-view.

This switch does not, however, prevent (Moles claims) allusions to Thucydides and Livy in the body of the narrative (as well as the preface). The promise of *asphaleia* ('truth' or 'safety') in Luke 1.4 then functions to assert the superiority of his narrative both over that of the imperial domination celebrated in Roman historiography and over the efforts of his Christian predecessors. In contrast to Alexander, then, Moles sees the Lukan preface as a masterpiece of classical historiography. While this high evaluation of Luke's ability may well prove controversial, it finds further support from recent studies by Michael Martin and Heather Gorman that emphasize the rhetorical skill with which Luke structured his composition in accordance with progymnastic topic lists (preliminary instruction for both rhetoric and prose writing).[41]

On Alexander's view Luke's preface suggests that he is a professional such as a doctor, architect or engineer, while Moles' view would make Luke the beneficiary of a more advanced rhetorical education. Luke's background may well have been much as Alexander suggests, for while Luke–Acts has more narrative shaping and more rhetorical intent than the kind of technical literature or anecdotal collections that are more typically the literary deposits of technical school settings

[39] Bauckham, *Eyewitnesses*, 118, citing David Aune, 'Luke 1:1–4: Historical or Scientific *Prooimion?*' in A. Christopherson, C. Clausen, J. Frey and B. Longenecker (eds), *Paul, Luke and the Graeco-Roman World: Essays in Honour of Alexander J. M. Wedderburn* (JSNTSup, 217; Sheffield: Sheffield Academic Press, 2002), 142.

[40] John Moles, 'Luke's Preface: The Greek Decree, Classical Historiography and Christian Redefinitions', *NTS* 57 (2011), 461–82.

[41] Martin, 'Progymnastic Topic Lists', 36–41; Heather M. Gorman, 'Crank or Creative Genius? How Ancient Rhetoric Makes Sense of Luke's Order' in John C. Poirier and Jeffrey Peterson (eds), *Marcan Priority without Q: Explorations in the Farrer Hypothesis* (LNTS, 455; London: Bloomsbury T. & T. Clark, 2015), 62–81.

(on which see further Chapter 4 below), *pace* Moles, Luke hardly writes to the standard that might be expected of someone who had undergone a full tertiary education in rhetoric. Of all the Evangelists, Luke's method of working is the most likely to resemble that of elite literary authors, but he is not among their number.

How far all this advances our understanding of Luke's reasons for writing is another matter. Alexander does not dispute Aune's view that Luke–Acts is intended as a work of history.[42] While Thatcher sees the Lukan preface as stressing an archival rather than a rhetorical function,[43] this could itself be a rhetorical move designed to give Luke's work the same air of historical 'objectivity' that Thatcher suggests John was aiming for. Aune sees Luke–Acts as presenting Jesus and the Apostles as paradigms of Christian life and thought; when Luke wrote, Christianity needed definition, identity and legitimation, and Luke–Acts provided all three, which more or less takes us back to the formative and normative functions described by Assmann.[44]

Conclusions

Matthew, Mark, Luke and John are no longer around to tell us precisely why they wrote, and there are limits to how far we can enter into the minds of people who died 20 centuries ago and about whom we know very little. A discussion of why they wrote their Gospels is thus bound to be at least partly speculative, and risks crediting them with more media awareness than they may have in fact possessed. That said, the following conclusions all seem reasonably probable: whatever more specific reasons the Evangelists had for writing what they did, reasons for *writing* will have included a desire to give relative fixity to their form of the Christian message, to propagate that form of the message through time and space, and to use the prestige accorded to written texts to lend authority to their own views. Moreover, each of the Evangelists was concerned to promote their particular answers to such key questions as: Who are we? Why are we here? What are we to believe? What should we do? Or, to borrow Aune's terminology, the Gospels were written to provide a sense of Christian identity, some models of Christian life and thought, and legitimation of their authors' notion of the true form of the faith.

Absent from this list is any suggestion that the Evangelists wrote to enhance their own literary reputations. With the questionable exception of the Fourth Gospel (depending on what one makes of the Beloved Disciple), the Evangelists

---

[42] Aune, *Literary Environment*, 77–8.
[43] Thatcher, *Why John WROTE*, 43.
[44] Aune, *Literary Environment*, 136–7.

all hide behind a cloak of impersonal anonymity. This may have been due more to a rhetorical strategy than any great sense of modesty: the very impersonality of the Gospel narratives makes them appear all the more objective, not simply one writer's view but simply the way it was. Moreover, while the Gospels do not appear to be composite works in the same way as the book of Isaiah, say, their composition was probably rather more of a joint effort than would be the case for a modern monograph or novel, as we shall be exploring further in Chapter 4.

The lack of any obvious literary ambition on the part of the Evangelists may be significant for their method of writing, but there is an ambiguity in the term 'literary' here. To the extent that the Gospels were intended to reach a relatively wide audience (more than just a small circle) and to influence people's beliefs and behaviour, the Gospels may be said to be 'literary' rather than documentary. Moreover, to the extent that Matthew and Luke both improve on Mark's style (on the thesis of Markan priority), or at least write better Greek than Mark, they may be said to be more literary than Mark. To that limited extent the Evangelists may be credited with at least some kind of literary ambitions. In a high culture sense, however, the Gospels would not have been (and subsequently were not) well regarded as 'literature' in comparison with the works of elite Graeco-Roman authors. We may assume that they were never intended to compete at this level and that the Evangelists were not seeking any kind of reputation as authors. This being so, we cannot assume that they would have gone about the task of composition in precisely the same way as elite authors typically did, although Luke may have aspired to. Thus, when we come in Chapter 4 to investigate how the Evangelists may have gone about composing their works, the methods of elite Graeco-Roman authors will be considered alongside two other models. But before we discuss how the Evangelists worked we should first consider what they had to work with, and this will form the subject of the next chapter.

3

The Evangelists' raw materials

Assuming the Evangelists did not simply invent their accounts from scratch (which virtually no one supposes), they must have got their material from somewhere: but where? The answers typically given to this question usually include some combination of written sources and oral tradition, but could potentially also include eyewitnesses, the Evangelists' own imagination and the creative use of Jewish Scriptures. As the present chapter will argue, alongside and underpinning all these resources will have been the Evangelists' use of memory. The discussion of compositional techniques will be left to the next chapter; here we shall confine ourselves to reviewing their raw materials and the more mechanical aspects of their use. Note, incidentally, that we are speaking of 'materials' rather than 'sources', since the latter term has potentially misleading implications, not least that the Evangelists employed their materials in the manner a detached scholar might use an historical source, rather than being existentially engaged with their material as a stream of living tradition in the context of communal memory.

Written materials

Broadly speaking, the written sources potentially used by the Evangelists may be divided into two classes: other complete Gospels (for example, Matthew's and Luke's use of Mark, and possibly Q, on the most common view of the Synoptic Problem), and more fragmentary material, such as collections of controversy stories or miracle stories sometimes thought to be used by Mark, sayings collections, or notes written down by interested persons.[1] At this point, however, we are not concerned to specify *which* written sources were used by any of the Evangelists, but rather what might be implied by the claim that they used any.

Assuming for example that Matthew used Mark as a substantial source for his own Gospel, what might such use actually have amounted to? Until the end of the last century it would be fair to say that, with one or two exceptions, most scholars effectively assumed that Matthew would have worked with Mark more or less as we would work with a modern printed text. Of course it has always

---

[1] See, e.g., Paul J. Achtemeier, 'Toward the Isolation of Pre-Markan Miracle Catenae', *JBL* 89 (1970), 265–91; Francis Watson, *Gospel Writing: A Canonical Perspective* (Grand Rapids, MI and Cambridge: Eerdmans, 2013), 249–85; Alan Millard, *Reading and Writing in the Time of Jesus* (The Biblical Seminar, 69; Sheffield: Sheffield Academic Press, 2000), 185–229.

been understood that any copy of Mark used by Matthew would have been hand-written and that first-century manuscript scrolls and codices are rather different from modern printed books, but the predominant assumption has been that Matthew worked with a copy of Mark open in front of him, consulting it by eye and then choosing to copy or edit its wording much as we would if we were working from a printed text.

This way of viewing the Evangelists' working practices has come under increasing challenge both from studies of how ancient authors actually worked and from a questioning of print-culture assumptions.[2] For present purposes it will be helpful to start from an essay by Andrew Gregory on what literary dependence between two Gospels might actually mean.[3]

Gregory's essay is primarily concerned with the question of literary dependence in relation to the Synoptic Problem. He points out that literary dependence need not necessarily mean that an author has sight of a text on which he is dependent while composing his own text. He considers the possibility that similar passages in synoptic parallels may be due to the use of a common, stable oral tradition, but suggests that such a model need play only a subsidiary role in a theory of synoptic relationships. While acknowledging that we lack precise criteria to determine how far the wording of two texts must agree to necessitate a literary relation between them as opposed to dependence on common oral tradition, he cites work suggesting that extensive verbatim memorization of primary oral material is rare.[4]

Gregory next points out that, particularly in antiquity, use of a source text did not necessarily mean having it open in front of one as one wrote, but could also mean using it from memory. Gregory cites the work of Christopher Pelling on Plutarch to the effect that while ancient authors read widely before composing their own work, they tended to follow only one source at a time (in the sense of having visual contact with it), relying on their memory for the use of other sources. Gregory also cites the work of Jocelyn Small and Mary Carruthers noting, among other things, the memory feats managed by some ancients and the role memory played in ancient (and mediaeval) literary composition.[5] As we shall see in Chapter 5, ancient and mediaeval authors often knew all their sources by heart

---

[2] For the former, see, e.g., R. A. Derrenbacker, *Ancient Compositional Practices and the Synoptic Problem* (BETL, 186; Leuven: Peeters-Leuven, 2005).

[3] Andrew Gregory, 'What Is Literary Dependence?' in Paul Foster, Andrew Gregory, John S. Kloppenborg and J. Verheyden (eds), *New Studies in the Synoptic Problem* (BETL, 139; Leuven: Leuven University Press, 2011), 87–114.

[4] Gregory, 'Literary Dependence', 93.

[5] Gregory, 'Literary Dependence', 95–103; Jocelyn Penny Small, *Wax Tablets of the Mind: Cognitive Studies of Memory and Literacy in Classical Antiquity* (Abingdon: Routledge, 1997); Mary Carruthers, *The Book of Memory: A Study of Memory in Medieval Culture* (2nd edn; Cambridge Studies in Medieval Literature; Cambridge: Cambridge University Press, 2008).

(at least in terms of content, if not verbatim). It is thus possible that the Evangelists had memory command of all their written sources, and so made little or no use of direct eye contact with any of them while composing their own work.

One factor which could suggest this is that while it would be relatively simple for an author to follow a scroll of Mark in Markan sequence (say) while composing his own work, it would be rather more cumbersome to access Mark out of sequence as Matthew would have to have done, for example, in composing Matthew chapters 8 and 9 (which collect together a number of miracle stories taken from various places in Mark). While it would not be impossible for an author already familiar with Mark to track down these various miracle stories from different parts of the scroll, it would not have been entirely straightforward given the lack of visual aids to doing so in a typical scroll, so anyone already conversant with the text of Mark would have found it easier to work from memory, especially in a culture which placed little value on the modern scholarly habit of checking references to ensure exact quotation, and in which reliance on memory was commonplace. The process would be eased if Matthew were using a codex of Mark (which cannot be ruled out), but while a codex, being in the form of a modern book, facilitates random access rather better than a scroll, it still lacks the kind of visual aids we have come to rely on in modern printed books.

John Poirier has nevertheless argued that the difficulty of consulting physical scrolls by eye has been exaggerated (in the context of defending the theoretical possibility of Michael Goulder's picture of Luke taking material from Matthew in reverse order by moving backwards through a scroll). Marking one's place in a scroll might not be all that difficult, especially if both ends roll together at the passage in question. Moreover, although there is good evidence that people in the first century did not use desks or tables to write on, this does not mean that they never used tables or lecterns to support their source texts.[6]

These arguments have been challenged in turn by Robert Derrenbacker, on the grounds that the example Poirier cites of one author (Clement of Alexandria) apparently using the text of another (Philo) in reverse order does not stand up to scrutiny, and that the evidence of a supposed 'table-like structure' in one of the rooms discovered at Qumran is uncertain at best (although Poirier does adduce some other evidence to suggest the possible use of stands or tables to support reading materials). Moreover, even if a table or stand were used to support a writer's source texts, they would not be readily visible to the writer while he sat with the text he was writing on his knees.[7] This latter objection has

---

[6] John C. Poirier, 'The Roll, the Codex, the Wax Tablet and the Synoptic Problem', *JSNT* 35 (2012), 3–30.

[7] Robert A. Derrenbacker, 'Texts, Tables and Tablets: A Response to John C. Poirier', *JSNT* 35 (2013), 308–87.

considerable force for authors who act as their own scribes, but is irrelevant for anyone who dictated their composition to someone else, since such authors could be standing or sitting at a table inspecting their sources while dictating. But at this point the issue of stands and tables becomes secondary, since authors who dictate would be free to hold a source text in their hands. The difficulty of consulting sources by eye in the act of composing may thus not be as great as the typical ancient writing posture might suggest.

It should thus not be denied that the Evangelists could have consulted written sources (including notes, sayings collections and the like) from time to time in the course of composition. The point being made here is rather that the use of written sources does not *necessarily* imply that the Evangelists had eye contact with those sources when they wrote. Given what is known of the ancients' use of texts and their reliance on memory, compositional dependence on memory may well be a better default assumption than visual dependence on a written text constantly consulted during the process of composition, as will be argued more fully in Chapter 5.

Oral tradition

Strictly speaking, oral tradition is something handed down by word of mouth over several generations, usually in a form or setting particularly suited to the purpose (for example, words crafted into poetic or other memorable form and performed on particular ritual or ceremonial occasions). In this strict sense, it is to be distinguished from oral history, which is the oral transmission of reminiscences either directly from an eyewitness or via one or two people broadly contemporary with those eyewitnesses (for example, stories my father told me about his father, who died when I was only two). When 'oral tradition' is suggested as a possible source for the Evangelists' compositions, it is often not entirely clear which of these two senses is meant, or whether it just means anything passed on by word of mouth in any form or situation whatsoever.

A definition of oral tradition that might be applicable to the Jesus tradition is material that is transmitted orally over a sustained period of time and that has achieved a measure of stability through being mnemonically crafted for that purpose. The language of the transmission of traditions found in Paul (together with supposedly pre-Pauline material found in Paul's letters, such as the tradition incorporated at 1 Corinthians 15.3–7) suggests the existence of some oral traditions of this sort, but these need not have been the only type of oral material with which the Evangelists were familiar or of which they made use. Loveday Alexander has suggested that anecdotes about Jesus' words and deeds may have been passed on in Christian 'schools' in a manner analogous to that in which

Hellenistic schools handled their traditions in order to promulgate both the teaching and the ethos of their founder.[8]

Whether in a strict or in some vaguer sense, oral tradition is instantiated only in performance. Oral transmission only occurs when one or more performers are actually speaking to an audience. The setting may be relatively formal, one in which a suitably authorized person performs a relatively stereotyped version of some part of the tradition to a receptive audience in a special setting (such as one of formal worship), or it may be completely informal, one person passing on his or her own reminiscences of the tradition to another in private conversation, or it may be something in between, such as a group discussion or teaching session. In any of these cases the performance will consist of rather more than the words as they appear when reduced to writing. Facial expression, gesture, bearing, intonation, pacing, pausing and the like all form essential parts of any oral performance. To take an example, someone performing Mark's Gospel orally need not be reliant on the words alone to characterize the people who appear in it, but would potentially have all the means of a good actor (mimicry, tone of voice, facial expression, gesture and the like) to bring all the different characters to life. An author making use of Mark in his or her own composition might be influenced not only by the words spoken but also by recollection of previous performances, the writer's understanding of Peter or Pilate (say) being strongly influenced by the way these characters had been performed, and not merely by the words attributed to them or used to describe their actions.

When oral tradition is proposed as a potential source for the Evangelists, there is presumably no implication that the Gospels were composed during an actual performance. What is envisaged is surely that the Evangelists employed their memory of oral performances, perhaps checking their own memories against that of their friends and collaborators as the need arose. Such memories may have taken several forms depending on what precisely was being recalled: a particular performance, a particular performance tradition or the impression left by a sequence of performances. In addition to the Evangelists' episodic memory of one or two particular performances may have been their semantic memory of the gist of one or more performances and of the ambient tradition in which they took place. These will in turn have been enmeshed in the collective memory of the Evangelist's community, a notion that will be explored more fully in Chapter 6.

In any case the Evangelists should not be seen as mere passive recipients of oral tradition; even if they were not performers of this tradition themselves (as some of them may well have been), they would surely have been heavily

---

[8] Loveday Alexander, 'Memory and Tradition in the Hellenistic Schools' in W. H. Kelber and S. Byrskog (eds), *Jesus in Memory: Traditions in Oral and Scribal Perspectives* (Waco: Baylor University Press, 2009), 113–53.

engaged in oral use of the material through teaching, discussion and debate. We should not fall into the trap of envisaging oral tradition as a one-way stream flowing from Jesus through the primitive Church only to be swallowed up by the Gospels. The Gospels were not the end products of the oral traditions that preceded them; rather they would have been composed in interaction with the traditions that enveloped them, and which they would have in turn influenced in their future course.

We might also question the form in which any oral tradition reached the Evangelists. The form-critical answer, which has become the default assumption of many New Testament scholars, is that the oral tradition originally circulated in the form of individual units such as *chreiai* (brief anecdotes), miracle stories, parables and other sayings, which may have coalesced over time into collections of like material; but there are reasons to question this model. An isolated parable, saying or miracle story of Jesus would have little point for an audience who had no idea who Jesus was. This might not matter so much for a performance to audiences familiar with other parts of the tradition, but that then presupposes a tradition of performances in which other parts of the tradition had been presented in a more or less coherent manner. Whether or not anyone had ever performed something like a complete story of Jesus' ministry prior to the composition of the first Gospel, it would be odd if no one had come up with some kind of rough outline (say along the lines of Acts 2.22–24, fleshed out in a bit more detail), or, indeed, if audiences were not left with some (if vague) impression of the overall course of Jesus' ministry, at least to the extent that he went around preaching and healing and teaching until he went up to Jerusalem where he was crucified and raised from the dead. It would be even stranger if the people who performed the Jesus tradition, and those who heard them, made no attempt to interpret its significance, so that it was left entirely to the Evangelists to supply their own interpretation independently of the tradition that preceded them.

It should not be supposed that oral tradition is some kind of uniform phenomenon that works in the same way in all times, places and cultures, and here it has been possible only to give the very briefest sketch of some of the issues it raises for the composition of the Gospels.[9] The main point to be borne in mind is that 'oral tradition' is intimately connected with memory.

Eyewitness testimony

The use of either written sources or oral tradition suggests authors who were at some remove from the events they describe. An alternative model might be that

---

[9] For fuller treatments see Eric Eve, *Behind the Gospels: Understanding the Oral Tradition* (London: SPCK, 2013) and Rafael Rodriguez, *Oral Tradition and the New Testament: A Guide for the Perplexed* (London and New York: Bloomsbury T. & T. Clark, 2014).

the Evangelists obtained their material directly from eyewitnesses. This appears to be suggested by the preface to Luke's Gospel (Luke 1.2) and by certain passages in John (John 19.35; 21.24). It also seems initially plausible on the basis that eyewitness testimony would surely have been preferred had it been available, and there seems to be no compelling chronological reason why it could not have been (particularly in the case of Mark).[10] Indeed, an ingenious case has been argued by Richard Bauckham for eyewitness sources behind the Gospels of Mark, Luke and John.[11]

Bauckham's work has not won general acceptance, however, and while Byrskog's more modest proposal concerning Mark (that it contains some pericopae derived from Peter's teaching) may have something to commend it, in practice Byrskog identifies only a few potential Petrine pericopae in Mark.[12] Moreover, little or nothing in the Gospels appears to have the character of eyewitness reminiscence. On Bauckham's theory what Mark had access to were the *chreiai* (pointed anecdotes) Peter used in preaching, suggesting material that had already been worked up for a particular use, and unless one sees the Evangelists as mere recorders of tradition any eyewitness material they received will have been further reworked in the interests of the Evangelists' design. What the Gospels contain is not eyewitness reminiscences of what Jesus liked for breakfast or the colour of his favourite cloak, but an account of words and deeds carefully shaped to perform formative and normative functions for church communities.

This suggests that if the Evangelists did have access to eyewitness testimony it would most likely have been in the form of hearing an eyewitness preach (as Papias supposes in the case of Mark and Peter). On this scenario, from the point of view of the process of Gospel composition it is hard to see how such testimony would differ greatly in kind from oral history or from memory. When it came to writing the Gospels, the Evangelists' own *use* of any eyewitness testimony to which they had access would have been similar to that of any other oral tradition, oral history or remembered material (or perhaps of any notes they had made). It would be different only if eyewitnesses were more directly involved in the process of composition, say by being available to an Evangelist for questioning along the lines of the preferred methods of the elite historians discussed by Byrskog, for at this point two additional factors would need to be taken into account: the memory of the eyewitnesses and the skill of the

---

[10] On the first point, see especially Samuel Byrskog, *Story as History – History as Story: The Gospel Tradition in the Context of Ancient Oral History* (Leiden and Boston: Brill, 2002), 64–107, 272–99.

[11] Richard Bauckham, *Jesus and the Eyewitnesses: The Gospels as Eyewitness Testimony* (Grand Rapids and Cambridge: Eerdmans, 2006).

[12] For criticisms of Bauckham see David R. Catchpole, 'On Proving Too Much: Critical Hesitations about Richard Bauckham's *Jesus and the Eyewitnesses*', *JSHJ* 6 (2008), 169–81; Stephen J. Patterson, 'Can You Trust a Gospel? A Review of Richard Bauckham's *Jesus and the Eyewitnesses*', *JSHJ* 6 (2008), 194–210; Eve, *Behind the Gospels*, 143–58. On Byrskog see Eve, *Behind the Gospels*, 135–43.

John the disciple?

Peter?

Evangelists in cross-examining them and formulating an account on the basis of their testimony.

It may be that the precise nature and extent of eyewitness material available to the Evangelists is no longer recoverable. That eyewitnesses played some part in initiating, transmitting and maintaining traditions about Jesus for at least some time after his death seems highly probable. That the Evangelists had *direct* access to the eyewitness testimony of major players in the Gospel story at the time they wrote is at best unprovable and perhaps unlikely given the nature of their accounts.

Imagination and invention

Another possible answer to the question of where the Evangelists obtained their raw material is that they may simply have made things up. For example, it seems likely that Matthew invented the story about the dead saints rising from their tombs and walking around Jerusalem after the resurrection (Matthew 27.52–53) since this account does not appear in his source and looks highly implausible. Similarly, the story of Peter's attempt to walk on the water (Matthew 14.28–31) looks suspiciously like a Matthean addition to the account of Jesus walking on the sea, just as the healing of the ear severed at Jesus' arrest (Luke 22.51) looks suspiciously like Luke's own contribution.

The possible use of the Evangelists' imagination nevertheless raises a number of questions. First, how can we be sure that it was the Evangelists who invented material of this sort rather than someone earlier? One might hazard a guess along redaction-critical lines, by reckoning as Matthean or Lukan embellishments whatever appears to be characteristic of Matthew or Luke, but there is a danger of circularity here (since one identifies what is characteristic of Matthew or Luke in part from their supposed embellishments). It cannot simply be assumed that what is characteristic of any Evangelist was unique to him, so that he is the only person who could have thought of it.

This leads to a second question: how far was any invented material the work of individuals? The point of the question is not to deny that one or more individual person's imaginative creativity would have been active at some point, but rather to question the extent to which potentially made-up materials in the Gospels might be the work of a single individual (the Evangelist) or the result of a group effort (a number or persons contributing ideas and hammering them out between them, for example, or an initial idea being continually reworked over a series of performances).

This in turn leads to a third question, namely what the Evangelists (or their sources) thought they were doing if they invented material, and what they expected to get away with. To give a concrete example, Rafael Rodriguez does not believe that the account of Jesus' inaugural sermon at Luke 4.16–30 is historical in the sense of being a factual account of an event that actually took place as described, but he does suggest that it was based on earlier traditions about Jesus and was thus in some sense appropriate to his memory.[13] In the context of Luke's Gospel, Jesus' sermon at Nazareth is seen as programmatic for his ministry. If Luke invented this incident from his own imagination, presumably his reason for doing so was to guide his target audience's understanding of Jesus. This might suggest that one important aim of such imaginative material was to interpret what was already there. This could well seem appropriate to people who understood truth not so much as strict correspondence with facts (the goal of positivist historiography) as bringing out the correct significance of events.[14]

The question whether and to what extent the Evangelists may have employed their imagination to invent (or radically reshape) their material is obviously related to the purposes for which they wrote. The Gospels hardly read as imaginative literature written for pure entertainment, so we should certainly not envisage the Evangelists indulging in the kind of creative storytelling a modern novelist might, even if they may have employed some imaginative touches in the interests of telling a good story. For the Gospels to have successfully performed the purposes suggested in the previous chapter, and in particular for them to have provided normative and formative guidance for the shaping of their target communities, they would have to have appeared at least reasonably plausible to their target audiences. That is, any invented material would have needed to chime in some way with existing collective memory (on which see Chapter 6). Conversely anything the Evangelists invented would have come, not from nowhere at all, but from the resources of their own (private and shared) memory. Thus (as the ancients well appreciated), invention and memory would have been closely related.

Scripture

One obvious source of material to use as a basis for invention would have been the Hebrew Scriptures (or at least, the traditions reflected therein). That Scripture was in some sense an important resource for the Evangelists is hardly to be doubted.[15] All the Evangelists explicitly quote Scripture at some point, and

---

[13] Rafael Rodriguez, *Structuring Early Christian Memory: Jesus in Tradition, Performance and Text* (LNTS, 407; ed. M. Goodacre; London: T. & T. Clark, 2010), 138–73.

[14] Compare the discussion of the understanding of memory in John's Gospel in Tom Thatcher, *Why John WROTE a Gospel: Jesus – Memory – History* (Louisville, KY: Westminster John Knox Press, 2006), xvii, 23–36.

[15] To suggest just two of the many relevant studies that could be cited in this connection, see Dale C. Allison, *The New Moses: A Matthean Typology* (Edinburgh: T. & T. Clark, 1993); and Joel Marcus, *The Way of the Lord: Christological Exegesis of the Old Testament in the Gospel of Mark* (Studies of the New Testament and Its World; ed. J. Riches; Edinburgh: T. & T. Clark, 1993).

the Gospels are replete with references and allusions to figures and events in the Old Testament. One may, of course, debate the extent to which particular Old Testament passages have shaped the Gospel accounts, or have merely been employed to provide colouring or scriptural depth to existing Jesus traditions. Thus, for example, while the influence of scriptural passages such as Psalms 22 and 69 on Mark's Passion narrative is widely recognized, views differ on whether this means that Mark's account of the crucifixion is almost entirely constructed out of Scripture, or whether scriptural language is being employed to express tradition.[16] It certainly appears that many of Mark's more spectacular miracle stories, such as the Feeding of the Five Thousand, Stilling the Storm and Walking on the Sea, have been heavily shaped by related passages in the Old Testament, if not almost entirely created out of them.[17] The birth and infancy narratives in Luke and Matthew seem to owe more than a little to 1 Samuel in the former case and Genesis–Exodus in the latter.

That the Evangelists made use of the Hebrew Scriptures is not at issue. The chief issue here is *how* they might have done so. Related to this is whether in every case where a modern reader might identify an allusion or reference to Scripture the Evangelist in fact had any specific scripture in mind, or whether he was in fact calling on wider Israelite tradition (or collective memory).

Where an Evangelist explicitly cites Scripture (for example, with a formula such as 'it is written') then we can be reasonably certain that a specific scripture is intended, but even then there are problematic cases, such as the mixed quotation that Mark 1.2–3 attributes to Isaiah, or the notorious formula quotation 'He shall be called a Nazarene' at Matthew 2.23, which corresponds to no identifiable passage. It is also often the case (particularly in biblical quotations peculiar to Matthew) that an Old Testament passage cited in the New corresponds to no known standard text form, such as the proto-Masoretic text or the Septuagint. Given the lack of printed texts that might have standardized text forms in the first century, this should be no great surprise; certainly the scriptural texts found at Qumran suggest that the textual tradition of several books was still quite fluid. But the imprecision of some quotations also suggests what is in any case likely, namely that the Evangelists cited the scripture from memory. This is in any case likely because it would have been awkward to keep looking up passages in scrolls to check their precise wording, a time-consuming procedure that would have appeared neither necessary nor desirable to anyone who already more or less

---

[16] See, e.g., Mark Goodacre, 'Scripturalization in Mark's Crucifixion Narrative' in Geert van Oyen and Tom Shepherd (eds), *The Trial and Death of Jesus: Essays on the Passion Narrative in Mark* (Leuven: Peeters, 2006), 33–47 (39–42).

[17] See, e.g., Eric Eve, *The Healer from Nazareth: Jesus' Miracles in Historical Context* (London: SPCK, 2009), 150–6; Eric Eve, 'The Growth of the Nature Miracles' in Graham Twelftree (ed.), *The Nature Miracles of Jesus: Historical and Theological Perspectives* (Eugene, OR: Wipf & Stock, forthcoming).

knew what he was looking for. Moreover, it is unlikely that the Evangelists would have had ready access to complete sets of scriptural scrolls which they could check. Conversely, the kind of person with the skill and authority to compose a Gospel is quite likely to be someone sufficiently conversant with the traditions and Scriptures of Israel to be able to quote a selection of passages from memory.

It is sometimes suggested that the Evangelists may have used *testimonia* collections, that is, convenient excerpts of scriptural passages that were felt to be particularly useful to the preaching, mission and instruction of the primitive Church. At least three considerations suggest such a possibility: first, the fact that certain passages such as Psalm 2.7; 8.6; 110.1; Isaiah 8.14; and Jeremiah 31.31–34 seem to have been particularly popular (which could be explained on the basis that such passages had been excerpted into a *testimonia* collection that was widely circulated in the primitive Church); second, the existence of such *testimonia* collections among the Dead Sea Scrolls discovered at Qumran (showing that such a thing could readily exist at this time); and third, the wider use of summary or digest versions of literature in contemporary Graeco-Roman culture.[18]

While this is a possibility, it is by no means a certainty. The recurrence of certain scriptural verses in the New Testament and other early Christian literature could be explained by their frequent use in early Christian preaching, reflection and instruction (in the sense that passages that were found to be serviceable by some people were quickly taken up by others). Even if such *testimonia* collections existed, the Evangelists may well have cited them from memory when they came to compose their Gospels. Moreover, the Evangelists' use of the Jewish Scriptures (or Israelite traditions) is far more wide-ranging than the passages they explicitly quote, ranging over a wide selection of biblical events, persons and themes employed in a manner that suggests considerable familiarity with the material on the part of both the author and the target audience. Thus, while we cannot exclude the possibility that one or more of the Evangelists read through a *testimonia* collection or some portion of Scripture to refresh their memories prior to the task of composition, it is far more likely than not that in the act of composition the Evangelists relied primarily on their memory for their use of Scripture (possibly aided by the memories of anyone assisting them in their task).

Memory

As indicated at the start of the chapter, each potential source of Gospel material turns out to be related to memory. For present purposes we are not concerned with how accurately memory may have transmitted the 'real' Jesus to the Evangelists,[19]

---

[18] See, e.g., Harry Y. Gamble, *Books and Readers in the Early Church: A History of Early Christian Texts* (New Haven and London: Yale University Press, 1995), 25–7.

[19] For a discussion of this point, see Eve, *Behind the Gospels*, 86–158.

but with the role it may have played in the composition of the Gospels. To this end, several aspects of memory may prove relevant.

The first relevant aspect is the extent to which the individual Evangelists (together, perhaps, with their assistants and collaborators) had memory command of any written sources they employed (such as the Jewish Scriptures, *testimonia* collections, previous Gospels, or various forms of notes, sayings collections and the like). This will be explored further in Chapter 5, but the factors considered here already suggest that rather than assuming that the Evangelists largely worked with their written sources open in front of them, we might do better to assume that they would have worked largely from memory. This should by no means be taken as a dogmatic assumption that all four canonical Evangelists worked *entirely* from memory. It is certainly not intended to exclude the possibility that the Evangelists consulted one or more texts before starting to compose (or during breaks in the actual composition process) or even that they may have had eye contact with a manuscript from time to time during the actual composition process. The point is rather that we should take the use of texts from memory as our default working hypothesis, while being open to consider challenges that may cause us to modify it (such as a particularly high degree of verbatim agreement between particular Synoptic parallels).

The second aspect is the way in which the Evangelists accessed oral tradition from memory. Most of the relevant questions about this have already been indicated above. To summarize, was the Evangelists' memory of oral tradition primarily episodic (i.e. of particular performances that made a strong impression) or semantic (i.e. a memory that such-and-such had been said without any recollection of any particular occasion on which it was said)? To what extent was the Evangelists' recollection purely verbal (i.e. simply of the words that were spoken) and to what extent was it influenced by the non-verbal aspects of performance, such as intonation, emotional tone, gesture, facial expression, bearing, pacing, timing and audience response, all factors that make a face-to-face oral performance so much more than the words that survive in manuscript?[20] To what extent were the Evangelists remembering their own performances, or the performances of others? Indeed, how far were the Evangelists remembering 'performances' in the sense of occasions (such as meetings for worship) specially marked off for an authorized person to perform some part of the tradition to an audience, or less formal occasions when oral material was passed on through informal conversation or chewed over in the course of discussion and debate? If the Evangelists were remembering performances, were they recalling specific performances or

---

[20] See, e.g., Ruth Finnegan, *Communicating: The Multiple Modes of Human Interconnection* (London: Routledge, 2002), 59–136, 223–9; Ruth Finnegan, *The Oral and Beyond: Doing Things with Words in Africa* (Oxford: James Currey, 2007), 78–81, 205–10.

the general impression left by a whole series of performances? Since there seems no clear way of arriving at definitive answers to any of these questions, it may be that we need a different route into the issues they raise.

The third aspect is the recognition that memory is not simply a matter of storage and retrieval, as if the brain were a kind of organic filing cabinet or computer hard disk, but rather a process of reconstruction based on memory traces, present interests, habits of thought and social circumstances. The implications of this for the individual memory of the Evangelists will be explored further in Chapter 5. But none of the Evangelists would have been remembering in isolation. All human memory has a social dimension, and this would be particularly true of memories of Jesus that were constantly being rehearsed in Christian communities. This leads to a further aspect of memory we need to consider: collective memory, which may provide an alternative route into the issues raised by oral tradition, and which will be the subject of Chapter 6. But before we delve any deeper into the workings of any kind of memory, we should first explore how the Evangelists may have worked with their material in the act of composition. This will form the subject of the next chapter.

4

Models of composition

The previous chapter looked at the various types of raw material that may have been available to the Evangelists as they wrote, but, as Christopher Pelling has said, 'until we know *how* an author used a particular source, we know very little indeed'.[1] In an oft-criticized passage, Burton Mack describes Mark as a scholar working in his study surrounded by books.[2] A rather more recent description of Matthew's working methods is equally anachronistic:

> Strewn upon his tabletop would no doubt have been a copy of some form of Mark, possibly another document of a collection of written traditions (Q), and papyri and other items upon which were inscribed bits of the Jesus tradition, sayings, miracle stories, parables etc. Additionally, he would have had scrolls of OT texts (e.g. MT, Aramaic, LXX or some other Greek translation of Isaiah, Jeremiah, Psalms, etc.) or, at the very least, testimony collections.[3]

Perhaps this passage should not be taken entirely at face value, since its author goes on to say that the composition of Matthew would have involved rather more than the use of written sources, but the picture it presents is deeply problematic, since it portrays an isolated author working on a tabletop with multiple texts before him. This looks suspiciously like a projection of modern writing practices back into the first century, when there were no writing desks, authorship was generally not an isolated activity, and authors seldom worked from several texts at a time in the manner suggested.

This thoroughly anachronistic picture needs to be replaced with something rather different. But while quite a bit of work has been done on how ancient authors worked, most of it relates to Graeco-Roman authors who were part of the literary elite, and we cannot automatically assume that the Evangelists worked in precisely the same way. The working methods of Graeco-Roman authors nevertheless provide a rather better starting point for understanding how the Evangelists may have worked than do our own.

---

[1] C. B. R. Pelling, 'Plutarch's Method of Work in the Roman *Lives*', *JHS* 99 (1979), 74–96 (96) (emphasis original).

[2] Burton L. Mack, *A Myth of Innocence: Mark and Christian Origins* (Philadelphia: Fortress Press, 1988), 321–3.

[3] Richard C. Beaton, 'How Matthew Writes' in Markus Bockmuehl and Donald A. Hagner (eds), *The Written Gospel* (Cambridge: Cambridge University Press, 2005), 116–34 (116).

Several New Testament scholars have, however, proposed a very different model of Gospel composition, namely one that views one or more of the Gospels (typically Mark) as oral-traditional literature. A third possible model taken from ancient compositional practice might be termed the scribal-school-memory-tradition model. This chapter will therefore consider all three models and draw some tentative conclusions on their applicability to the Gospels.

Graeco-Roman authors

Information on how elite authors went about their task is relatively limited, and there is a danger of arriving at an artificial composite from what is known of different authors who may have worked differently, not least by conflating Greece and Rome. Since our primary interest here, however, is with the composition of the Gospels rather than elite literature, a general description of elite working methods should suffice.

Discussions of the working methods of Graeco-Roman authors often describe two or more phases, a 'research' phase in which the author gathered his (or occasionally her) material, and a 'composition' phase in which he wrote it up (at *Inst.* Intro. 2–3 Quintilian states that the first phase took him far longer than the second). There is also a 'publication' phase, discussed in Chapter 1, while the 'composition' phase may itself be broken down into a number of stages, such as producing a rough draft, seeking feedback and making a final version.[4] In none of these phases did authors typically work alone; instead they made use of research assistants and secretaries whose contribution to the final product might be substantial, if rarely acknowledged. Ancient authorship was thus rather more of a collective activity than authorship usually is today.

The research phase often consisted of being read to by a slave (or perhaps a freedman assistant). The older Pliny, for example, is said by his nephew to have had a slave read to him when he was in the bath, or dining, or on a journey, to make the best use of his time (Pliny, *Letters* 3.5.10–15), although such extreme dedication to literary pursuits was no doubt exceptional.[5] Notes might be made either by annotating the scroll that was being read, or separately in a notebook (a wax tablet might typically be used for the purpose) or scroll. Some authors may have made their own notes, but they were probably often dictated to a secretary. Authors may also have sometimes dispatched research assistants to look up information and gather notes on their behalf (from texts held in archives or libraries, for example). Such note-taking was usually not as thoroughgoing as it

---

[4] Cf. the list of stages in Rex Winsbury, *The Roman Book: Books, Publishing and Performance in Classical Rome* (London: Bristol Classical Press, 2009), 102.

[5] Jocelyn Penny Small, *Wax Tablets of the Mind: Cognitive Studies of Memory and Literacy in Classical Antiquity* (Abingdon: Routledge, 1997), 171–2.

might be today, however, since greater reliance would be placed on memory, and given that wax tablets were fairly unwieldy compared with modern note-cards or notebooks it seems more likely that authors would have read through their notes before starting to compose than that they would have consulted their notes in the actual course of composition.[6]

Once an author had gathered his material, the next phase would be to produce a rough draft. This would normally be done by dictation, with one or more secretaries taking down the text. It may be that wax tablets were used for this purpose, since they readily allowed erasures and corrections; but it may be questioned how much of a lengthy composition would actually fit on a reasonable number of tablets, which may suggest that this stage had to proceed in relatively short sections, or that it may not have been the method most commonly employed. Since neither papyrus nor secretarial labour (which was often slave labour)[7] would have seemed that costly to an elite author, dictation of drafts, even multiple drafts of the same work, may more normally have been onto scrolls, which the author would then correct. It appears that at least some quite lengthy works were transcribed from wax tablets, but the more normal use of such tablets may have been for note-taking or as a drafting tool for authors who preferred to write their own material rather than dictate (as Quintilian, *Inst.* 10.3.20–22, 31–33 recommends).[8]

The speed of dictation probably varied according to the inclination of the author and the ability of the secretary. There apparently were some scribes capable of taking shorthand, while others may have been obliged to take only sketchy notes that they would write up later. Conversely, some authors may have been readier than others to slow their speech to dictation speed, not only to allow their secretaries time to keep up, but to allow themselves more time to think.

An author dictating a rough draft in this fashion would have had his hands free to consult either his notes or his source texts by eye, but it would have been awkward to keep juggling between several such texts. An alternative would have been to have a slave or other assistant read a short passage from a source text or notes, on the basis of which the author could then proceed to dictate to his scribe, but it is unknown whether any authors chose to work this way. In all probability most authors worked from memory, both because they trusted their memory more than modern authors do and because they were far less concerned about verbatim accuracy in the reproduction of a source.[9]

---

[6] Small, *Wax Tablets*, 188–9; Catherine Hezser, *Jewish Literacy in Roman Palestine* (Texts and Studies in Ancient Judaism, 81; Tübingen: Mohr Siebeck, 2001), 422–3.

[7] Winsbury, *Roman Book*, 20, 79–85.

[8] Small, *Wax Tablets*, 143, 146; F. Gerald Downing, 'Waxing Careless: Poirier, Derrenbacker and Downing', *JSNT* 35 (2013), 388–93 (391); Robert A. Derrenbacker, 'Texts, Tables and Tablets: A Response to John C. Poirier', *JSNT* 35 (2013), 380–7 (384–5); Winsbury, *Roman Book*, 103.

[9] Small, *Wax Tablets*, 185, 189, 192.

The existence of this stage of composition is attested in a number of sources, such as Lucian's advice to would-be historians to first gather their material into an ordered set of rough notes, or a rough draft (the exact meaning of the Greek term is not clear), in order to 'get the facts straight', and then work up the rough draft into a polished literary product (Lucian, *quom. hist.* 48).[10] That said, Lucian gives this advice after lampooning the efforts of a number of (in his estimation) quite poor historians, so it can hardly be assumed that everyone followed the procedures he recommends. Moreover, his advice appears principally aimed at people writing histories of recent wars, so some caution may be needed in generalizing it to every kind of literary composition.

Once a rough draft was available, an author might try it out on a group of friends, presumably by reading them extracts (or the complete draft) and inviting comments and suggestions. Or it may be that the author's scribal assistant (secretary) would first write up a fair copy of the notes/draft onto a scroll before this stage, perhaps doing a considerable amount of tidying up of the text in the process. Further corrections might be made on this copy before a final fair copy was made for 'publication'.

Exactly how many stages and iterations this process would go through would presumably depend on the nature of the work, the aspirations of the author, and the resources available. Papyrus was not in such limitless supply that the less affluent could readily afford to make multiple drafts, and, of course, the business of producing handwritten drafts would have been time-consuming and expensive. Thus, in order to go through all the steps just described, one would either have to be wealthy oneself (as most elite Graeco-Roman authors were) or else be the client of a wealthy patron who was prepared to support one's literary efforts.

When it comes to the way Graeco-Roman authors used their sources, it is frequently emphasized that they would typically follow only one source at a time, at least for any single incident, relying on their memory of other sources for any supplementary details they might wish to include; they seldom if ever substantially conflated two or more accounts into their own account.[11] This is not to deny that ancient authors might employ multiple sources in the course of a single work, but rather to assert that for the purposes of composing a particular passage, they might read (or have read to them) the relevant passage in a number of sources, but then choose the one they preferred, and make that one the basis

---

[10] See, e.g., Small, *Wax Tablets*, 177; Pelling, 'Plutarch's Method', 94; R. A. Derrenbacker, *Ancient Compositional Practices and the Synoptic Problem* (BETL, 186; Leuven: Peeters-Leuven, 2005), 39–42.

[11] Derrenbacker, *Ancient Compositional Practices*, 116–17; F. Gerald Downing, 'Compositional Conventions and the Synoptic Problem', *JBL* 107 (1988), 69–85 (71–82); repr. in F. Gerald Downing, *Doing Things with Words in the First Christian Century* (JSNTSup, 200; Sheffield: Sheffield Academic Press, 2000), 152–73 (154–68).

for their own account (even though they might remember, and possibly use, the odd detail from other sources). The common supposition, then, is that ancient authors typically composed with only one source open in front of them at a time, and based each portion of their composition principally on a single source. Pelling's article on Plutarch's use of sources in his Roman Lives is often cited in support of this position, so it may be helpful to put this in the context of what else Pelling has to say about Plutarch.[12]

Pelling's first point is that Plutarch *needed* to research the writing of his Roman Lives, since he did not start out familiar with Roman history. Part of Pelling's evidence for this is that Plutarch's Roman Lives do not exhibit the same depth of cultural and literary background as his Greek ones. More specifically, what Pelling takes to be the two earliest of Plutarch's Roman Lives, *Lucullus* and *Cicero*, appear far less well informed than the remaining six.[13] This implies that Plutarch would not simply have obtained the odd detail here and there from his recollection of sources other than the one he was currently following, but must have been relying on his memory of a breadth of reading to inform his whole account, particularly in the later Roman Lives once he had carried out more research.

Second, part of Pelling's concern is to argue that the six later Roman Lives were worked on more or less together, since they often show similarities of content and even wording, although, conversely, the same incidents are often treated differently in different Lives in order to fit Plutarch's literary presentation of the particular subject he was writing about in any given Life.[14]

From there Pelling goes on to consider what sources Plutarch may have used, and suggests that while the Pollio-source was one major influence, Plutarch must have used many other sources in addition, including some oral tradition.[15] It is then that Pelling states that Plutarch nevertheless appears to have employed the Pollio-source alone for the majority of his composition, and that he was far from alone among Graeco-Roman authors in working in such a manner, Cassius Dio, Livy and Tacitus being other examples.[16] According to Pelling (and the scholarship he cites), all these authors followed a single source at a time for a single section. In Pelling's view,

> The curious fidelity to a single source for individual episodes is most easily understood if we make a simple assumption: that, following this initial wide reading, an author would generally choose just one work to have before his eyes when he composed, and this work would perform the basis of his narrative.[17]

---

[12] In Pelling, 'Plutarch's Method'.

[13] Pelling, 'Plutarch's Method', 75.

[14] Pelling, 'Plutarch's Method', 75–83.

[15] Pelling, 'Plutarch's Method', 83–91.

[16] Pelling, 'Plutarch's Method', 91–2.

[17] Pelling, 'Plutarch's Method', 92.

An author might switch to another source when it was more appropriate (for example, when it dealt with material not contained in the main source being followed), or he might combine items from his previous reading with the account in his main source, without, however, going back to check any other written text. The reason for this method of working, in Pelling's view, was the physical difficulty of working with a scroll, and the awkwardness of working with more than one scroll at a time. Pelling acknowledges that it may have been possible to compare two written accounts by making use of a bookrest or a slave to hold the second scroll, and he even states that 'no doubt it was sometimes done', but he at once goes on to add: 'But it would be very inconvenient, and it would not be surprising if authors preferred to rely on their memory.'[18] Pelling then goes on to cite examples of signs of the use of memory in Plutarch's work, concluding that Plutarch appears to have made little use of notes.[19] Jocelyn Small further suggests that some of what Pelling takes to have been deliberate literary variation between the representation of similar source material in different Lives may instead be due to memory errors.[20] Whether this suggestion adequately takes into account either Pelling's argument that the later six Roman Lives were composed simultaneously or his discussion of why the various versions of the same events fitted their different literary contexts is debatable, but we shall return to Small's suggestion in Chapter 5.

Pelling concludes by pointing out that his analysis applies specifically to the Roman Lives, and that Plutarch may not have needed to conduct such extensive research for his Greek Lives, for many of which 'he would already be sufficiently familiar with the material'.[21] While, for example, he may have had a historical source such as Herodotus or Thucydides open in front of him when writing *Themosticles* (which seems to be heavily dependent on those two historians), many of the 'supplementary' items may come from information Plutarch had known from his youth, and would not explicitly have needed to research.

While Pelling's work is helpful, it is important to note what it does not establish. In particular it does not establish that all classical authors wrote (or dictated) with one source open in front of them at a time. What Pelling actually argues is that Graeco-Roman authors preferred to *follow* one source at a time, and that it would have been difficult (though neither impossible nor totally unheard of) to work with more than one. He does not equate following a source with necessarily having eye contact with it at the point of composition, since he also suggests the possibility that 'an author, immediately before narrating an episode, would *re*read one account, and compose with that version fresh in his

---

[18] Pelling, 'Plutarch's Method', 93.
[19] Pelling, 'Plutarch's Method', 93–4.
[20] Small, *Wax Tablets*, 193–4.
[21] Pelling, 'Plutarch's Method', 96.

mind', a procedure that would account for what may well be slips of memory in the resultant text.[22]

That at least some authors worked without any immediate visual contact with written sources is suggested by a letter of the younger Pliny in which he describes how he liked to work by planning his composition in his head while lying in the dark on waking up in the morning, and then dictating the result to an assistant (*Letters* 9.36.1–3).[23] Small points out that in working in this manner Pliny was following both the advice of his teacher Quintilian and a method used by other writers such as Demosthenes and Plotinus.[24] She concludes that, 'If we pull together our information so far, our average ancient historian should first read through his notes, then order them in his memory, and finally write down the ordered contents of his memory.'[25] Indeed, given that the ancient literary ideal was not to reproduce the wording of one's sources but to rework them in one's own literary style, attempting to dictate one's own differently worded version while simultaneously looking at one's source may have felt more difficult than reworking that source from memory.

Applicability to the Gospels

While it is useful to know something about how contemporary Graeco-Roman authors worked, we cannot simply assume that all the Evangelists worked in precisely this way. The Gospels were not Graeco-Roman historiography, and even if they partially resembled *bioi*, they were not literary Lives like those of Plutarch, but rather what we dubbed 'biblical *bioi*', narratives that owed as much to biblical as to Graeco-Roman models, and which deliberately related themselves to the great sweep of biblical 'history'. Moreover, the social location of the Evangelists was probably very different from that of elite Graeco-Roman authors such as Plutarch or Pliny. Not only is their educational level likely to have been somewhat different, but they are unlikely to have had access to the same resources such as slave labour, the use of which seems in any case to have been characteristic of Roman rather than Greek authors.[26] So before discussing how far the compositional techniques of the literate elites may illuminate those of the Evangelists, we should first set out some of the principal differences between the two cases.

First, the Gospels were not written with (elite) literary intent. That is, they were not written to provide entertainment in elite circles, or to enhance the reputation

---

[22] Pelling, 'Plutarch's Method', 92 (emphasis original).

[23] Small, *Wax Tablets*, 181; Pieter J. J. Botha, *Orality and Literacy in Early Christianity* (BPC, 5; ed. H. E. Hearon and P. Ruge-Jones; Eugene, OR: Cascade, 2012), 107.

[24] Small, *Wax Tablets*, 182–3.

[25] Small, *Wax Tablets*, 185.

[26] Winsbury, *Roman Book*, 84.

of their authors, or to be made available to the wider reading public through either the book trade or a network of fellow elites. This is in part indicated by their unpretentious style, which was unfavourably commented on by pagan critics.[27] It is also suggested by their content, which implies that their primary purposes were more pragmatic (as discussed in Chapter 2). Luke may be a partial exception here, but even Luke's writing does not come up to the standard expected of Graeco-Roman literature.

Second, the degree of verbal agreement between the Synoptic Gospels is highly atypical of the level of agreement one finds between a piece of Graeco-Roman literature and the source or sources it employed, not least because a literary author would be expected to rework his sources into his own literary style (although it may be that some authors were not, after all, entirely scrupulous about paraphrasing what they borrowed; some may simply have copied from sources we no longer possess).[28] The practice of the Evangelists may in part be due to factors such as, on the one hand, a conservative desire to retain what was regarded as authoritative material in the source text(s) or, on the other hand, a more radical desire to displace the source text(s) by absorption. But whatever explanation we give for this phenomenon, it does suggest a method of using sources different from that of elite Graeco-Roman authors.

Third, the social composition of the first-century Church makes it unlikely that it would have contained many persons wealthy enough to command the resources of a Pliny or educated to elite literary standards.

These differences reduce the confidence with which what we know about the working methods of elite Graeco-Roman authors can be directly applied to the composition of the Gospels, but a few tentative suggestions can nevertheless be offered about how what we know of the former may be adapted to the circumstances of the latter.

The collaborative nature of authorship could quite readily have been replicated in a first-century church setting either if its members clubbed together financially to provide the resources an Evangelist might need (for example, by jointly employing secretarial assistance) or, perhaps more likely, by finding the requisite skills from within its own ranks (with church members offering their scribal skills for free). The writing of the Gospels could well have been a collaborative enterprise, not in the sense that the Gospels were written by committees, but rather that the Evangelists might well have tried out their drafts on friends or fellow church-members before producing a final version, and may have discussed what they planned to write before setting pen to papyrus or getting their amanuensis to do so.

---

[27] Harry Y. Gamble, *Books and Readers in the Early Church: A History of Early Christian Texts* (New Haven and London: Yale University Press, 1995), 1, 103.
[28] Winsbury, *Roman Book*, 133.

We cannot assume that each of the Evangelists produced their texts via dictation just because that is how most elite authors worked; the Evangelists may not have had that luxury. Nevertheless, the fact that Paul is known to have used an amanuensis for at least some of his letters shows that secretarial assistance was available to at least some church leaders, and this makes it more probable that the Gospels could also have been composed by dictation. But probability is as far as the evidence takes us.

The relatively unliterary (by elite standards) nature of the Gospels casts some doubt on their having gone through all the stages recommended by Lucian for would-be historians. At the very least it is hard to see how so many of Mark's linguistic infelicities would have survived a serious attempt to produce a polished final product. So (again tentatively) we could perhaps envisage Mark dictating (or possibly himself writing) his version of the Gospel having perhaps discussed what he was going to say with other people, and Luke perhaps producing a rough draft before writing up a more polished version, with Matthew perhaps dictating or inscribing his expanded (and thoroughly revised) version of Mark after several years of reading that Gospel (and Q?) for his own community, but it must be stressed that these suggestions are highly tentative, and should only be taken as illustrative of how elite methods may have been adapted for church use.

Before settling on a model based on extrapolating from elite literary practices, however, we should first consider a radical alternative, namely one that sees the Gospels, and especially Mark, not as the product of literary authorship but as a by-product of oral tradition.

The Oral Composition Hypothesis

The notion that the Gospels were oral (folkloric) rather than literary compositions is one with a long history.[29] As an overall theory about the Gospels it founders on the strong indications of some sort of literary relationship between Matthew, Mark and Luke, but this does not rule out the possibility that the earliest of the Gospels originated as an oral rather than a literary composition. The suggestion that Mark might have been composed orally gains some initial traction from the supposedly 'oral' features that a number of New Testament scholars have claimed to find in it. To assess this alternative model for the composition at least of Mark we shall look at the work of three of these scholars: Pieter Botha, Antoinette

---

[29] For some twentieth-century examples, see Albert B. Lord, 'The Gospels as Oral Traditional Literature' in William O. Walker (ed.), *The Relationships among the Gospels: An Interdisciplinary Dialogue* (Trinity University Monograph Series in Religion, 5; San Antonio: Trinity University Press, 1978), 33–91; Alan Dundes, *Holy Writ as Oral Lit: The Bible as Folklore* (Lanham, MD and Oxford: Rowman & Littlefield, 1999).

Clark Wire and Joanna Dewey. But first it will be helpful to say something about oral-traditional composition in general.

The model of oral-traditional literature that has proved particularly influential is that developed by Milman Parry and Albert Lord in connection with Homeric and South Slavic epic poetry. Parry noticed that much of Homer's verse was made up of recurring formulas such as 'rosy-fingered dawn', 'wine-dark sea' or 'swift-footed Achilles'. Such formulas (in Greek) fit conveniently into one half of a hexameter (the metre used in the Homeric poems). From noting that such formulas appeared to be traditional, Parry subsequently went on to suggest that they were also oral, and that their formulaic nature enabled an oral poet to compose in performance by slotting ready-made sequences of words (such as the noun–epithet pairs exemplified above) into the appropriate portion of a line. In conjunction with his student Albert Lord (who continued his work after his death) Parry conducted extensive fieldwork in what was then Yugoslavia that appeared to confirm this thesis, since traditional Balkan bards were found to compose and perform their epic poetry in much the same manner as Parry and Lord proposed for Homer.[30]

In its classic form, the oral-formulaic theory of Parry and Lord held that one could tell whether a work had been composed in performance by calculating the density of the formulas it employed (although this is an aspect of the theory that has since come in for considerable criticism).[31] While on the Parry–Lord theory the Homeric poems were considered to be highly formulaic in the manner just described (by always employing the same set of words to express the same idea in the same metrical context), the notion of formula was also extended to themes and scenes, so that, for example, a scene in which one of Homer's heroes armed for battle would tend to follow a set sequence.

On this understanding of epic poetry, 'composition in performance' is to be understood in contrast to 'prior composition and memorization'. In their research into Balkan epic poets Parry and Lord found that even when traditional performers claimed to be rendering the 'same' poem 'word for word', there were always notable differences from one performance to the next (and generally even more so between the performances of the same poem by different singers). This led Parry and Lord to the conclusion that there was no such thing as the 'original'

---

[30] For a classic statement of this thesis, see Albert B. Lord, *The Singer of Tales* (2nd edn; Harvard Studies in Comparative Literature, 24; Cambridge, MA and London: Harvard University Press, 1960). For a later treatment, see John Miles Foley, *The Theory of Oral Composition: History and Methodology* (Bloomington and Indianapolis: Indiana University Press, 1988).

[31] For assessments of the oral-formulaic theory from other viewpoints, see, e.g., Ruth Finnegan, *Oral Poetry: Its Nature, Significance and Social Context* (Bloomington and Indianapolis: Indiana University Press, 1992), 58–72; and Rosalind Thomas, *Literacy and Orality in Ancient Greece* (Key Themes in Ancient History; ed. P. A. Cartledge and P. D. A. Garnsey; Cambridge: Cambridge University Press, 1992), 29–51.

version of an oral poem, and also to question the previously held notion that oral tradition of this kind relied primarily on the verbatim memory of a fixed text. Far from memorizing a fixed text, the traditional singer of tales recreated the poem anew each time it was performed. The recreation was, however, far from being a new work made out of nothing; rather it was based on traditional themes and traditional formulas that the singer had mastered, and was, in a sense, a rendering of the 'same tale' in that the same principal characters and basic story line would be preserved.

Pieter Botha argues that instead of seeing Mark as the product of tradition and redaction, it should be viewed as a piece of oral-traditional literature on the Parry–Lord model.[32] Botha is well aware that Mark is not epic poetry, so he does not expect to find recurrent noun–epithet formulas of the kind Parry and Lord identified in Homer, but he does suggest that Mark employs formulaic themes in the manner described by the oral-formulaic theory and he further identifies what he regards as a number of stereotypical phrases in Mark analogous to the metrical formulas of the Parry–Lord theory.[33] Botha does not go on to argue that these features *demonstrate* that Mark is an oral-formulaic composition, since he is aware that this cannot be proved from a statistical analysis of supposedly formulaic elements. He instead argues that the oral characteristics he finds in Mark support a view that is probable on other grounds, given the likelihood that in that culture stories of Jesus would have circulated orally long before being written down, and in particular that 'It is absurd to think that an extended narrative about Jesus became a reality outside the initial followers of Jesus and only after a long period of time.'[34]

For Botha, then, Mark was not an *author* so much as an oral-traditional storyteller re-composing a traditional story about Jesus using the method of composition in performance. On this understanding Mark did not just use oral tradition as a source, since his entire Gospel *is* oral tradition.[35] Botha is not quite so clear, however, on how Mark ended up as a written Gospel. He first suggests that 'It is quite possible that the gospel of Mark is a casual transcription of what had been performed *orally*' and then states a few pages later that the reason 'we have a written copy today is probably due to the traditional narrator having dictated his story at some stage', without apparently noticing that he has just proposed two rather different things.[36] A 'casual transcription' suggests a stenographer taking

---

[32] Botha, *Orality and Literacy*, 163–90; originally published as Pieter J. J. Botha, 'Mark's Story as Oral Traditional Literature: Rethinking the Transmission of Some Traditions about Jesus', *HTS* 47 (1991), 304–31.

[33] Botha, *Orality and Literacy*, 178–85.

[34] Botha, *Orality and Literacy*, 186.

[35] Botha, *Orality and Literacy*, 187–8.

[36] Botha, *Orality and Literacy*, 185, 187 (emphasis original).

notes of an oral performance which he or she subsequently writes up, while 'dictation' suggests a deliberate attempt by the performer to set down a particular version of the text, and would imply a slower speed of performance (to allow the scribe to keep up) which would in turn allow rather more time for the performer to think of what he was going to say and how to say it than would typically be the case for composition in performance. Botha does try to address the latter point, just as he also notes that 'almost *all* writing done at the time was by dictation',[37] although this second point simply emphasizes what Mark would have had in *common* with an elite Graeco-Roman author. The conclusion Botha wishes to draw is that instead of seeing Mark as 'literature' or 'narrative' (by which he presumably means the deliberate narrative creation of a single authorial mind), we should see it as traditional storytelling.

A similar approach to that of Botha is presented in a book-length study by Antoinette Clark Wire.[38] Wire's main proposal is that the Gospels 'were composed, not by individual authors with pens in hands, but orally in performance'.[39] In Wire's view, whereas an author can employ tradition to his or her own ends, performers of tradition are constrained by their audiences to remain faithful to that tradition (at least in overall gist). She suggests that it is pointless to look for some moment when the tradition was first narrated; instead we should envisage a process of gradual growth with each performer making only minor changes to the version he or she received and each performer concerned not to innovate, but simply to preserve and pass on the tradition. Mark's Gospel should thus be heard 'as the story of a community told by several favored oral performers rather than the product of a single writer'.[40]

Like Botha, Wire appeals to the work of Parry and Lord on Homer's epics, but she also brings in Foley's work on metonymic referencing, and recent research into folklore and ethnopoetics by scholars such as Dennis Tedlock and Dell Hymes.[41] After briefly considering the role of 'oral torah' in early rabbinic Judaism and oral recitation of the Qur'an, in which she points to a growing shift in scholarly assumptions about speech and writing in these areas, she gives a brief survey of the study of the oral Jesus tradition from form criticism to James Dunn, ending with a complaint that the default setting remains a literary paradigm. Wire then reiterates that the time has come to make the case for Mark being an oral-traditional composition, and specifically, one whose text was generated by composition in

---

[37] Botha, *Orality and Literacy*, 187 (emphasis original).

[38] Antoinette Clark Wire, *The Case for Mark Composed in Performance* (BPC, 3; ed. H. E. Hearon and P. Ruge-Jones; Eugene, OR: Cascade, 2011).

[39] Wire, *Mark*, 2.

[40] Wire, *Mark*, 3–5.

[41] Wire, *Mark*, 6–9. For a convenient summary of some of this material see Eric Eve, *Behind the Gospels: Understanding the Oral Tradition* (London: SPCK, 2013), 103–7.

performance.[42] She then sets out a number of possible objections to this thesis which the bulk of her book is concerned to rebut.[43]

We cannot follow all Wire's arguments and counter-arguments in detail here. But to give one example, she suggests that the variability in the early textual tradition of Mark indicates that there may never have been an authoritative original, so that the fluidity of the textual tradition may be a sign of the fluidity of the oral performative tradition that lay behind it.[44] It is far from clear, however, that the manuscript evidence for Mark (which in any case is quite sparse for the first few centuries after its composition) exhibits the same degree of variation as Parry and Lord found in the performance of oral epic poetry, however fluid it may appear compared with a printed text. Wire also considers a number of objections relating to the nature of Mark's text, first that Mark is a prose narrative rather than memorable poetry, second that it concerns recent events rather than ancient identity-shaping legends of the sort we might expect to find in oral-traditional literature, and third that the coherence of Mark suggests its composition by an individual author rather than its growth through a series of performances.

Yet Wire does not so much meet these objections head-on as provide a further series of arguments for seeing Mark as an oral composition. The first of these is that the language of Mark resembles speech rather than writing.[45] It is unclear, however, whether a written text can be *proved* to have an oral origin by such means, since writing can always imitate speech. The second is that Mark is made of a number of scenes that tend to follow a set pattern, and that these are analogous to the themes that Lord suggests occur in epic poetry.[46] But this analogy again only suggests that Mark may have been composed orally, not that it must have been; episodic composition could also have been employed as a written technique (not least when intended for oral performance), as Mary Ann Tolbert suggests it was in ancient romances.[47] The third is that the story pattern of Mark is more indicative of composition in oral performance than of the literary work of a single author, in part because it exhibits oral storytelling patterns and the kind of metonymic referencing of traditions (such as biblical stories of the prophets) that Foley finds to be indicative of oral-derived texts.[48]

Yet even suppose we grant all these points. What they amount to is a case for regarding Mark as oral storytelling. They do not show that the story told must

---

[42] Wire, *Mark*, 9–18.

[43] Wire, *Mark*, 18.

[44] Wire, *Mark*, 31–40.

[45] Wire, *Mark*, 73–89.

[46] Wire, *Mark*, 90–109.

[47] Mary Ann Tolbert, *Sowing the Gospel: Mark's World in Literary-Historical Perspective* (Minneapolis: Fortress Press, 1989), 65–6.

[48] Wire, *Mark*, 110–34.

have taken shape over many decades by a process of composition in performance. In particular, they do not address the kind of literary-critical analyses of Mark that suggest that his Gospel looks like the result of deliberate design rather than the endpoint of numerous performances by anonymous performers concerned only to pass on their tradition. Wire apparently falls into the trap of contrasting a modern conception of literary authorship with a particular model of oral composition as if these were the only two alternatives available, but they are not.

The final stage of Wire's argument is to sample a number of prominent features in Mark's Gospel (such as the coming of the kingdom, the use of parables and the enigmatic ending) and to suggest how these can be better interpreted on her understanding of the genesis of the text.[49] Here, though, it is unclear how her interpretations differ from those of scholars using more conventional literary-critical or redaction-critical approaches, or why they should be preferred where they do differ; in any case identifying something as an oral-derived text tells us next to nothing about its mode of composition.[50]

While Joanna Dewey also wishes to argue for an oral-derived Mark, she does not claim to know whether Mark was in fact composed in performance or was composed by dictation or writing; she does, however, maintain that it was composed in an oral style for oral performance.[51] In an article exploring why Mark's Gospel survived at all (given its near absorption by Matthew and Luke) she argues both that Mark's Gospel built on a previously existing narrative tradition and that its subsequent oral transmission was what helped to ensure its survival.[52] In this connection she points to the ubiquity of oral storytelling in antiquity, not least in connection with synagogue worship, which meant it was likely to be prevalent in early Christian worship (and other early Christian activities too). While manuscripts might be used to support oral performance, Dewey (following Richard Rohrbaugh and Richard Horsley) believes that the social location for the earliest performances of Mark would have been peasant villages, where the use of manuscripts was rare.[53]

Furthermore, both the length and the style of Mark made it well suited for oral performance, not least because it was composed of vivid and thus highly memorable incidents, so it would not be that difficult to remember on the basis

---

[49] Wire, *Mark*, 135–74.

[50] John Miles Foley, *The Singer of Tales in Performance* (Voices in Performance and Text; ed. J. M. Foley; Bloomington and Indianapolis: Indiana University Press, 1995), 60–98.

[51] Joanna Dewey, 'The Gospel of Mark as Oral Hermeneutic' in Tom Thatcher (ed.), *Jesus, the Voice and the Text: Beyond the Oral and the Written Gospel* (Waco: Baylor University Press, 2008), 71–87 (72, 86).

[52] Joanna Dewey, 'The Survival of Mark's Gospel: A Good Story?', *JBL* 123 (2004), 495–507.

[53] Richard L. Rohrbaugh, 'The Social Location of the Marcan Audience', *BTB* 23 (1993), 114–27; Richard A. Horsley, *Hearing the Whole Story: The Politics of Plot in Mark's Gospel* (Louisville, KY: Westminster John Knox Press, 2001), 178–83.

of hearing it performed. In deference to Foley's insistence that there is no way of proving whether a written text was first composed orally or in writing, Dewey allows that it is possible that Mark started out as a written composition in oral register, but believes that it is more probable that it was an oral composition. In any case, she maintains, however Mark's Gospel was composed, it was transmitted through oral performance.[54]

Dewey next examines the nature of the traditions that must have been available to Mark in order for him to have composed his narrative, and counters the form-critical assumption that these would have formed isolated units of tradition.[55] Instead, Dewey insists that traditions about a hero generally coalesce quite quickly into connected narratives rather than circulating independently for decades. While individual storytellers may well have narrated individual incidents on particular occasions, the general trend would have been for the early growth of a connected story about Jesus, with each performance of this tale building on previous ones. On the basis of parallels in folklore and other oral literature Dewey suggests that the general outline of such a story would quickly become quite stable, but that individual performers would nevertheless put their own creative stamp on the traditional material on which they drew. Mark's version gained prominence because he was a particularly gifted storyteller, whose version was dictated (and hence put into writing) either by Mark or by someone who knew his version. That Mark's Gospel nevertheless had predecessors is suggested to Dewey by the sophistication of its narrative in contrast to the roughness of its Greek and the oral-performative nature of its structure. It seems unlikely that Mark would have been able to do such a good job in one go if he had been starting from scratch, and much more likely that he was improving on earlier efforts.[56]

The third stage of Dewey's argument concerns the use and transmission of Mark's Gospel. While she acknowledges that the existence of a written version would tend to fix the text, she also doubts that the manuscripts of Mark made much difference to its use and transmission for the first few decades or so. This is in part because of the fluidity of the manuscript tradition: so far as we can tell, the early copying of Mark's text was not carried out with particularly scrupulous care, so there are limits on how far it could have fixed the text. In part it is also because Dewey conceives of Mark as being *performed* (from memory) rather than read aloud, which, she thinks, would have been difficult to do from a manuscript written in *scriptio continua*. Moreover, the existence of a written version would

---

[54] Dewey, 'Survival', 497–500; Foley, *Singer of Tales*, 60–98.

[55] On form criticism see Christopher M. Tuckett, 'Form Criticism' in W. H. Kelber and S. Byrskog (eds), *Jesus in Memory: Traditions in Oral and Scribal Perspectives* (Waco: Baylor University Press, 2009), 21–38; and Eve, *Behind the Gospels*, 15–32; on the isolation of individual pieces of tradition see especially 31–2.

[56] Dewey, 'Survival', 500–3.

not of itself have interrupted a tradition of oral performance. Furthermore, Dewey argues, the variability we expect to find in oral performance could explain the relatively high degree of variability we apparently find in the early manuscript tradition of Mark (in comparison with the other three canonical Gospels), on the assumption that a continuing tradition of oral performance would have affected the copying of the manuscripts. Finally, the relative scarcity of manuscripts of Mark (compared with the other Gospels) and the noticeable decrease in patristic citations of Mark from the second to the third centuries suggest to Dewey that Mark ceased to be of much interest once the tradition of oral performance ceased and the Fathers' interests became more literary. Thus, Dewey concludes, it was only Mark's continued success as oral performance up until the time when the Church began to fix upon a fourfold Gospel that ensured its survival.[57]

Evaluation

One major problem with the oral-compositional approach just outlined is that the first-century Roman Empire was far from being a purely oral-traditional society. According to a recent article by Larry Hurtado, arguments for an orally composed Mark of the sort just summarized rest on oversimplifications and misunderstandings of the media dynamics of Roman antiquity.[58] While not denying the value placed on oratory, Hurtado insists that writing played a larger and more distinct role in the Roman Empire than advocates of oral composition and performance allow. Moreover, Hurtado insists, reading aloud was an activity that was carefully distinguished from acting or oratory; in particular a reader would not mimic the dramatic style of an actor, not least because he or she would not wish to be mistaken for an actor (someone pretending to be someone they were not).[59] Furthermore (as noted in Chapter 1 above) the difficulty of reading from a manuscript written in *scriptio continua* is often exaggerated, not least because it fails to take account of the fact that people in antiquity would have been thoroughly trained in reading manuscripts written in this format. Also, many ancient Christian manuscripts appear to have incorporated features designed to aid the reader (such as larger than usual lettering or rudimentary punctuation), indicating that they were probably intended to be read aloud to groups (rather than performed from memory); there are references to material being read to Christian gatherings, but none to anything being performed. — *good point*

---

[57] Dewey, 'Survival', 503–6.

[58] Larry W. Hurtado, 'Oral Fixation and New Testament Studies? "Orality", "Performance" and Reading Texts in Early Christianity', *NTS* 60 (2014), 321–40.

[59] Cf. Holt N. Parker, 'Books and Reading Latin Poetry' in W. A. Johnson and H. N. Parker (eds), *Ancient Literacies: The Culture of Reading in Greece and Rome* (New York: Oxford University Press, 2009), 186–229 (188).

Addressing the notion that one or more Gospels may have been composed orally, Hurtado suggests that this is to confuse the practice of dictation as one stage in the production of a literary work with that of composition in performance, which is nowhere attested of an ancient literary text:

> I know of no Roman-era evidence that any extended literary work was actually *composed* in 'performance'. That a work such as the Gospel of Mark is written in a kind of oral 'register' (i.e. reflecting some of the syntactical traits of spoken Koine Greek) is not a basis for asserting that it was *composed* in/through 'performance'.[60]

These are all important points, but while they do call the Oral Composition Hypothesis into question, its proponents could perhaps accuse Hurtado of begging the question on the grounds that their point is precisely that Mark should not be considered a 'literary work'. It could also be pointed out that, as Hurtado indeed allows, at least some kinds of written compositions (namely speeches and plays) *were* intended for memorization and performance in antiquity. While Mark is clearly not a speech, it is not inconceivable that it could originally have been intended as a script for dramatic performance, even if it is not formally a play; proponents of the oral-composition/performance thesis point to features of Mark's narrative that particularly suit it to such use. Moreover, the fact that there is evidence that texts were subsequently read (rather than performed) to Christian groups does not conclusively prove that this was Mark's original intention, or that all the Gospels were read rather than performed right from the start. Again, the concern to distinguish reading from acting may have been more pressing to elite persons than to the kind of people likely to have constituted Mark's target audience. Thus, while Hurtado's criticisms raise a number of serious questions for the Oral Composition Hypothesis, they do not quite dispose of it. There are, however, a number of other reasons for doubting aspects of the Oral Composition Hypothesis, in particular the notion of Mark as a mere performer of traditional oral narrative and the thesis that his Gospel is a mere transcript of oral performance rather than a written text in its own right, and these should now be examined in more detail.

First, second-century writers such as Papias (as cited in Eusebius, *Hist. eccl.* 3.39.14–15) and Irenaeus (*Haer.* 3.1.1) apparently regarded Mark as a specific individual who obtained the material for his Gospel from Peter. This information may well have been inaccurate, and it may be that it originated in an attempt to find an apostolic authority behind Mark's Gospel, but the point is not what patristic writers actually knew about Mark, but what they supposed to be plausible, and they seemed to have thought it plausible to regard Mark not as the scribal deposit of a long tradition of oral performance, but as the written

---

[60] Hurtado, 'Oral Fixation', 335 (emphasis original).

work of a specific individual. Of course this could just be put down to their own literate bias, but it is suggestive that people much closer to the time and place of Mark's composition than we are did not apparently regard it as an oral-traditional tale, and that any literate bias on Papias's part did not prevent his claiming to prefer the living and abiding voice to what he could find in books or from regarding Mark as composed on the basis of orally performed material (Peter's preaching).

Second, while the textual tradition was fluid, it was not so fluid as to have caused the Gospels to lose their distinct identities. Despite the fact that in a few places there are, for example, as many textual variants between different manuscripts of Luke as there are between some of these manuscripts and the corresponding passages in Mark,[61] overall what survives in the manuscript tradition is not a composite Gospel or a continuum of Gospels but four quite distinct Gospels, each with its own distinctive point of view and narrative structure. While the textual tradition of the Gospels is indeed fluid in comparison with the fixity of printed texts, it is still remarkably stable compared with the kind of oral-performance variations expected on the Parry–Lord model.

Whatever the degree of textual fluidity in the early textual transmission of Mark's Gospel, what remains is still a text that is quite distinctive compared with Matthew and Luke, including the very features of Markan style that have led scholars such as Dewey, Wire and Botha to argue for its oral origins. Among some of the peculiarities of Markan style noted by Craig Evans are frequent parataxis, redundancies, the use of the historic present, misplaced *gar* clauses, and intercalations ('sandwiches').[62] While some of these may be put down to an 'oral' style, it is curious that all of them (including the misplaced *gar* clauses and intercalations) would survive if the early manuscript tradition of Mark were a series of transcriptions of oral performances rather than the result of copying one manuscript from another. A series of oral performances by different performers would be unlikely to repeat precisely those oddities of verbal style.

The distinctiveness of Mark in terms of structure, tone and narrative presentation also tells against seeing it as the product of anonymous oral performers primarily concerned with passing on the tradition. The observations of redaction and literary critics on the distinctive stances of each Gospel cannot simply be wished away by impugning their allegedly anachronistic media assumptions. It may well be that we should not regard Matthew and Luke as redacting (or editing) Mark as we might edit a modern printed text, but it can hardly be denied

---

[61] David C. Parker, *The Living Text of the Gospels* (Cambridge: Cambridge University Press, 1997), 46–7.

[62] Craig A. Evans, 'How Mark Writes' in Markus Bockmuehl and David A. Hagner (eds), *The Written Gospel* (Cambridge: Cambridge University Press, 2005), 135–48.

that the Gospels reflect particular points of view and are not simply repositories of tradition. This in turn would seem to require a particular creative mind behind each Gospel, even if not exactly an author in the modern sense.

The argument is complicated by the fact that proposals for an oral Mark concern three distinct phases: the oral antecedents of Mark, the composition of Mark and the subsequent transmission of Mark, and that alleged media differences between orality and writing can be employed on both sides of the argument. Our evaluation has tended to favour the transmission of Mark as a written text. This is not to deny that most people would have become acquainted with it through hearing it rather than reading it for themselves, or that oral renditions of Mark might have had some influence on the written textual tradition, although this is probably not strictly necessary to explain textual variants that could just as well be the product of loose scribal copying. We can speculate that some scribal errors or changes were caused by scribes' recollections of what they had heard, but this remains speculation.

The conflation of the first two phases envisaged on the model of composition proposed by Botha and Wire is also suspect. Both Botha and Wire rely heavily on the oral-formulaic model of Parry and Lord, but this raises the question why this should be seen as an appropriate model for the composition of the Gospels. Botha points to what he regards as formulaic elements of Mark's compositional style, but he does not show that these could only have come about by the mechanism of composition in performance proposed by Parry and Lord. Moreover, it is hardly a consequence of the Parry–Lord theory that oral poetry is composed by no one in particular but is simply handed down by traditional singers from the dawn of time. On this understanding it would be hard to see how any oral epic ever came into being in the first place. It completely ignores Lord's observations on the skill and creativity of some of the best singers, such as Avdo Međedević, who was able not just to repeat a poem of several thousand lines after one hearing, but completely transform it in the process, for example not only expanding one scene from 176 lines to 558, but stamping it with 'his own understanding of the heroic mind'.[63] He was able to do this mainly because he could draw on the vast store of other traditional material he knew which he could use to supplement the version he had just heard, but this still makes Međedević far more than a mere transmitter of traditional poems.

It would seem, then, that the Parry–Lord theory does not in fact support the notion that composition in performance implies a strongly conservative handling of existing tradition by a series of anonymous performers of strictly limited creativity. Such a view is more characteristic of the romantic notion of folklore employed by form criticism, and identified and criticized as such by Erhardt

---

[63] Lord, *Singer*, 78–9.

Güttgemanns (and also, incidentally, by Ruth Finnegan).[64] Moreover, the Parry–Lord theory is far from being the only available model of oral composition; there are societies in which oral poets are recognized as creative individuals.[65] At the end of her assessment of the Parry–Lord theory in the context of ancient Greece, Rosalind Thomas notes that 'The oral poet, then, could have had various techniques at his disposal, and we should avoid the idea that oral poets can only function before an audience and through totally formulaic and traditional language.'[66] Indeed a 'society with little or no writing is not necessarily the homogeneous and totally traditional one that one might infer from some literature on oral poetry. Creativity, individuality and innovation did exist.'[67]

Furthermore, perfectly reasonable doubts have been raised whether the Parry–Lord theory can adequately account for the artistry of the *Iliad* and the *Odyssey*, the very Homeric epics the theory was created to explain.[68] Thus, quite apart from the other considerations advanced, the appeal to Parry's and Lord's work on Balkan bards and their theories about Homer do not justify the picture of oral-traditional composition propounded by Botha and Wire.

This does not, however, dispose of other aspects of the oral-composition theory. In particular it could still be the case that the oral tradition available to Mark was not a collection of isolated anecdotes and sayings, and that Mark had previously worked on his narrative orally before his Gospel was set down in writing (although, as we shall see later, Loveday Alexander suggests that isolated anecdotal material was frequently used to transmit traditions in Hellenistic schools without any automatic tendency for them to coalesce into connected narratives). In other words, Mark could still be Dewey's particularly gifted storyteller who had perhaps taken a previous (oral) version of the story of Jesus and had managed to transform it into something far more compelling, rather as Avdo Međedević was apparently able to do with an epic poem. In doing so, like Međedević, Mark may well have called on other traditional material he had at his disposal. That is, he could have called on a wider social memory of his community than was encapsulated in any particular performance of the Jesus story he had heard.

Another plank in Dewey's argument is that if (as she supposes) Mark was originally addressed to rural communities in Galilee and Syria (as Horsley and Rohrbaugh argue), then it is much more likely to have been performed orally than committed to writing, since there would be little use for manuscripts in

---

[64] Erhardt Güttgemanns, *Candid Questions Concerning Gospel Form Criticism: A Methodological Sketch of the Fundamental Problematics of Form and Redaction Criticism* (Pittsburgh Theological Monograph Series, 26; Pittsburgh, PA: Pickwick Press, 1979), 127, 184–93; Finnegan, *Oral Poetry*, 30–41.

[65] Finnegan, *Oral Poetry*, 52–87, 170–213.

[66] Thomas, *Literacy and Orality*, 50.

[67] Thomas, *Literacy and Orality*, 51.

[68] Thomas, *Literacy and Orality*, 34–40.

peasant villages. Part of the difficulty with this argument is that Horsley and Rohrbaugh both suppose that the communities depicted in the Gospel are more or less the same as the communities addressed by the Gospel, but it surely cannot be assumed in general that the target audience of a narrative is quite so straight-forwardly reflected in the setting of that narrative. To be sure, narratives may reveal something about their target audiences, and Rohrbaugh's analysis of the social location of Mark's audience makes a good case for placing it at the lower rather than the upper end of the social spectrum; Mark does appear to represent a perspective 'from below' rather than an elite one. But it is less clear whether the predominantly rural setting of Mark's narrative represents that of his target audience or simply that of the traditions with which Mark worked.[69] While on the face of it Mark may appear to be particularly addressing the concerns of rural communities, this could simply be because that is what Jesus did (or was believed to have done). Dewey is almost certainly right to insist that rural communities would be better served by oral performances than by written manuscripts, but the only evidence we have for the existence of Mark comes in the form of written manuscripts, whose existence becomes hard to explain if Mark was in fact com-posed for oral performance in a rural setting.

This leads to the final problem with the oral-compositional view of Mark, namely the difficulty any version of this theory has in explaining why Mark's Gospel should ever have been written down at all. Dewey's model of ongoing oral performances of Mark in which written texts played only a subordinate role and the written tradition was controlled by the oral leaves the written texts strangely redundant: why would anyone go to the trouble and expense of producing written texts that had no apparent function? The Botha–Wire model suffers from a similar problem: if our Mark's Gospel were in reality just a transcription of an ongoing tradition of composition in performance, why was the transcription made? One might argue that someone thought Mark's tale worth preserving, but then on the Botha–Wire model it was preserving itself perfectly well through a tradition of oral performance, so what would be the need to fix it in writing?

Chapter 2 examined a number of reasons why someone might commit a Gospel to writing, but none of these possible reasons features in any version of the oral-composition model. Taken in conjunction with the other doubts raised about this model, this would seem to make the oral-composition model overwhelmingly improbable (except in the limited sense in which oral performance may have preceded or aided in the written composition of Mark), and if it does not work for Mark, it is even less likely to work for any of the other Gospels.[70]

---

[69] Cf. Richard Bauckham, 'For Whom Were Gospels Written?' in Richard Bauckham (ed.), *The Gospels for All Christians: Rethinking the Gospel Audiences* (Edinburgh: T. & T. Clark, 1998), 9–48 (25–6).

[70] See also Christopher Bryan, *A Preface to Mark: Notes on the Gospel in Its Literary and Cultural Settings* (Oxford: Oxford University Press, 1993), 67–162 (esp. 153–4).

The scribal-school-memory-tradition model

A third possible model of textual composition is that attributed to some ancient Near Eastern scribes, who were neither authors (in either the modern or elite Graeco-Roman sense) nor oral-traditional performers in the sense just discussed above, but rather literate shapers of traditional material. The primary aim of writing on this model is not publication but education, that is to say the training and enculturation of the next generation of scribes (in the sense of administrative and intellectual retainers rather than low-level secretaries or clerks), and the typical kind of writing produced is that known as 'wisdom literature', a form of instructional material that apprentice scribes would be expected to copy and learn by heart, both in order to learn to write, but also, and just as importantly, to internalize the values and precepts contained in such texts so that they became inscribed on the tablets of their hearts, not only in the sense of memorizing what they said, but of adopting their stance to the world and becoming socialized into the scribal ethos. While the majority of scribes might be content with learning and copying their exemplars, a few older and more experienced scribes might try to make their own contribution by composing their own texts on the basis of previous models. These scribes would see themselves not as authors (in the sense of authorities promoting original ideas) but as conduits of an older tradition (which they might nevertheless be adapting) and hence as spokesmen for the authoritative voices of the past. On this model one's sources would be not so much texts one consulted in a deliberate research phase as material one had absorbed through enculturation and reflection over a long period.

This is essentially the model derived from scribal practices as described by Jan Assmann and Richard Horsley, although there are differences in emphases between the two.[71] Assmann's discussion of scribal enculturation comes in the context of contrasting oral and written means of addressing the expanded situation, and so emphasizes the role of writing, while Horsley appears anxious to correct print-culture assumptions and so emphasizes that the primary mode of scribal education was through oral repetition and memorization rather than reading and writing texts. While this may be something of an over-correction, the emphasis on memorization is sound (and shared with Assmann), and Horsley is no doubt also correct in asserting that oral recitation played an important role in memorization. Horsley in any case acknowledges that written texts may sometimes have

---

[71] Jan Assmann, *Religion and Cultural Memory* (tr. Rodney Livingstone; Stanford, CA: Stanford University Press, 2006), 101–17; Richard A. Horsley, *Scribes, Visionaries and the Politics of Second Temple Judea* (Louisville, KY and London: Westminster John Knox Press, 2007), 90–108; cf. David M. Carr, *Writing on the Tablet of the Heart: Origins of Scripture and Literature* (Oxford: Oxford University Press, 2005), 40–1.

been used as aids to recitation and memorization, even though he sees this use as very much subordinate to the role of oral recitation.[72]

While such instructional texts would typically result in what has come to be termed 'wisdom literature', Horsley envisages a similar process underlying the composition of texts in other genres. In Horsley's view, the composition of much covenantal and legal material happened in the process of its cultivation by priests, Levites and scribes and of its adaptation to developing social–political circumstances, while prophetic oracles were remembered and similarly adapted. These 'traditional oral cultivated materials (which may also have been written) then formed the basis for further development by the more creative scribes, which might be called composition'. In Mesopotamia, for example, 'creative scribes could adapt, combine, or reconfigure those blocks of traditional material in the process of creating a text that was both new and traditional'. Horsley views this composition as more akin to oral-traditional composition in performance than literary authorship, although he allows that the text so composed 'was eventually dictated and written'. Thus, in Horsley's view, this type of composition need not involve writing but did involve 'literacy in various ways, some more subtle and others more obvious'. Examples include psalms and wisdom literature structured as acrostics (where each successive line starts with the next letter of the alphabet), 'the arrangement of materials in books such as Isaiah, Deuteronomy, or Nehemiah' and the use of the books of Samuel and Kings in the composition of Chronicles.[73]

In applying these insights to the composition of Ben Sira, Horsley goes on to suggest that rather than seeing the echoes of earlier wisdom literature in Ben Sira as literary allusions, they should rather be taken as indications of composition in a traditional register, meaning the use of a particular kind of language (style, phraseology, choice of vocabulary, etc.) appropriate to particular topics or occasions (for example, the register appropriate to a eulogy delivered at a memorial service would be very different from that appropriate to an academic lecture on the Synoptic Problem).[74] The same principle might apply to scribal compositions in other genres as well. On this model scribal composers of new wisdom, prophetic, legal and hymnic (or psalm) texts were not citing or alluding to earlier texts in the same genre, but rather composing in the traditional style of that genre on the basis of their thorough familiarity with it (which includes not just typical themes but typical turns of phrase employed in the tradition, enabling a new composition to sound rather like a traditional text, although it may also contain innovations).

It is perhaps no accident that this model looks somewhat akin to the Parry–Lord model outlined above. One reason for this may be that Horsley views scribal

---

[72] Horsley, *Scribes*, 101–4.
[73] Horsley, *Scribes*, 105.
[74] Horsley, *Scribes*, 133–44.

composition as an essentially oral process that somehow ends up in writing, although he also makes concessions to some essentially literary aspects of the process. It is hard to tell whether this apparent tension is due to a desire to emphasize the difference between ancient scribal and modern print culture or a tendency (found also in some other writers) to associate memory more with oral than with written modes of verbal production.

For Assmann, on the other hand, the written production of cultural texts previously stored in memory alone is something quite distinct from oral tradition:

> What this involves – as a rule – is *not* the writing down of a living, oral corpus. The oral tradition remains unaffected. What develops in the medium of writing by way of cultural texts is something quite different. Instead of proverbs we have wisdom literature, instead of myths, elaborately artistic and highly didactic narratives, like the Gilgamesh epic or the Story of Sinuhe. We are looking at texts that are conceived as written, not with traditional works subsequently put into writing.[75]

Rather than getting drawn into the complex debate over whether there is a fundamental difference between oral and written modes of expression (to which the short answer is probably that it depends on what sort of material one has in mind), it may be simpler to cut this particular Gordian knot by pointing out that our present purpose is not to determine the precise configuration of orality, memory and writing in the practice of ancient Near Eastern scribes but to sketch out a model that is distinct from both the elite authorship model and the oral-composition model. For this purpose it will be convenient to lean more towards Assmann than Horsley (where the two differ) while drawing on many of Horsley's suggestions. The model that then emerges is one in which scribes compose a new written work on the basis of their thorough knowledge of a tradition that includes earlier written texts, many of which they have committed to memory, along with the oral–memorial cultivation of those texts and related oral traditions. Such scribal composers are not authors in the modern (or even ancient elite) sense, since they do not aim to be original so much as to be purveyors of a tradition (albeit a tradition they may in fact be actively reconfiguring to meet new needs) and they do not see themselves as the authorities standing behind their works, which are thus usually either anonymous or attributed to some great authority figure of the past.

To see how this might apply to the writing of the Gospels we may take Matthew as an example. H. Benedict Green has written a study of the poetic material in Matthew (such as the Lord's Prayer and the Beatitudes), arguing that it works well poetically in *Greek* (suggesting therefore that this must have been the language

---

[75] Assmann, *Religion*, 111 (emphasis original).

it which it was composed) and seems to be in a style distinctive to Matthew. Green also points to multiple instances where these poetic compositions employ (or echo) phrases found in the Greek Old Testament. He then concludes that this sayings material was composed by Matthew on the basis of scriptural material.[76] This model seems implausible if we are meant to imagine Matthew hunting among Scripture scrolls for phrases to stitch together, and may look a little odd if we imagine Matthew deliberately alluding to a number of scriptural texts. It would, however, fit the scribal-tradition-memory model quite well if we picture Matthew composing fresh material in a register with which he was thoroughly familiar and then attributing it to the most important figure in his tradition (i.e. Jesus). The point here, though, is not so much to argue that this is what actually happened as to illustrate the model.

On this model, Matthew would presumably be trying not to pass off his own ideas as Jesus', but rather to give expression to what he believed Jesus' teaching to have been. The register in which he composed would thus be influenced as much by the Jesus tradition with which he was familiar as by his knowledge of Israelite Scripture and tradition. His ability to merge the two streams of tradition so seamlessly would doubtless have been helped by his sense of deep congruity between them; after all, for Matthew Jesus was the true fulfilment of the Law and the Prophets.

This raises the question of how Matthew's use of Mark might appear on this model. One of the seemingly odd features of the Synoptic Gospels is the extent to which the Evangelists take over the wording of their sources. While it is often suggested that antiquity lacked any notion of plagiarism, this statement requires nuance. It is perfectly true that there were no copyright laws governing the use of one author's work by another, but it would do little to enhance a would-be elite writer's reputation were he to be caught copying someone else's work more or less verbatim and trying to pass it off as his own. Plagiarism might thus attract moral censure even though it broke no laws.[77] Elite authors therefore generally made the effort to rewrite the material they took from their sources in their own words. But if Matthew's (and possibly Luke's) ethos was more scribal than elite-authorial, originality in wording would have been less of a concern; the use of a substantial amount of wording taken from a source would be fully compatible with standing in the same tradition as that source. If Matthew's aim was not to author an original text but to reconfigure the tradition he had received to meet his own situation, there would be little reason for him not to recycle

---

[76] H. Benedict Green, *Matthew, Poet of the Beatitudes* (JSNTSup, 203; Sheffield: Sheffield Academic Press, 2001).

[77] F. Gerald Downing, 'Writers' Use or Abuse of Written Sources' in Paul Foster, Andrew Gregory, John S. Kloppenborg and J. Verheyden (eds), *New Studies in the Synoptic Problem* (BETL, 139; Leuven: Leuven University Press, 2011), 523–48 (524); Winsbury, *Roman Book*, 132–3.

wording that he found perfectly serviceable for his purpose, particularly if that wording was already starting to be invested with some aura of authority.

Matthew's use of Mark nevertheless suggests at least a slight move away from a purely scribal model. The fact that some of Matthew's changes (such as the addition of infancy and resurrection narratives) bring his Gospel a little closer to a typical *bios* than Mark's suggests some appreciation of Graeco-Roman literary culture, just as his improvements to Mark's Greek coupled with his tendency to tie up Markan loose ends and correct dubious Markan theology appears indicative of at least some literary sensibilities. The tendency of such changes is in part to make Matthew's Gospel better suited than Mark's to stand on its own feet without so much support from an ambient tradition; in other words, to function more securely as a literary text in an expanded situation. Matthew may have been a scribe, but if so he was a scribe with at least some inclination towards authorship.

The 'scribal' model just discussed is quite closely related to what might be called a 'school' model, in the sense of the Hellenistic schools responsible for the production of technical literature (*Fachprosa*) for philosophical and professional groups, which passed on technical learning in areas such as medicine, architecture, engineering and (at a higher social level) rhetoric. It is in the written production of this kind that F. Gerald Downing finds the closest parallel to the extent to which the Synoptic Evangelists borrow the wording of their sources (as opposed to the paraphrasing that would be expected of a more literary author), and it is this kind of school setting that Loveday Alexander suggests might be the most appropriate context for Luke–Acts (and quite possibly the other Gospels as well).[78] In this setting philosophical, ethical and technical (craft) teaching are often handed on by means of anecdotes, both orally and in written collections, which might be frequently reworked to meet changing needs. Particularly in situations where it might seem important to preserve the ethos of a teacher, these anecdotes might sometimes be arranged in the form of a *bios* (though this was far from inevitable), and in situations where the school tradition had already taken *bios* form one might expect revisions to stick to that form.

Whereas the scribal model drawn from Horsley and Assmann is based on the practices of ancient Near Eastern scribes, the setting adumbrated by Downing and Alexander is based on Hellenistic schools. Yet scribal schools were, after all, one form of school, and by Roman times the ancient Near East doubtless shared many features of the common Mediterranean culture, so these may be not so much two distinct models as variations on a common theme. Alexander

---

[78] Downing, 'Writers' Use', 524–36; Loveday Alexander, 'Luke's Preface in the Context of Greek Preface-Writing', *NovT* 28 (1986), 48–74 (59–74); Loveday Alexander, 'Memory and Tradition in the Hellenistic Schools' in W. H. Kelber and S. Byrskog (eds), *Jesus in Memory: Traditions in Oral and Scribal Perspectives* (Waco: Baylor University Press, 2009), 113–53.

envisages the school model as one in which existing traditions are continually adapted rather than the scribal process of composing on the basis of older material, but there is only a thin line between the two.

Alexander appears to be proposing two applications of the school model: first as the literary background to the Evangelists' efforts and second as the matrix in which the Gospels took shape. The first part of this proposal is then that Luke (and perhaps the other Evangelists) wrote the kind of prose they did in the way they did because, coming from such a craft or professional setting themselves, this was the model that most immediately suggested itself to them for writing about a serious subject. The second is that Jesus' deeds and teaching were rehearsed and passed on in the form of memorable anecdotes which came to be committed to writing for use as instructional handbooks (or aids to memory) in a specifically Christian school setting (such as church meetings for teaching and worship). But as Alexander at once goes on to acknowledge, 'the canonical Gospels are clearly more complex literary creations than the disconnected anecdote collections that we see in the papyri, with a much stronger narrative connection' and so she goes on to suggest that this is because the Gospels 'may owe as much to the Bible as to Greek biography'.[79] This in part supports the suggestion that the Gospels be seen as *biblical* bioi, but at the same time throws doubt on the second part of Alexander's proposal.

It may be that sayings collections or miracle-story collections (if they existed) came about as memory aids in Christian 'schools' as Alexander suggests, but the Gospels appear to be a different kind of composition, put together with at least some degree of rhetorical intent (aiming to persuade by the shape of their overall narrative, and not simply to provide a quarry for sermon material). Thus while the 'school' model may provide a further refinement to the 'scribal' model, it remains the case that the composition of the Gospels belongs somewhere between this kind of model and a more rhetorically informed model associated with the literary elites.

Conclusions

This chapter has considered three possible models for the composition of the Gospels, which may be termed the authorial, the oral and the scribal school. These should be seen more as ideal types than three discrete buckets into which all of the Evangelists must be placed. The actual working methods of each Evangelist may have had elements from more than one of these models, and since all three models imply substantial reliance on memory (as well as at least some interpenetration with orality) the lines between them may often be blurred.

---

[79] Alexander, 'Memory and Tradition', 150.

Susan Niditch has proposed an oral–literate continuum along which she places four possible models for the composition of the Hebrew Bible.[80] The three models considered here for the composition of the Gospels do not, however, fit so neatly along a continuum. While it may be useful to think of a continuum between the authorial and scribal models, there is both contact and disjunction between the scribal and oral ones, for while scribes' rendering of their tradition has several points of affinity with the Parry–Lord model of composition in oral performance, there are fundamental differences in the media, methods and material employed. Instructional, prophetic and legal material is not epic poetry, and lacks the mnemonic support of a good story. Scribal training requires conscious and deliberate memorization in a manner that is quite alien to the methods of the Balkan bards studied by Parry and Lord. And however much scribal writing is tied up with oral recitation, writing does make a difference.

The four Evangelists should probably all be placed a little differently in relation to our three models, although any placement can only be tentative at best. The working methods of the Evangelists are likely to be related to their backgrounds, educational attainments, social locations and purposes in writing, all of which have to be deduced from what they wrote coupled with a considerable amount of guesswork informed by what we think we know about the primitive Church and first-century media. Our estimates of their level of education are likely to be guided in part by our evaluation of how well they wrote, which inevitably involves an element of subjective judgement (although the opinions of other ancient authors provide some guidance here).

Those caveats made, we may tentatively suggest that Matthew lies somewhere towards the scribal end of the scribal–authorial axis (although, as suggested above, at least some way towards the authorial pole), whereas Luke lies closer to the authorial model (at least in aspiration and working method) than any of the other Evangelists. John may perhaps be placed somewhere between Matthew and Luke. Mark is harder to place, in part because without access to his raw materials there is no way of determining how he employed or transformed them in the course of composition.

A further puzzle with Mark is the apparent contradiction between the relative sophistication of his narrative construction and the relative crudity of his Greek. One might try to explain this by suggesting that Greek was not his first language, but it is also worth bearing in mind that admiration for Mark's narrative achievement seems to be rather more prevalent among his modern than his ancient critics; Papias, for example, apparently felt it necessary to apologize for Mark being 'not in order'. It may, however, be that Mark's Greek appears relatively rough

---

[80] Susan Niditch, *Oral World and Written Word: Orality and Literacy in Ancient Israel* (Library of Ancient Israel; ed. D. A. Knight; London: SPCK, 1997), 117–29.

since he never troubled to revise a first draft dictated to a scribe. This may be less an indication of Mark's ability or aspiration than of the resources at his disposal; unlike an elite author he would not have had access to slave secretarial assistance and may well not have been able to afford the quantity of papyrus needed to make multiple drafts. One might alternatively hazard a guess that Mark was an able storyteller of modest scribal attainments trying his hand at a written composition (probably via dictation) while being more at home in an oral register. This is not the same, however, as suggesting that Mark's Gospel is simply the written version of an oral performance; on this understanding it remains something intended as a written composition (for reasons already discussed above), but it may have had oral antecedents (as Dewey suggests) or have first been tried out orally before being committed to writing. This perhaps leaves Mark with a foot in all three camps (if one may be permitted a tripedal Mark), but tells us little about his working methods for the reason already given: we do not know what he had to work with.

In sum, the Evangelists could well have employed a variety of compositional methods drawn from a number of available models, and not just in the way the literary elites made use of written sources in writing history or biography. But what is common to all three models of composition discussed here is their heavy reliance on *memory*, which will be the subject of the next two chapters.

5

Memory and writing

The previous two chapters have argued that memory is likely to have been central to the composition of the Gospels, but saying that tells us very little unless we go on to explore the implications. The present chapter will look at issues surrounding memory from the perspective of the individual author, while, since both human memory and Gospel authorship are socially embedded, the following chapter will go on to explore social, collective or cultural memory. The present chapter's discussion of individual memory will encompass three aspects: the extent to which and the purposes for which ancient writers used their memories, the workings of individual memory and ways in which memory interacts with the process of writing.

Ancient uses of memory

Memorization played a far larger role in ancient education than it does today. This applies not least to the ancient use of written texts, which were often used for students to memorize as part of their enculturation into the traditions and values of their society.

According to David Carr this was the case throughout much of the ancient world, as he demonstrates with evidence of the use of texts for recitation, memorization and enculturation from Mesopotamia, Egypt, ancient Israel, Hellenistic Greece (and Rome) and Second-Temple Judaism.[1] Various methods might be employed to aid memorization, such as having students copy the texts, or recite them by chanting or singing, and by mnemonic aids within the texts such as chiasms (sandwich patterns) and acrostics. Some of these were briefly mentioned in the previous chapter in connection with the training of scribes. Explicit training in memory techniques also formed part of a rhetorical education, which became increasingly important in the Hellenistic and Roman periods.

One of the most commonly taught memory methods was the method of *loci* (places), the invention of which was attributed to one Simonides of Ceos. Simonides is said to have left a banquet just before the building it was being

---

[1] David M. Carr, *Writing on the Tablet of the Heart: Origins of Scripture and Literature* (Oxford: Oxford University Press, 2005), 27–8, 64, 71–3, 74–5, 96–9, 125, 135–7, 156, 180–2, 209, 228–30, 236–7, 247–8.

held in collapsed, crushing those inside. He was able to remember who had been present (and thus identify the mangled corpses) by being able to picture where they had been sitting.[2] The method of *loci* thus consisted of first committing some scene to memory, typically a familiar building or street around which one could travel in one's imagination, and then mentally placing an image representing each item to be remembered in sequence in each distinctive memory *locus*, with the aim of creating a memorable conjunction of images. To recall the items in the required sequence (the sequence of topics comprising a speech one was to deliver, say), one then mentally visited each memory *locus* in turn and recalled the associated image.[3]

This method was recommended not only as a means of recalling a sequence of things or concepts, but also for remembering words, though Quintilian (*Inst.* 11.2.17–26) was sceptical of its value for the latter, suggesting that it might be more trouble than it was worth to think up images for each word and then try to recall them all; indeed, Quintilian opined, such a double strain on memory was unlikely to result in fluent speech. Quintilian thus suggested a number of other methods, such as breaking down a longer work into shorter sections and learning each in turn (*Inst.* 11.2.27–28) or learning a text from the same wax tablet on which one had written it, since the physical appearance of the line of writing on the tablet, including any alterations made to the text, should aid recall (*Inst.* 11.2.32–33).[4]

It thus appears first that educated persons were expected to learn a considerable amount of material, particularly culturally significant texts, by heart, and second that by the first century there was a widespread recognition, not only of the importance of memory, but of the need to train it (especially for the purposes of rhetoric). Texts were certainly read, but they were often read aloud, and often recited as part of the process of learning their content by heart:

> The focus was on inscribing a culture's most precious traditions on the insides of people. Within this context, copies of texts served as solidified reference points for recitation and memorization of the tradition, demonstrations of mastery of the tradition, and gifts from the gods.[5]

The question then arises how far down the social scale this kind of enculturation extended. Carr's evidence relates almost entirely to the education of the elites.

---

[2] Frances A. Yates, *The Art of Memory* (London: Pimlico, 1992), 17, 42–4.

[3] Mary Carruthers, *The Book of Memory: A Study of Memory in Medieval Culture* (2nd edn; Cambridge Studies in Medieval Literature; Cambridge: Cambridge University Press, 2008), 89–92, 172–86; Yates, *Art of Memory*, 17–62; Jocelyn Penny Small, *Wax Tablets of the Mind: Cognitive Studies of Memory and Literacy in Classical Antiquity* (Abingdon: Routledge, 1997), 81–116; Janet Coleman, *Ancient and Medieval Memories* (Cambridge: Cambridge University Press, 1992), 51–4.

[4] Yates, *Art of Memory*, 38–41; Carruthers, *Book of Memory*, 92–3; Small, *Wax Tablets*, 117–22.

[5] Carr, *Writing*, 6.

In his discussion of ancient Israel, for example, he expresses doubt over whether many people would have had mastery of the entire biblical corpus, although he acknowledges parallels in other cultures of elite mastery of similarly sized corpora as well as traditional Islamic recitation of the Qur'an.[6] He also points out that Josephus's assertions about the extent of Jews' education and knowledge of their law (*Ant.* 16.43; *Ag. Ap.* 1.60; 2.175, 204) are more likely to represent aspiration than reality.[7] We may assume that the vast majority of people who could neither read nor write were largely excluded from the learning of texts by heart (even if they could have been taught orally, there is little reason why they should have been, and it appears to be difficult for anyone to learn more than about 50 lines without the support of a written text).[8] We know little about the education of non-elite persons who were taught to read and write, whether as slaves in the service of a master, or for business purposes, or as members of the retainer class directly or indirectly in the service of the elite (for example, in some kind of administrative role), or as apprentices to a master possessed only of craft literacy. Yet it is most likely to have been from one of these classes of people that the Evangelists were drawn.

It may nevertheless be possible to deduce something about how such people would have been educated on the basis that educational practices seem to have been fairly uniform; according to Teresa Morgan, what was taught, 'at any given level, recurs again and again in the surviving evidence in remarkably similar forms across vast geographical distances, a wide social spectrum and a timespan of nearly a thousand years'.[9] Moreover, we do have some indications about the elementary stages. Verbatim rote memorization of texts was the basis of all education, and Quintilian advised starting it at an early age. According to Quintilian (*Inst.* 1.1.19), 'the elements of reading and writing are entirely a matter of memory', by which he meant not simply the ability to retain information but the ability to manipulate it in one's head. Quintilian (*Inst.* 1.1.36) was also keen that the material students used in learning to read, write and recite should be morally improving.[10] It would seem likely, then, that non-elite persons who received some education in reading and writing would have been educated in much the same

---

[6] Carr, *Writing*, 155; on recitation of the Qur'an see William A. Graham, *Beyond the Written Word: Oral Aspects of Scripture in the History of Religion* (Cambridge: Cambridge University Press, 1987), 79–115, especially 104–6 on memorization.

[7] Carr, *Writing*, 246–7.

[8] So Carr, *Writing*, 7; cf. David C. Rubin, *Memory in Oral Traditions: The Cognitive Psychology of Epic, Ballads, and Counting-out Rhymes* (Oxford and New York: Oxford University Press, 1995), 6–7, who states that there is no evidence of any text longer than 50 *words* being remembered verbatim in any oral tradition.

[9] Teresa Morgan, *Literate Education in the Hellenistic and Roman Worlds* (Cambridge Classical Studies; Cambridge: Cambridge University Press, 2007), 3.

[10] Carruthers, *Book of Memory*, 111, 135, 140–1, 221.

way as their elite contemporaries, though not to the standard required for successful oratorical performance. As has been mentioned before, memory played a major role in the training of (at least the higher-ranking) scribes, who would largely have been members of the retainer class rather than the elite.

The previous chapter indicated that memory was also employed in *writing*, or at least in the composition of texts, examples including how Pliny the Younger composed in his head and then dictated to a secretary, and Plutarch relying on his memory of background reading. It is also likely that educated persons who had learned a number of texts by heart would use their memory of those texts in their own writing rather than consulting a physical copy. This would partly be a matter of convenience, as has already been argued, but there is also a fair amount of evidence to show that this is how ancient (and mediaeval) authors generally worked.

Carr cites a number of examples. Sumero-Akkadian writers did not 'edit' texts or follow modern 'cut and paste' methods, but used previously memorized hymns as mental prototypes (as in the scribal model discussed in the previous chapter). Biblical quotations and the use of biblical material in other compositions in many of the scrolls discovered at Qumran also appear to be based on memory.[11] Quintilian's advice to writers included sorting one's material out in one's head and only then dictating it to a secretary (thereby avoiding producing hastily dictated material that had not been properly thought out).[12] Admittedly Quintilian also provided advice on the use of wax tablets in the process of composition, but this was aimed more at beginners, the idea being that more advanced students would learn to revise their material in their heads (*Inst.* 10.3.31–32; 10.6.1–4).[13] While this advice concerns the process of composition rather than the use of sources, the ability to arrange one's composition in one's head would seem to presuppose that one has memory command of one's raw material.

According to Mary Carruthers, composition continued to be primarily a mental activity well into the Middle Ages: it 'is not particularly an act of writing. It is rumination, cogitation, dictation, a listening and a dialogue, a gathering (*collectio*) of voices from their several places in memory.'[14] It was not, however, simply a matter of sorting things out in a logical way; parts of the process could be highly emotional, involving fierce concentration, more akin to meditation and mulling over than calculation and reasoning.[15] Moreover, it seems mediaeval

---

[11] Carr, *Writing*, 230, 236.

[12] Quintilian, *Inst.* 10.3.17–20; 10.6.1–2; Carruthers, *Book of Memory*, 241, 252; Small, *Wax Tablets*, 181–3.

[13] Carruthers, *Book of Memory*, 252–3.

[14] Carruthers, *Book of Memory*, 244.

[15] Carruthers, *Book of Memory*, 245–9, citing evidence from Augustine and Quintilian as well as Thomas Aquinas and Anselm.

authors often knew their sources by heart and continued to rely on their memories to access them. Thomas Aquinas, for example, is said to have composed in this way.[16] William of Ockham was forced to do so when he was exiled to Munich, where he had little access to books or to the latest documents. He was able to do so because he had memorized material from a wide range of sources as part of his normal education. Where Ockham apologized for imperfections in his work produced under these conditions, he was referring not to failures in his memory but to his inability to consult the latest works (and so to be completely up to date).[17] Peter of Ravenna, at the end of the fifteenth century, preferred to lecture on canon law from memory, even though printed books were then becoming available.[18]

These attitudes to reading and writing in the Middle Ages were by no means exceptional; they were instead typical reflections of mediaeval education. Monks, for example, were expected to memorize psalms, and some educated laypersons would have known some of them by heart. Augustine's sermons often appear to have presupposed such knowledge in his audience, and his own writings were steeped in the language of the Psalms, just as those of Pope Gregory the Great were later steeped in Augustine. Memory played a large part in mediaeval education, and was often identified not simply with mental storage but with creative thinking. Petrarch (e.g. *Secretum,* Dialogue 2) indicates that memorization was by no means left to chance, but was rather a learned technique; he made a point of learning valuable material by heart when encountering it in the course of reading, and placed marks in the text as an aid to memory. Not all material need be learned by heart (i.e. verbatim or *ad verbum*), however; for some purposes learning *ad rem* (to the matter, i.e. memorizing the gist) might suffice. Memorization was nevertheless often presupposed. Carruthers, for example, argues that Jerome's index and gloss of Hebrew names in the Bible would be much more useful to someone using the Bible from memory than someone working with a manuscript copy, and that the order of citations in Robert Grosseteste's topical concordance suggests that it was compiled from memory rather than from written texts. It was thus analogous in function to other mediaeval florilegia (collections of excerpts) that were intended to provide memory cues to material previously read.

The process of reading was meant to be one of 'dividing' (Hugh of St Victor, *Didascalion* 3.9), meaning that one learned a text by storing it and subsequently retrieving it as a series of short passages (as Quintilian advised). Composition was an extension of this, since it started in memorized reading. Seneca's advice (*Epistles* 84.3), which formed part of the standard mediaeval curriculum, was that

[16] Carruthers, *Book of Memory*, 113.
[17] Carruthers, *Book of Memory*, 113, 196–8.
[18] Carruthers, *Book of Memory*, 137.

one should imitate bees who gathered different kinds of nectar from different flowers and then sorted and stored them in separate cells. Composition was then a matter of producing one's own blend from the material carefully kept separate in one's memory, or, to vary the metaphor, one had to not simply ingest what one read but fully digest it, ruminating on what one had read through one's composition (compare the imagery of consuming a scroll at Ezekiel 3.1–3).[19]

The connection between reading, writing, composing and memory, the memorization of texts and reliance on memory in composition thus appear to have been constant features of educated culture from ancient Mesopotamia until at least the end of the European Middle Ages, and is well attested in Roman writers. It thus seems safe to assume that memory would have played a prominent role in the composition of most first-century texts, not least the Gospels. Although we remain ignorant of precisely what education the Gospel writers had undergone, it seems far more likely than not that it would have resembled at least the earlier stages of other contemporary training in reading and writing, and would thus have included a similar emphasis on the use of memory. The fact that the Evangelists almost certainly would not have received the full tertiary education in rhetoric reserved for the upper class does not mean that they would have received no memory training; neither does it mean that they would be any less inclined to rely on their memories. It implies only that they may have been less good at it, or at least, that they were unlikely to have been able to perform some of the more impressive feats boasted of by some of their better-educated contemporaries.

There is certainly no reason to suppose that non-elite authors would have been any more 'bookish' than their elite counterparts in the sense of being any more inclined to consult texts to check their references, although it could well be that they would have a smaller range of texts at their command in memory. On the other hand, non-elite authors such as those who wrote the Gospels would have had no less access to oral tradition and what we may call common knowledge, or, more specifically, the collective memory of the group for which they were writing. This all reinforces the view that the default way in which the Evangelists used their raw material (and composed their Gospels) would have been through memory.

This does not mean that we should altogether rule out the use of notes or the possibility that an Evangelist had eye contact with a source for at least part of the time in the course of writing, dictating or composing in his head. The point is rather that our assumption should be that the Gospel authors largely worked from memory for much of the time. Whether there is in fact any evidence of literary copying (in the sense of one Evangelist working with a copy of another Gospel in front of him) is a question to which we shall return in Chapter 7.

---

[19] Carruthers, *Book of Memory*, 112–15, 144–9, 195, 202–5, 217–19, 237–8.

The workings of memory

Having established the likelihood that the Evangelists relied heavily on memory in the course of composing the Gospels, we should next explore the implications. To this end we shall proceed in two stages, first taking a look at the workings of memory in general and then focusing on more specific issues concerning the use of memory in writing.

Although the present chapter is primarily concerned with the psychological aspect of memory as it relates to individual Gospel-writers, the first point to emphasize is that there is an irreducibly social dimension to human remembering (as Maurice Halbwachs insisted).[20] In order to explain our memories to others and even to ourselves, we must employ a language we learned from our surrounding culture. In order to make sense of our memories we frequently need to employ narrative patterns we share with those around us. We also employ basic frameworks (notions about the way the world works) that are not of our own making but are inherited from society. The world-view and schemata we use both to encode our memories in the first place and then to retrieve and interpret them are similarly borrowed from our social environment. Moreover, our memories are likely to be influenced by what we hear other people say. Different people may be more or less suggestible and more or less eager to conform, but none of us is a mnemonic island.

The social embeddedness of individual memory has both stabilizing and distorting effects. Human memory works well enough for most practical purposes, although that includes forgetting much of what we do not really need to remember, and compressing much of the rest from particular instances to general gist, both of which help make the contents of our memories more usable. Verbatim memory of (oral or written) texts may be something of a special case, however, since people certainly can reliably learn such material by heart (especially with the aid of a written archetype).

The next main point to emphasize is that memory is not a matter of storage and recall, as if the human brain were an organic filing cabinet or hard disk drive, but is instead largely a process of reconstruction based on memory traces. To be sure, something is encoded when we experience things, or there would be

---

[20] Maurice Halbwachs, *On Collective Memory* (The Heritage of Sociology; ed. D. N. Levine; tr. Lewis A. Coser; Chicago and London: University of Chicago Press, 1992), 53, 172–3; so also, e.g., F. C. Bartlett, *Remembering: A Study in Experimental and Social Psychology* (Cambridge: Cambridge University Press, 1995 [1932]), 239–300; James L. Fentress and Chris Wickham, *Social Memory* (New Perspectives on the Past; Oxford and Cambridge, MA: Basil Blackwell, 1992), 7; and more specifically in connection with the Gospels, Richard A. Horsley, 'Prominent Patterns in the Social Memory of Jesus and Friends' in Alan Kirk and Tom Thatcher (eds), *Memory, Tradition, and Text: Uses of the Past in Early Christianity* (SBL Semeia Studies, 52; ed. G. A. Yee; Leiden and Boston: Brill, 2005), 57–78 (65).

nothing to recall, but the process of recall generally entails the construction of a coherent memory from the fragments encoded. Such a reconstruction will inevitably be shaped to meet the needs of the present and may be biased by self-interest. To the extent that the memory traces being retrieved do not give a complete picture, the mind fills it in with its notion of what ought to have happened or what usually happens or what would otherwise make sense of the encoded fragments.[21]

This process of reconstruction is greatly assisted by *schemata*, which, roughly speaking, are the patterns or models we use to make sense of things. Two common kinds of *schema* are the *script* and the *frame*. A script is the sequence of actions that typically goes to make up an event. For example, when you visit the dentist you might typically report to the receptionist, take a seat in the waiting room, read one of the magazines there, be summoned to your appointment, sit in the dentist's chair for your check-up and treatment, and finally report back to the receptionist again to settle the bill and book your next appointment. Knowing this typical sequence may help you reconstruct what happened on any one occasion, so that, for example, if you recall reading a particularly interesting magazine article on your last dental visit, you will assume you found it in the waiting room, not under the dentist's chair. A frame is a piece of structural knowledge about some aspect of the world, for example that a car generally has wheels, seats, a chassis, a body and an engine, with variable elements (such as the shape and colour of the body, the number of seats, the size of the engine) that can be slotted into the structure.

Scripts and frames help both to encode information in the first place and reconstruct it when we need to recall it. In the main such schemata are helpful, since they help us to make sense of the world and to recall items from the past in a fairly economical manner, rather than becoming overwhelmed by a mass of information. But schemata can also mislead, especially when the event we are trying to recall does not conform to the standard schema. To be sure, such an event may be memorable precisely because it was atypical; schemata are by no means Procrustean beds which all memories are made to fit, and the exceptional may well stand out in our memory. On the other hand, schema-related memory errors do occur, in which our recollection of something is reshaped to conform more closely to the standard schema we expect.

This was famously illustrated in an experiment by the Cambridge-based psychologist Frederick Bartlett in the 1930s. Bartlett showed a Native American story called the 'War of the Ghosts' to a number of subjects and had them retell it (or rewrite it) after various intervals. He found that in what he called the *effort*

---

[21] Daniel L. Schacter, *Searching for Memory: The Brain, the Mind, and the Past* (New York: Basic Books, 1996), 88–97.

after meaning, the new versions of the story had been reshaped to make better sense to his subjects, who were unfamiliar with Native American culture. Elements of the story that made no sense to the subjects tended to be dropped or radically altered, and fresh elements and rationalizations introduced to make sense of them according to the subjects' world-view.[22] Although Bartlett's experimental methods have been criticized, his findings have been substantially confirmed; there is a tendency for recollective reconstruction to be guided (and often misled) by schemata. In particular, information that is consistent with one's schemata is more likely to be remembered than information that is not.[23] One would also expect there to be a tendency for writers relying on memory to conform their material to schemata that are familiar or important to them, although not all recollection is distorted in this way.

Narrative patterns form a particularly significant type of schema. In narrating our memories to ourselves or others we inevitably have to shape them into some conventional narrative form in order to make sense of them. Thus while repeated narration may serve to fix a memory, it may also serve to fix a distorted version of it or even introduce fresh distortions.[24] That is to say, if a narrator introduces changes into some account of an event, the repeated act of narrating the new version will tend to lead the narrator into remembering this altered version as the 'correct' one. This has implications for how the Evangelists might remember any material they were in the habit of narrating. For example, it would suggest that their own narrative embellishments or interpretations would tend to become incorporated into their memory of the material.

Schema-based errors are not the only kind of memory distortion that can occur. Another frequent type of error is source misattribution. We are not always very good at remembering where we learned something from. Sometimes we may forget whether we actually did something or merely intended to, or be uncertain whether we only dreamt it. We may misremember whether we heard something on the television or in face-to-face conversation or read it somewhere, and if so, where. We may misattribute what one person said to someone else. We may think we saw something happen when we were only told about it. In one bizarre case a woman accused a man of having raped her because she confused his face (which she had seen on television shortly before) with that of the rapist.[25] It is thus conceivable that where the Evangelists were trying to recall material they had

---

[22] Bartlett, *Remembering*, 63–94.

[23] Alan Baddeley, Michael W. Eysenck and Michael C. Anderson, *Memory* (Hove and New York: Psychology Press, 2009), 4–5, 94–6, 128–34, 320–2; Bartlett, *Remembering*, 199–214; Geoffrey Cubitt, *History and Memory* (Historical Approaches; ed. G. Cubitt; Manchester and New York: Manchester University Press, 2007), 81–2; Fentress and Wickham, *Social Memory*, 32–6;

[24] Cubitt, *History and Memory*, 96–106; Schacter, *Searching for Memory*, 110–12.

[25] Schacter, *Searching for Memory*, 114–18; Baddeley et al., *Memory*, 187–8; 322–3.

heard, something said or done by someone else could become misattributed to Jesus, particularly if it appeared to be a reasonably good fit to what was already believed about him. Such misattribution need not be conscious or deliberate at all, but simply a consequence of the vagaries of human memory.

As events recede into the past and other events of a similar type occur more recently, the older incidences tend to merge into a blur. If, for example, I do much the same at breakfast every morning (eat a bowl of cereal, drink a couple of cups of tea and listen to the news on the radio, say) then it will not be long before the memory of one breakfast merges with that of another, or rather with the memory of a typical breakfast, so that I no longer retain distinct memories of any of them for more than a few days. For the most part this is helpful, since my memory does not need to be burdened with the details of a great many similar events, and for most practical purposes it is easier to deal with the composite (the typical breakfast script).[26]

This (normally beneficial) blurring effect may, however, be related to another type of memory error known as *interference*, where the memory of one item interferes with our efforts to retrieve another. Interference can be either *retroactive* or *proactive*. In *retroactive interference* our memory of something we learned more recently interferes with our ability to recall something learned longer ago. For example, in trying to recall the details of your journey into work the day before yesterday it is quite likely that you will be impeded by your memory of details of yesterday's journey. *Proactive interference* works the other way around, when older knowledge gets in the way of something learned more recently, for example when we struggle to remember a new password because the old one keeps obtruding itself in our mind.[27] Proactive interference has also been found to affect scribal memory in the act of writing, for example the apparent occurrence of 'memory contamination' in some of the Dead Sea Scrolls.[28] Presumably there is no reason why retroactive interference should not also occur in this context. In either case the more strongly remembered wording might obtrude upon the text the scribe was trying to make use of.

Schemata can influence memory of words, not least by guiding the comprehension (and hence memory) of what we read (or hear). In particular, schemata (both scripts and frames) can help us to fill in the gaps, draw inferences, and thus make sense of the written or spoken text (or else, perhaps, to misconstrue them, as in the 'War of the Ghosts' example). This could easily lead a scribe or author who was using an oral or written source to recall what he thought it ought to

---

[26] Baddeley et al., *Memory*, 128–30; Schacter, *Searching for Memory*, 76.

[27] Baddeley et al., *Memory*, 202–5.

[28] Alan Kirk, 'Memory, Scribal Media, and the Synoptic Problem' in Paul Foster, Andrew Gregory, John S. Kloppenborg and J. Verheyden (eds), *New Studies in the Synoptic Problem* (BETL, 139; Leuven: Leuven University Press, 2011), 459–82 (463–4).

have said, rather than what it actually said, particularly if the source text was unclear or relied upon a different set of assumptions from that of the person using it.[29] This is in addition to any schematization of remembered material that might occur in the process of composition, where it may be largely gist rather than wording that is remembered.

Verbatim memory and gist memory are clearly not the same thing, and gist memory tends to be more vulnerable than verbatim memory to the memory quirks we have just been examining (although, as just noted, verbatim memory is not entirely exempt).[30] It seems, moreover, that mere repetition is not a particularly effective method of learning, particularly if what is to be learned is complex or unfamiliar.[31] Memorization works better with elaborate encoding strategies, as the ancients realized with their penchant for teaching memory techniques.[32] One example of memory for words is the technique employed by actors to memorize large parts. Recent studies suggest that this is achieved not by rote repetition but by analysing what motivates a character to speak as he or she does, so that verbatim recall springs from a deep understanding of the text.[33] It may also be helped by various forms of cueing.

A study by David Rubin examined how oral traditions manage to be as stable as they are, but his answers may apply equally well to words learned from written texts (especially for a culture such as that of the first-century Roman Empire in which speech and writing were so thoroughly intertwined). Rubin was concerned with such oral forms as epic poetry, folk ballads and children's counting-out rhymes, but this does not necessarily limit his main conclusions, which were first that such material is recreated in sequence by the performer, with one line cueing the next, and second that accuracy was greatly aided by the presence of multiple cues (such as rhythm, assonance, alliteration and rhyme, which turn out to be just as important as sense, gist and story structure). Or to put it more simply, if you are reciting a poem, you are far more likely to get the next line right if the current line contains multiple cues to what comes next than if it only contains one cue. Multiple cues used together are orders of magnitude more effective in prompting correct recall than individual cues used in isolation.[34]

Plainly, we cannot know for certain how the Evangelists went about recalling the material at their disposal, or what particular quirks of memory may have

---

[29] Baddeley et al., *Memory*, 129–31.
[30] Baddeley et al., *Memory*, 277–9.
[31] Baddeley at al., *Memory*, 76–8.
[32] Schacter, *Searching for Memory*, 46–50.
[33] Schacter, *Searching for Memory*, 49.
[34] David C. Rubin, *Memory in Oral Traditions: The Cognitive Psychology of Epic, Ballads, and Counting-out Rhymes* (Oxford and New York: Oxford University Press, 1995), esp. 39–193; cf. Baddeley et al., *Memory*, 170; for a brief summary and discussion see Eric Eve, *Behind the Gospels: Understanding the Oral Tradition* (London: SPCK, 2013), 100–2.

afflicted them (though we may be able to hazard the occasional guess). For example, even on the assumption that Matthew relied entirely on his memory of Mark in composing his own Gospel, we have no way of knowing whether he had learned the entire text verbatim, or whether he relied more on his knowledge of the gist of Mark's story together with certain phrases that stuck in his mind, or whether he got into the text in a manner analogous to actors getting into their parts, or in what ways he was guided in its reproduction by cues and schemata. We can, however, advance our understanding a little further by considering some more specific points about memory and writing in the remainder of this chapter.

Memory in writing

Writing is a cognitively demanding task, so much so that it can easily overload the limited working-memory resources available.[35] Different aspects of the writing process may make different demands, however. Planning (working out what to say and how to say it) is particularly demanding. Monitoring (reading and correcting what has just been written) can also demand a lot of attention. The physical process of writing, that is, programming and executing the actual muscle movements required to handwrite, type or dictate, typically makes lighter cognitive demands on writers who are sufficiently skilled in these activities to be able to perform them more or less automatically.[36] Dictation may make fewer cognitive demands than either writing or typing since it eliminates the need to attend to the mechanics of spelling and moving the pen; thus dictation can improve fluency.[37] While it may seem no surprise that writers who know what they are writing about will tend to write better, one possible explanation for this is that people with expertise in a particular area are able to supplement their normal (short-term) working memory with some kind of long-term working memory which operates through the reliable retrieval of information from their long-term memory of the subject matter. This would suggest that writers dealing with familiar subject matter place less demand on their cognitive resources.[38]

This rather brief and abstract summary of the memory demands on writing from the point of view of cognitive psychology is, of course, based on experiments with modern writers working under modern conditions and on models that are

---

[35] Mark Torrance and Gaynor Jeffery, 'Writing Processes and Cognitive Demands' in Mark Torrance and Gaynor Jeffery (eds), *The Cognitive Demands of Writing* (Amsterdam: Amsterdam University Press, 1999), 1–11 (1, 6); Michel Fayol, 'From On-line Management Problems to Strategies in Written Composition' in Torrance and Jeffery (eds), *Cognitive Demands*, 13–23 (13); Ronald T. Kellogg, 'Components of Working Memory in Text Production' in Torrance and Jeffery (eds), *Cognitive Demands*, 43–61 (49).
[36] Fayol, 'On-line Management', 14, 19; Kellogg, 'Components', 45–6.
[37] Kellogg, 'Components', 49.
[38] Kellogg, 'Components', 43–4, 55–8; Torrance and Jeffery, 'Writing Processes', 2.

largely hypothetical (though supported by experimental evidence). Nonetheless, since the structure of the human brain has not changed significantly in the last 2,000 years, and limitations on human memory would seem to be neurologically based, these results can be extrapolated back into the first century with due caution. One might suppose that the physical act of inscribing words on a page was, if anything, likely to have been rather more cognitively demanding then than it is now, given the use of more primitive writing materials and the need to balance the text on one's knees as one wrote and to manipulate a scroll from one column to the next by winding and unwinding it. It would thus appear that whatever the actual reason was for the ancient preference for writing by dictation, it was probably the method best suited cognitively to the writing technology of the age. By dictating rather than handwriting themselves, first-century authors would have freed up cognitive resources for composing their texts. On the likely assumption that the Evangelists were writing on subjects with which they were thoroughly familiar, they would further have been able to take advantage of long-term working memory to minimize demands on other cognitive resources. The Evangelists, then, may have been optimally placed in terms of the cognitive resources available to them for the task of manipulating material in memory in the course of composition.

This does not in itself tell us what memory operations they were able to perform. Presumably there would have been little difficulty in following a source that was already held in memory (for example, in Matthew or Luke recalling Mark from memory in Mark's sequence); the issue is how far they may have been able to do more than this, such as working from a memorized source out of sequence or combining it with other material.

Alan Kirk has suggested that the smallest whole units of discourse (however they might be defined) could not readily be broken down in memory or isolated from the coherent sequence in which they were originally located, since the narrative or topical sequence would function as a mnemonic script and the smallest units would only have been memorable insofar as they comprised meaningful sequences of words and phrases.[39] In this connection he cites (among other things) Rubin's work on serial cueing (mentioned above). It is not immediately clear, however, how exactly this applies. For example, it may be that I recall a line like 'Now is the winter of our discontent made glorious summer by this sun of York' as a single sense-unit, but having done so there seems nothing to prevent my plucking individual words or phrases such as 'winter of discontent' out of it for use in my own composition, and indeed a phrase like 'winter of discontent' may well act metonymically (*pars pro toto*, a part standing in for the whole) for any-one familiar with Shakespeare's play (quite apart from its more recent political

---

[39] Kirk, 'Memory', 463.

associations). Nor would anyone familiar with *Richard III* have to start from 'Now is the winter . . .' and work through the entire play in order to retrieve 'A horse, a horse, my kingdom for a horse!' or even 'I that am not shaped for sportive tricks, nor made to court an amorous looking-glass' a few lines further on in the opening soliloquy. Random access to pieces of text we know off by heart is not particularly difficult for us, which presumably is one reason why memory of texts was so highly valued in antiquity.

But perhaps Kirk's point is not so much about what can be retrieved in memory as what can readily be processed. It is easy enough to recall 'Now is the winter of our discontent' or 'A horse, a horse, my kingdom for a horse'; it is equally easy to extract isolated words such as 'winter' or 'horse' from these remembered lines; what would be far harder would be the mental word-by-word conflation of these two extracts into 'Now a is horse the a winter horse of my our kingdom discontent for made a glorious horse', or even into the marginally more meaningful 'Now is a horse, the winter horse of our kingdom discontent, made a glorious horse.'

Rubin's point about serial cueing is that it helps performers reproduce the wording of an oral text such as a ballad or an epic poem with a good degree of accuracy, particularly when what has just gone before (or is currently in progress) provides multiple cues for what is about to follow. This is a theory about how people's memories operate when they are reciting a text in its original sequence. It is not a theory that restricts memory to doing only this. In other words, in discussing one type of memory retrieval mechanism Rubin is not thereby excluding the existence of others.

In general terms, the process of retrieval is a progression from one or more *cues* to the *target memory* (the item we are trying to recall). Cues are believed to help the process of retrieval through *association* or *links* (by which one memory is linked to another), and retrieval can usually be achieved by a variety of cues. In principle, any memory content could serve as a reminder to a target memory; this does not mean that any cue will serve to retrieve any target, but simply that there are no restrictions on the kinds of link that can in fact be made, although in practice some will be far stronger than others.

Retrieval cues can fail for a number of reasons, for example if we do not attend to them, or attempt to retrieve the target memory through an inappropriate cue because we are asking ourselves the wrong question ('Where did I leave my keys?' may not help very much if it fails to trigger the appropriate association). Cues can also fail if they are relevant but weak. Conversely, cues can be strengthened by a number of factors. A cue is frequently stronger if it was present when the target memory was encoded even if it is not so obviously relevant (a kitchen table may be better as a reminder to buy something at the chemist than the chemist shop I happen to pass if it was the table I was staring at when I made a mental note to pick up my prescription). Moreover, as Rubin notes, cues work far better in combination than they do individually. The strength of the target memory can be another factor; it is usually harder to retrieve something that was not strongly encoded in the first place. Retrieval can also be aided by the use of an efficient strategy; for example, we are more likely to retrieve a target memory if it fits a currently active schema. Various types of context cue are also important, where *context* refers to the circumstances under which the target memory was encoded. The context can be a spatio-temporal one, but can also include mood, physiological state and cognitive state. For example, depressed people are more likely to recall sad memories, and experiments with divers showed that they had better recall of material memorized under water when they went back under water. Retrieval can also be affected by unconscious influences, such as prior priming.[40]

In other words, a great many things may be capable of cueing any particular target memory, and what will be effective in doing so is not always predictable. So, for example, while for someone who knows *Richard III*'s opening soliloquy off by heart the line 'But I, who am not shaped for sportive tricks' may indeed be cued by the immediately preceding line, 'He capers nimbly in a lady's chamber to the lascivious pleasing of a lute', it might also be cued by an idea such as 'Richard's resentment of his misshapen form' or perhaps just the phrase 'sportive tricks'. Or it might be cued at the point in the speech at which Richard turns from an (albeit ironic) celebration of the decisive Yorkist victory at Tewkesbury that has allowed war-making to be replaced by love-making to his bitter rejection of the pleasures of peace and his determination to seize the throne through villainous plots. The cue employed will largely depend on the reason for wanting to retrieve that particular line; but nothing prevents its being retrieved out of sequence.

Kirk does not in any case intend to say that a writer using a text from memory can *only* follow the order of his source (as we shall see in Chapter 7). Moreover, as intimated above, Kirk's point may be not so much about the possibilities of random retrieval as about random retrieval and recombination in the act of composition, which would indeed impose a larger cognitive load. He may also have in mind something along the lines of Small's assertion that it would have been impossible for ancient historians 'to dissect in memory contradictory variants into separate elements in order to produce a single, more logical version' since 'the ancient historian could deal only in wholes each of which came with its own indivisible set of elements'.[41] Small does not cite any evidence from experimental psychology to back this claim, which is probably not in any case intended to apply to human memory in general, since it would otherwise be hard to explain how modern historians manage to overcome these limitations, for

---

[40] Baddeley et al., *Memory*, 165–80.
[41] Small, *Wax Tablets*, 185–6.

whatever advantages are supplied by printed books and information technology, at some point even modern scholars have to manipulate material in memory to notice and attempt to reconcile discrepancies. Her argument seems to be based more on ancient memory techniques and habits of thought, which may well account for why ancient historians worked the way they did. The extent to which the Evangelists were faced with significant discrepancies between parallel accounts of the same incident (and so may have come up against precisely this kind of limitation) is, however, far from immediately clear.

We have probably reached the limit of what appeals to cognitive psychology can tell us, so it may be more helpful to look at what relevant authors actually managed to achieve. As previously noted, it seems likely that the New Testament authors mostly quoted Scripture from memory. It is most unlikely, for example, that Paul hunted through a series of scrolls in the course of dictating Romans. Yet at Romans 3.10–18 he compiled a catena of quotations drawn from Psalms 14.1b–3 (or 53.1b–3); 5.9; 140.3; 10.7; Isaiah 59.7–8 and Psalm 36.1 (in that order). It is sometimes suggested that he used a catena that was already in existence, but this is by no means certain.[42] Even if this were the case, then the catena would almost certainly have to have been put together by someone else from memory, since it is most unlikely to have been compiled by anyone trying to manipulate scrolls of the Psalms and Isaiah. On the more likely assumption that Paul compiled his catena himself in the course of composing Romans, this shows that he was well able to pull verses from their original context and reassemble them in an order of his own making.

To be sure, it is not hard to find a strong associative link (on the theme of unrighteousness) between the scriptural passages Paul deploys here, but that simply confirms the point that cueing can work by means other than the order of the original source. Another example from the same letter would be Romans 10.18–20 where Paul cites Psalm 19.4 followed by Deuteronomy 32.21 followed by Isaiah 65.1. Presumably he is able to do this in part because this sequence fits his train of thought at this point in Romans.

To take an example from the Gospels, Mark 1.2b–3 is generally thought to be a composite quotation from Exodus 23.20, Malachi 3.1 and Isaiah 40.3. That Mark was quoting from memory is suggested not only by the impracticability of assembling this quotation from three different scrolls, but also by its apparent misattribution to Isaiah *in toto* and the fact that the wording agrees with no known Greek or Hebrew version.[43] Whether or not Mark was making a mistake,

---

[42] John Ziesler, *Paul's Letter to the Romans* (TPI New Testament Commentaries; ed. H. C. Kee and D. Nineham; London/Valley Forge: SCM Press/Trinity Press International, 1989), 103; James D. G. Dunn, *Romans 1—8* (Word Biblical Commentary, 38A; Milton Keynes: Word Books, 1988), 145.

[43] John R. Donahue and Daniel J. Harrington, *The Gospel of Mark* (Sacra Pagina, 2; Collegeville, MN: Michael Glazier, 2002), 60–1.

or simply attaching the name of the most important authority to his consciously conflated quotation, this would appear to indicate an ability not only to combine different sources in memory (if only by accident) quite apart from their original contexts, but also to combine quite fragmentary texts. This is also suggested by Mark 1.11, which is often seen as a combination of Psalm 2.7 and Isaiah 42.1, perhaps also with an echo of Genesis 22.2 (the offering of the beloved son Isaac) in the space of just a few words, although this example is more questionable. Nonetheless, there is no evidence here that either Mark or Paul was labouring under the kind of mnemonic constraint seemingly suggested by Kirk.

Given what else we know of the ancients' emphasis on memory not simply as a retrieval system but as an instrument of manipulation, this is just what we should expect. According to Mary Carruthers:

> One accomplishment which always seems to have been greatly admired by both ancient and medieval writers was the ability to recite a text backwards as well as forwards, or to skip around it in a systematic way, without becoming lost or confused. The ability to do this marked the difference between merely being able to imitate something (to reproduce it by rote) and really knowing it, being able to recall it in various ways. Such reports are common enough throughout the period of my study. For example, Augustine describes a school friend named Simplicius:
>
>> an excellent man of remarkable memory, who, when he might be asked by us for all the next-to-last verses in each book of Virgil, responded in order quickly and from memory. If we then asked him to recite the verse before each of those, he did. And we believed that he could recite Virgil backwards. If we desired a common-place concerning any topic, we asked him to make one and he did. If we wanted even prose passages from whatever of Cicero's orations he had committed to memory, that also he could do; he followed in order however many divisions (*versus*) we wanted, backwards and forwards. When we wondered (about his abilities), he testified that he had not known God could do this before this proof from his experience.[44]

According to Carruthers, what Augustine finds remarkable here is not that his friend had good memory command of Virgil and Cicero, nor that he could manipulate bits of them in his memory, but rather the *extent* to which he was able to do so. Thus, 'The proof of a good memory lies not in the simple retention and regurgitation even of large amounts of material. Rather, it is the ability to move it about instantly, directly, and securely that is admired.'[45]

To be sure, Simplicius is presented as exceptional in his abilities, but this account shows what could be done, and not only in antiquity. Mary Carruthers describes

---

[44] Carruthers, *Book of Memory*, 21, citing Augustine, *De natura et origine animae* 4.7.9 (CSEL, 60, 389, lines 7–19).
[45] Carruthers, *Book of Memory*, 21–2.

how she went about memorizing psalms using the method described by Hugh of St Victor by attaching psalm verses to a mental numerical grid corresponding to modern chapter and verse divisions.

> I realized quickly that doing so gave me complete flexibility and security in finding the verses again in whatever order I chose. I could reverse the order, pull out all the odd-numbered verses, or all the even-numbered ones, or alternate reciting the odd-numbered verses in forward order and the even ones in reverse. I could also mentally interleave and recite the verses of one psalm with those of another.[46]

In reflecting on her success, Carruthers goes on to say that the numerical grid was a device not so much for memorizing the material as for accessing material she already knew. In effect the grid provided cues for retrieval, allowing the material to be accessed in any desired sequence.

In commenting on the same passages from Carruthers, Andrew Gregory remarks:

> I do not wish to equate any of the evangelists with Simplicius, nor to claim that what they may have done required the same degree of control that so impressed Augustine. But the sort of thing that Simplicius and Carruthers were able to do, and that the *Rhetorica ad Herennium* commends, shows in practice how an author like Livy or Plutarch may have composed his work.
>
> In general terms, it also shows how a synoptic evangelist may have worked, provided that we may assume that he was able to use the mnemonic technique advocated in the *Rhetorica ad Herennium* in order to retrieve material that he already knew by heart.[47]

To be sure, whether the Evangelists actually had been trained in quite such sophisticated memory techniques remains uncertain. The probability is, as we have already argued, that they would have received some memory training in the course of being taught to read and write. Moreover, we have just seen that both Paul and Mark appeared to be able to retrieve and combine scriptural passages as the need arose (although in Mark's case it may equally have been an accidental conflation of passages he had heard). It thus appears that a writer working from memory would not be constrained to follow the narrative order of his source. The argument that memory is aided by the logic of the narrative or the topical sequence of a source is effectively a schema-based one; the schema supplied by the source provides the cues for retrieval. But this is only a constraint on composition to the extent that the author lacks any alternative schemata to cue retrieval. Thus, while it is impossible for us to know with any certainty what

---

[46] Carruthers, *Book of Memory*, xiii.

[47] Andrew Gregory, 'What Is Literary Dependence?' in Paul Foster, Andrew Gregory, John S. Kloppenborg and J. Verheyden (eds), *New Studies in the Synoptic Problem* (BETL, 139; Leuven: Leuven University Press, 2011), 87–114 (101).

was psychologically possible for any given individual in antiquity, the balance of probability is strongly in favour of the Evangelists being able to reproduce and manipulate their source material in memory in the course of composing their own Gospels, and for that manipulation to include at least some reordering and recombining of source material. To what extent this may be so and what the consequences might be for understanding the specifics of Gospel composition are questions to which we shall return in Chapter 7.

A different question about the use of memory in writing is how accurate it might be. As was mentioned in Chapter 4, what Pelling interpreted as Plutarch's literary adaptation of source material Small interpreted as memory error. The particular example cited by Small comes from Plutarch's Life of Caesar, where the number of senate sessions taken to condemn the Catilinarian conspirators is reduced from three (as stated in Plutarch's other Lives) to one.[48] According to Pelling, this was a deliberate use of the literary technique of abridgement by conflation, since in this context, 'Plutarch found it tedious to distinguish the three final senatorial debates on the Catilinarians. He was, after all, concerned with Caesar's role, and that was confined to the final session.'[49]

Small, however, points out that this conflation of similar but separate incidents is similar to one of the kinds of memory error exhibited by John Dean in his testimony to the Senate over Watergate.[50] She nevertheless acknowledges that we have insufficient information to determine whether such a case is one of deliberate literary technique or one of memory error, or even a combination of the two. Given that recollection is generally reconstruction for present use, it is perfectly possible to misremember something in a way that suits one's present purpose. Pelling nevertheless elsewhere describes a number of what he does consider to be memory errors in Plutarch, for example where according to *Caesar* 22.1–5, 400,000 barbarians were killed in Caesar's slaughter of the Usipetes and Tencteri, whereas *Cato* 51.1 and the *Comparison of Nicias and Crassus* 4.2 both give the figure as 300,000. Here there seems to be no literary reason to change the figure, especially as the higher figure is supported by Plutarch's likely source and there would be little motive for lowering it.[51]

One possible example of a memory error in Luke's writing occurs at Acts 21.38, when, having arrested Paul just outside the Temple the tribune Claudius Lysias asks him, 'Are you not the Egyptian, then, who recently stirred up a revolt and led the four thousand men of the Assassins (*sikariōn*) out into the wilderness?' This looks suspiciously like a muddled conflation of what Josephus says at *J.W.*

[48] Small, *Wax Tablets*, 194.
[49] C. B. R. Pelling, 'Plutarch's Adaptation of His Source-Material', *JHS* 100 (1980), 127–40 (127).
[50] Small, *Wax Tablets*, 194.
[51] C. B. R. Pelling, 'Plutarch's Method of Work in the Roman Lives', *JHS* 99 (1979), 74–96 (93).

2.254–63 where Josephus first described the *sicarii* (urban terrorists who killed collaborators with daggers), then some imposters who led people into the desert (with no suggestion that these people had anything to do with the *sicarii*) and finally the Egyptian imposter who led a crowd of people to the Mount of Olives from where he proposed to launch an assault on Jerusalem and overpower the Roman garrison (cf. *Ant.* 20.169–72).[52] In this instance we need not assume that Luke had necessarily *read* Josephus's *Jewish War*; he may instead have simply heard part of it being read by someone else.

A rather different type of memory error is suggested by the phenomenon of 'editorial fatigue', in which a later Evangelist (Matthew or Luke) starts by making an alteration at the beginning of a pericope taken from Mark, but then fails to carry it through consistently, leading to apparent inconsistencies (or 'inconcinnities') in their version of the story. For example Luke's version of the Healing of the Paralytic (Matthew 9.1–8 || Mark 2.1–12 || Luke 5.17–26) fails to mention at the outset that Jesus entered a house, instead beginning, 'On one of those days, as he was teaching, there were Pharisees and teachers of the law sitting by' (Luke 5.17). It is thus unclear on Luke's account why the four men who bring the paralytic on a stretcher need to let him down through the roof (Luke 5.19), although this is made perfectly clear in Mark 2.1–4. One might also observe that by omitting the account of the paralytic being let down through the roof, it is rather less clear in Matthew 9.2b than in Mark 2.5 what exactly is being referred to by the words, 'when Jesus saw their faith'.

Another Matthean example given by Mark Goodacre is the story of the Cleansing of the Leper (Matthew 8.1–4 || Mark 1.40–45 || Luke 5.12–16) where Matthew's introduction has Jesus followed down the mountain by a crowd; since Jesus then proceeds to cleanse the leper in front of this crowd, the command to silence that follows (Matthew 8.4, apparently taken from Mark 1.44) looks pointless (although the command to secrecy following the raising of Jairus's daughter at Mark 5.43 would seem equally pointless, but can hardly be due to editorial fatigue).[53]

Goodacre offers 'editorial fatigue' as an argument for Markan priority, and this may very well be right, although the term 'editorial fatigue' rather suggests one Evangelist editing the work of another that lies open before him. But an alternative way to view this phenomenon may be as one of memory error, taking 'memory' in the broad sense of recall plus processing. On this model it may

---

[52] Steve Mason, *Josephus and the New Testament* (Peabody, MA: Hendricksen, 1992), 212–13; Eric Eve, *The Jewish Context of Jesus' Miracles* (JSNTSup, 231; Sheffield: Sheffield Academic Press, 2002), 299–301.

[53] Mark Goodacre, *The Case against Q: Studies in Markan Priority and the Synoptic Problem* (Harrisburg, PA: Trinity Press International, 2002), 40–3; Mark Goodacre, 'Fatigue in the Synoptics', *NTS* 44 (1998), 45–58.

be, not that Matthew deliberately decided to omit the lowering down of the paralytic through the roof as described in Mark 2.4, but that he forgot to include it, or that in the course of manipulating Mark's version in his memory he focused on what was, to him, the more interesting detail about faith at the expense of the less interesting detail about roof excavations. Similarly, Luke may simply have forgotten to add the Markan detail about being inside a house when he came to write his introduction to the pericope at Luke 5.17. The phenomenon would then be less one of fatigue causing errors later in the pericope than of errors of omission earlier in the pericope at the point where the later Evangelists' cognitive resources were most tied up in composing a new introduction to suit the context they were providing.

It may also be relevant that the two Matthean examples just cited come from a portion of his Gospel where he is not following Mark's order. Matthew's account of the Cleansing of the Leper (Matthew 8.1–4 ‖ Mark 1.40–45) follows directly on from the Sermon on the Mount. It is followed by a story with no Markan parallel, the Healing of the Centurion's Servant (Matthew 8.5–13 ‖ Luke 7.1–10), then the Healing of Peter's Mother-in-Law (Matthew 8.14–15 ‖ Mark 1.29–31), then a very loose parallel to the Sick Healed at Evening (Matthew 8.16–17 ‖ Mark 1.32–34) with which after the opening phrase 'that evening' (*opsias de genomenēs*) it has very little wording in common, then another non-Markan pericope, On Following Jesus (Matthew 8.18–22 ‖ Luke 9.57–62), then the Stilling of the Storm (Matthew 8.23–27 ‖ Mark 4.35–41), then a highly compressed account of the Gadarene Demoniac, which does come next in Mark (Matthew 8.28–34 ‖ Mark 5.1–20) and then the Healing of the Paralytic (Matthew 9.1–8 ‖ Mark 2.1–12), where Matthew follows the Markan sequence for three pericopae before once again going his own way with the story of Jairus's Daughter and the Woman with a Haemorrhage (Matthew 9.18–26 ‖ Mark 5.21–43), again greatly abbreviated, before concluding the chapter with material that has only a fairly loose connection with anything in Mark (Healing of Two Blind Men – Matthew 9.27–31 ?‖ Mark 10.46–52, the Dumb Demoniac – Matthew 9.32–34 ?‖ Mark 3.22, The Harvest is Great – Matthew 9.35–38 ?‖ Mark 6.6b, 34 ‖ Luke 8.1; 10.2). It seems highly unlikely that Matthew would have scrolled back and forth in his copy of Mark to compose this sequence, and much more likely that he was working from memory.

In this connection it is noteworthy how often Matthew provides a highly compressed or substantially rewritten version of Mark in these pericopae; the wording only tends to become closer (though not identical) in proverbial material attributed to Jesus such as the sayings about the folly of patching an old garment with a piece of unshrunk cloth or putting new wine into old wineskins (Matthew 9.14–17 ‖ Mark 2.18–22), which is precisely the sort of material one might expect to be more memorable. Thus, whether or not Matthew relied on his memory of

Mark throughout, on the assumption of Markan priority it seems quite likely that he did so when composing Matthew 8—9.[54]

Conclusions

This chapter has been concerned to establish three points: first that ancient authors made extensive use of memory (whether of gist, wording or some of each), second that this use of memory involved not simply recollecting material but manipulating and reordering it in the course of composition, and third that the Evangelists are more likely than not to have conformed to this ancient practice. The implications of all this for relations between the Synoptic Gospels will be considered further in Chapter 7. The present chapter has focused largely on the use of a writer's individual memory in handling sources. The next chapter will consider how collective memory may have affected composition.

---

[54] On the composition of Matthew 8—9, see Walter T. Wilson, *Healing in the Gospel of Matthew: Reflections on Method and Ministry* (Minneapolis: Fortress Press, 2014).

6

Collective memory

The Evangelists did not work as isolated individuals but as persons embedded in one or more social contexts, and individual memory in any case has a social dimension. To think about memory and composition, therefore, we should also think about collective memory, but this is a notion that can be hard to pin down, so before attempting to define it we shall start with an example.

In March 2015 King Richard III was finally laid to rest in Leicester Cathedral, after his remains had been discovered in a nearby car park three years before. The event attracted extensive television coverage, and judging by the size of the crowds lining the streets, considerable public interest as well, with some people having travelled from as far away as Australia to be there. It is hard to imagine any other English monarch whose reburial would have attracted quite such attention. Many in the crowd tossed white roses at his coffin as it passed by, apparently keen to honour the last Yorkist king, and at least one of their number interviewed for the television coverage said she was there because Richard had such a great story (although she was given no opportunity to elaborate on what she took that story to be). Richard III, it seems, is not just a remote figure from mediaeval history but one who resonates powerfully in contemporary collective memory.

He is, of course, a highly controversial figure. Perhaps no other monarch has ever aroused such sharp disagreement. He is the only English king with a society dedicated to restoring his reputation, yet many regard him as the arche-typal evil schemer who usurped the throne and then, to secure it, ordered the murder of the princes in the Tower (his young nephews Edward V and Richard, Duke of York). It seems people either love him or hate him; in his case (as in many others) collective memory is also contested memory. In the judgement of many he was a malign monster; in the judgement of others he is a greatly maligned king who, had he lived longer, might have come to be regarded as our greatest mediaeval monarch. The idea that he may simply have been a man of his time, behaving much as others of his class behaved, has far less traction on the imagination, since it is far less emotionally satisfying. It is as if we need Richard to be either a hero or a villain, and not just another mediaeval monarch caught up in the exigencies of his time.

In part this may be because his story has all the ingredients of a classic tragedy, whether one sees him as a good man corrupted by ambition, an evil schemer getting his just deserts, or a noble king struggling against impossible odds and betrayed by those around him. All views of Richard converge on Bosworth, where even his detractors allow that he fought and died bravely, one of only two English kings ever to die in battle. According to Philip Schwyzer, the earliest collective memory of Richard III would have been of his broken and bloodied body being taken from Bosworth, an ambiguous image meant to emphasize his total defeat by the victorious Henry but at the same time evoking (in late mediaeval piety) the image of Christ's broken, bloodied and naked body being taken down from the cross.[1] Significantly, Richard's father Richard Duke of York had similarly been defeated in battle by his enemies and put to death, having first, so the story went, suffered the indignity of a mock crown being placed on his head, which could also be seen as an echo of Christ's Passion. To his enemies, however, Richard III's death in battle was not the sacrifice of a martyr but God's judgement on a usurper.

It is perhaps Shakespeare's *Richard III* that has done most to cement Richard's place in collective memory. Even for people who can scarcely quote a line of the play or provide more than the vaguest summary of its plot, Shakespeare's Richard sticks in the mind as a witty but ruthless hunchback, devoid of all charity while brimming with charisma.

Collective memory is often said to be tied up with community identity. Richard's reputation was clearly tied up with the legitimacy of Tudor rule, but it is not immediately obvious what might be at stake today. And yet the extended ceremonies surrounding Richard's re-interment, and the public response to them, suggest that chords were being struck. Perhaps it was because this most memorable of mediaeval kings symbolizes a depth of continuity to England's history, monarchy and hence sense of national identity, or even, perhaps, because the death of this particular king marked the turning of an age, the English Middle Ages supposedly ending with Richard's death at Bosworth and Early Modernity dawning with the accession of Henry VII. To be sure, no one who woke up on the morning of 23 August 1485 would have been aware of any such transformation, but for collective memory myth and symbol have rather more resonance than mundane historical facts. But perhaps, most profoundly, the battle over Richard's reputation has to do with values we wish to admire or condemn as part of our own self-understanding and which we are accordingly keen that such a weighty figure should embody.

This extended example conveniently illustrates several facets of collective memory. First, collective memory is not simply knowledge of the past, but involves the way people evaluate and feel about that past. Second, even though we may talk about the collective memory of a community, collective memory is often disputed. Third, collective memory is often solidified in powerful stories and

---

[1] Philip Schwyzer, *Shakespeare and the Remains of Richard III* (Oxford: Oxford University Press, 2013), 19–21.

larger-than-life figures. According to Iwona Irwin-Zarecka, 'A "good story" . . . has a much better chance of entering collective memory' where 'a "good story" is usually the one where the protagonists are at once universally human and historically concrete, where their actions can be understood without the need to delve too deeply into cultural complexity'. Good stories are stories that possess a mythic resonance, and can be helped by claiming to be historical even when they are fictional.[2] Mythic resonance may in turn be aided by the process of keying and framing, whereby more recent events (such as the death of Richard III) are viewed through the lens of earlier salient events (either the death of Christ, as suggested above, or, probably more commonly in Tudor times, biblical stories of God's defeat of Israel's enemies or of fall and redemption, the cycle of chaos initiated by the deposition and murder of Richard II finally being redeemed by the Tudor messiah's defeat of Richard III).

Finally, collective memory has an ambiguous relationship with the past, reconfiguring it to meet present needs or answer to present interests but never entirely parting company with what actually happened. Had Richard III not died at Bosworth, there would have been no Tudor dynasty. Had Richard not declared his nephews to be illegitimate and claimed the throne for himself, he would not have gone down in either history or collective memory as King Richard III. Yet between these undisputed facts there are many others that remain disputed and more than one way of filling in the gaps to create a story.[3] Richard's reputation has always been tied to what he actually did, but never wholly determined by it. Shakespeare's *Richard III* is an excellent example of how a good story, in this case a particularly powerful drama, can shape collective memory for generations to come, yet his play is a curious mix of historical fact, popular legend, unjustified calumny and dramatic invention.

This discussion of King Richard III has attempted to introduce the idea of collective memory in concrete rather than purely abstract and theoretical terms, but before applying the notion of collective memory to the composition of the Gospels we should first take a more formal look at what the term 'collective memory' actually means.

What is collective memory?

Whatever else collective, social or cultural memory may be, none of these terms is intended to refer to a form of mental storage in some kind of mysterious

---

[2] Iwona Irwin-Zarecka, *Frames of Reference: The Dynamics of Collective Memory* (New Brunswick and London: Transaction, 2009), 154–5.

[3] Contrast, for example, Charles Ross, *Richard III* (new edn; Yale English Monarchs; New Haven and London: Yale University Press, 1999) with Annette Carson, *Richard III: The Maligned King* (updated edn; Stroud: History Press, 2013).

group-psyche. It is harder to say precisely what these terms do refer to, however, since different writers use them in different ways. As David Manier and William Hirst remark, 'The elasticity of the concept "collective memory" renders coherent treatment of the topic difficult.'[4] For Barry Schwartz, social memory 'refers to the *distribution* throughout society of what individuals believe, know, and feel about the *past*, how they judge the *past* morally, how closely they identify with it, and how they commemorate it.'[5] For Michael Schudson, collective memory is 'the preservation of the past for current use in a variety of cultural forms and formulae.'[6]

Jeffrey Olick emphasizes the role of collective memory in the identity formation of 'imaginary communities', by which he means communities that are too large for every member to interact with every other member, so that some kind of imaginative construction is needed to bind the community together. For Olick collective memory is not a thing but a process. It involves social frameworks (that help shape individual memories) and public representations, but it is far from monolithic, and comes down to a variety of mnemonic products and practices, such as stories and rituals (among many other products) and reminiscence and commemoration (among many other practices).[7] Ritva Williams similarly sees social memory in terms of process, defining it as 'those processes by which persons and groups are shaped by the past, consciously and unconsciously, in establishing, affirming and maintaining particular social identities'.[8]

One way to distinguish 'social' and 'collective' memory in a way that remains close to Maurice Halbwachs's original usage is to use the former to refer to the impact of socially provided frameworks on the memory of individuals and the latter to the way in which the group as a whole commemorates the past.[9] 'Collective memory' then denotes the external means by which a group makes use of the past to construct its own identity through ritual, monuments, oral traditions, texts, accepted ways of behaving and so forth.

An alternative division proposed by Jan Assmann (and touched on in Chapter 2 above) is between 'communicative memory' and 'cultural memory'. The former

---

[4] David Manier and William Hirst, 'A Cognitive Taxonomy of Collective Memories' in Astrid Erll and Ansgar Nünning (eds), *A Companion to Cultural Memory Studies* (Berlin: De Gruyter, 2010), 253–62 (253).

[5] Barry Schwartz, 'Where There's Smoke, There's Fire: Memory and History' in Tom Thatcher (ed.), *Memory and Identity in Ancient Judaism and Early Christianity: A Conversation with Barry Schwartz* (SBL Semeia Studies, 78; ed. G. O. West; Atlanta: SBL, 2014), 7–37 (10) (emphasis original).

[6] Michael Schudson, *Watergate in American Memory: How We Remember, Forget and Reconstruct the Past* (New York: Basic Books, 1992), 4.

[7] Jeffrey K. Olick, 'Products, Processes, and Practices: A Non-Reificatory Approach to Collective Memory', *BTB* 36 (2006), 5–14.

[8] Ritva Williams, 'Social Memory', *BTB* 41 (2011), 189–200 (190).

[9] Chris Keith, 'Social Memory Theory and Gospels Research: The First Decade (Part One)' in *EC* 6 (2015), 354–76 (360); cf. Geoffrey Cubitt, *History and Memory* (Historical Approaches; Manchester and New York: Manchester University Press, 2007), 13–14.

refers to the transmission of personal memories of an originating event by informal face-to-face conversations, which can span no more than three or four generations, or at most 80–100 years. Once this limit is reached, the memory must be transformed into 'cultural memory' if it is to survive into the future. At this point, the informal communication processes give way to institutionalized means of preservation that must be maintained by specialists. There are various ways in which this can be achieved, but in cultures that possess writing, this is generally through the production of written texts. In fact the use of writing usually starts earlier, since (as was discussed in Chapter 2) a crisis or rupture in the tradition (*Traditionsbruch*) frequently occurs at around 40 years after the originating event, as the original witnesses start to die out.[10]

Manier and Hirst helpfully propose a taxonomy of different types of collective memory based on analogy with individual memory systems. *Collective episodic memory* is the memory of a group of people rehearsing their personal memories of a shared experience. *Collective semantic memory* refers to common knowledge (or perceptions) of facts about the recent or more distant past. *Lived semantic memories* are those of roughly contemporary events (such as the destruction of the Twin Towers on September 11, 2001) that are widely known about by people who did not directly experience them, but who learned about them at the time; *distant semantic memories* are current perceptions of the more remote past, such as the horrors of trench warfare in the First World War. *Collective procedural memories* comprise community traditions, practices and rituals which members of a community know how to perform (such as the celebration of the Mass by many Roman Catholic parishioners). Such knowledge may be unconsciously *embodied* but may still exercise considerable influence on people's lives, extending to many areas of daily life in which members of a social group do certain things (for example eat, drink and wash) in certain ways.[11]

The term 'collective memory' may thus refer (1) to the *processes* by which a given social group recalls and interprets the past; (2) the *purposes* for which the past is recalled; (3) the ways in which beliefs about and interpretations of the past undergo *change* within a given social group; (4) the *content* of beliefs about the past that members of a social group largely hold in common; (5) the way the past is *evaluated* and so helps to shape a sense of common identity; and (6) the shared *frameworks* that members of a social group use to talk about the past. What all these senses have in common is that in none of them is 'memory' used to denote objective knowledge of what exactly happened in the past; it is instead

---

[10] Jan Assmann, 'Communicative and Cultural Memory' in Astrid Erll and Ansgar Nünning (eds), *A Companion to Cultural Memory Studies* (Berlin: De Gruyter, 2010), 109–18.

[11] Manier and Hirst, 'Cognitive Taxonomy', 257–9. On embodied memories see also Paul Connerton, *How Societies Remember* (Themes in the Social Sciences; ed. J. Dunn, J. Goody, E. A. Hammel and G. Hawthorn; Cambridge: Cambridge University Press, 1989).

used to mean beliefs about the past, ways of talking about and interpreting the past, and ways of using the past in the interests of the present (and in particular, of a group's identity and self-understanding, of creating a world of shared meanings). From all this it should be apparent that collective memory has emotive and evaluative dimensions as well as cognitive ones; it is not simply a matter of what groups believe about the past, but also how they feel about it and how they take it to embody or contradict present values.

Continuity and change in collective memory

The mechanisms by which collective memory reshapes a community's view of the past may be complex, but many of them are widely recognized. Since collective memory helps to shape individual memory through the frameworks it supplies, and is in turn shaped by the individual memories of those most influential in communicating collective memory, it should come as no surprise that many of these mechanisms resemble those identified by psychologists in relation to individual memory.

Societies often remember their past in the form of stories. Stories help make sense of the past by providing a natural way to order events and explain them in a meaningful way.[12] Moreover, stories are easier to remember than a collection of otherwise unrelated facts; the logic of the plot serves to provide some kind of stability to what is being encoded and later recalled.[13] But the needs of storytelling can also distort what is recalled, since stories are generally cast into a socially familiar form (employing a plot structure familiar to the culture in which it is told), and this often requires simplification and adaptation of the material being emplotted. Moreover, the very act of casting our memories into some socially recognizable narrative form may affect the way we remember them. While the internal logic of a story may aid its preservation in changing social circumstances, a change in circumstances, particularly one to a substantially different social setting, may well result in changes to the story to fit the new setting, especially if the story contains elements that no longer make sense or have ceased to be relevant.[14] Producing a compelling narrative, then, would be one way an Evangelist might seek to shape the collective memory of his community, while the Evangelists would in turn be influenced if not also constrained by any stories already in circulation, as well as by the particular situation they were trying to address.

---

[12] James L. Fentress and Chris Wickham, *Social Memory* (New Perspectives on the Past; Oxford and Cambridge, MA: Basil Blackwell, 1992), 49–51; Ann Rigney, 'The Dynamics of Remembrance: Texts between Monumentality and Morphing' in Astrid Erll and Ansgar Nünning (eds), *A Companion to Cultural Memory Studies* (Berlin: De Gruyter, 2010), 345–53 (347–8).

[13] Fentress and Wickham, *Social Memory*, 50, 71–2.

[14] Fentress and Wickham, *Social Memory*, 73–6.

An important factor in social (as in individual) memory is the process of *framing*, or the application of schemata. How we understand both the present and the past is conditioned by the conceptual frameworks we employ in order to interpret our past and present experiences. Such frameworks might include a shared sense of time (how we date things in a publically shared calendar), how we classify objects and how particular types of story should be narrated. Such shared frameworks help us both to communicate with others and to make sense of things for ourselves by drastically reducing the need to explain masses of extraneous detail and by helping us to focus on and give order to what is significant in a great jumble of data. The previous chapter described how we tend to remember best what fits our habitual frameworks and tend to reshape the unfamiliar to better fit our commonly used schemata. Not surprisingly, these tendencies apply as much to collective memory as they do to individual memory. Collective memory tends to conform to the predominant conceptual frameworks of the group to which it belongs, although the fit can often be imperfect, and there is always the possibility of some events being recalled precisely because they are so strikingly different from the norm.[15] The shared frameworks of Christian groups would both constrain the Evangelists (their narratives would have to make sense within those frameworks) but also empower them (since a shared framework could help to ensure that their texts were interpreted in the manner intended).

Closely related to the idea of framing is that of *keying*, which means understanding one set of events in terms of another, or, to put it more fully, using our understanding of a significant episode at one point of time (the more distant past, say) to make sense of a striking but potentially puzzling or unsettling episode at another (the present or the more recent past, say). According to Barry Schwartz, 'Keying transforms the meaning of activities understood in terms of one primary framework by comparing them with activities understood in terms of another.'[16] Thus, for example, the story of Jesus might be keyed to (in other words, presented in terms of) parts of the sacred history of Israel, and to salient figures such as Moses, David, Elijah and Elisha. The stories of kings, prophets and other leading figures from Israel's epic past might become the basis of messianic and prophetic *scripts* or *schemata* which in turn could help organize the way Jesus was remembered and understood.[17]

---

[15] Barbara A. Misztal, *Theories of Social Remembering* (Theorizing Society; Maidenhead and Philadelphia: Open University Press, 2003), 82–3; Barry Schwartz, 'Memory as a Cultural System: Abraham Lincoln in World War II', *ASR* 61 (1996), 908–27 (911).

[16] Schwartz, 'Memory as a Culture System', 911; cf. Misztal, *Theories*, 96–7.

[17] Barry Schwartz, 'Jesus in First Century Memory – A Response' in A. Kirk and T. Thatcher (eds), *Memory, Tradition, and Text: Uses of the Past in Early Christianity* (SBL Semeia Studies, 52; ed. G. A. Yee; Atlanta: SBL, 2005), 249–61 (250–2); Cubitt, *History and Memory*, 208; Richard A. Horsley, *Hearing the Whole Story: The Politics of Plot in Mark's Gospel* (Louisville, KY: Westminster John Knox Press, 2001), 231–53; Richard A. Horsley, *Jesus in Context: Power, People, and Performance* (Minneapolis: Fortress Press, 2008), 36–42, 119–23, 139–45, 156–61.

Conversely, one might see Matthew as keying the Pharisees and other opponents of Jesus in his Gospel to the opponents (perhaps early rabbis) his own community faced (see, e.g., Matthew 10.24–25). On this understanding Matthew does not simply use the Pharisees as ciphers for the Jewish leaders of his own day, neither does he straightforwardly identify pre-70 Pharisees with post-70 rabbis; rather he sets up a typological correspondence between the two so that his understanding of Jesus' opponents in the traditions that came to him and his understanding of the contemporary opposition he now faces mutually inform and shape each other.

Shifts in collective memory are not limited to attempts to make sense of the past in terms of familiar cultural patterns or in the light of changed circumstances. They may also be due to the desire to appropriate the past to serve the needs of the present. It may often be a matter of rewriting or at least radically reinterpreting the past in order to legitimate some present interest.

This raises the question of how far any society or group is able to rewrite the past in collective memory to suit present needs. On Halbwachs's model, collective memory is a reconstruction whose primary function is to serve the interests of the group that maintains it. This model can be pressed to a 'constructivist', 'presentist' or 'invention of traditions' approach that sees the past almost entirely as an invention of the present.[18] Opposed to this model are various 'continuity' approaches that, while recognizing that the present reshapes our view of the past, nevertheless insist that the past remains immanent in the present. For one thing, the shared language and frameworks we employ to interpret the past did not spring into existence just now, but are themselves derived from the past. For another, the past lives on in the present in many of its effects, not least in its physical remains and its institutions. Given the way things are today, certain versions of the past simply *could not* be true; had Hitler won the Second World War, the world would be a very different place today.

Moreover, a radical constructivist position does not allow for the resilience of individual memory. While individual memories can certainly be reshaped to some extent by social interaction, there are limits to the extent that most people are likely to misremember their own pasts; the idea that the collective past can be wholly reshaped at will is psychologically implausible. In addition, the 'presentist' approach overlooks the extent to which the interpretation of the past is likely to be contested by people who are unwilling to accept the 'official' view.[19] That said, the past that continues to influence the present is not necessarily 'what actually

---

[18] Misztal, *Theories*, 56–61; Alan Kirk, 'Social and Cultural Memory' in A. Kirk and T. Thatcher (eds), *Memory, Tradition, and Text: Uses of the Past in Early Christianity* (SBL Semeia Studies, 52; ed. G. A. Yee; Leiden and Boston: Brill, 2005), 1–24 (11–14); Barry Schwartz, 'Christian Origins: Historical Truth and Social Memory' in Kirk and Thatcher (eds), *Memory, Tradition, and Text*, 43–56 (44–6).

[19] Misztal, *Theories*, 54–5, 61–74; Kirk, 'Social and Cultural Memory', 10–17.

happened'; it may be constituted as much by previous interpretation of the past, for one aspect of the past that can frequently survive into the present is its interpretative frameworks. So while the 'continuity' model of collective memory allows for a more complex interaction of past and present than a straightforward constructivist model, even on the continuity model collective memory remains a construction, an interpretation of the past from the perspective of the present, or a dialogue between past and present in which each shapes the perception of the other, and in which the past the present interacts with is frequently a previous interpretation of the past.

Pneumatic memory in the Fourth Gospel

To return from abstract theory to concrete example, it may be helpful to revisit Tom Thatcher's treatment of John's Gospel, since Thatcher explicitly relates John's notion of charismatic (or Spirit-guaranteed) memory in John to collective memory. As was discussed in Chapter 2, according to Thatcher one reason why John felt he needed to write a Gospel was to counter the claims of a dissident group within his own community, the so-called 'Antichrists'. Part of John's difficulty was that both he and the Antichrists shared the same view of charismatic memory, so that the Antichrists could not be countered simply by appealing to the oral tradition; something weightier was needed, and a written Gospel was the answer.

Thatcher points to a number of places in John (e.g. 2.17, 22; 12.16) where the disciples' remembrance of Jesus is a matter not so much of recalling what happened as coming to a subsequent understanding of the true significance of what Jesus said or did in the light of faith and Scripture. For John, then, memory was not primarily a matter of retrieving empirical facts from the past but rather of coming to a correct understanding of the past. That does not mean that what Jesus actually said and did was unimportant, but the memory of these things was in any case guaranteed by the work of the Spirit in the community, whose task it was both to remind Jesus' disciples of his teaching and to lead them into a correct understanding of it (John 14.16–17, 26; 15.26; 16.13–14). On this understanding, 'witness' in the Fourth Gospel is not simply the relating of facts about Jesus' life, but of proclaiming the correct interpretation of those facts in the light of the way Jesus' identity and destiny came to be understood.[20]

Thatcher proceeds to map this theory of charismatic memory onto a notion of collective memory in which the past is primarily important for maintaining a particular dogmatic position in the present. On this understanding, the collective memory of John's church was not so much a set of data about the past as the

---

[20] Tom Thatcher, *Why John WROTE a Gospel: Jesus – Memory – History* (Louisville, KY: Westminster John Knox Press, 2006), 23–36.

capacity of church members to tell stories about Jesus in ways that made sense within the common frameworks shared by members of the group. The shared memory of Jesus was then not a fixed body of data but the potential to talk about Jesus in accordance with an accepted performance tradition, that is, an agreement among the members of the group about *how* stories about Jesus should be told so as to generate images of the past that were relevant to the group's current social situation. Insofar as this shared memory was stable, it was stable not at the level of a fixed content but at the level of shared meanings and images. Particular items could be dropped and new ones added, provided they fitted the existing pattern.[21]

At first sight this may all seem a little abstract, and one may want to question the separation of framework from content, as if the two could be completely independent. The collective memory in question is after all the collective memory of a particular person, Jesus, who moved among people in particular places (Judaea, Galilee and Samaria) at a particular time (when Pilate was governor of Judaea) and did particular kinds of things (taught, performed signs, came into conflict with the authorities, suffered death by crucifixion and was then raised from the dead). It is hard to see how this content can be removed from the tradition or substantially altered without losing sight of the person the tradition is meant to be about, and indeed Thatcher goes on to acknowledge that 'Such historical facts, and past understandings of such facts, will to some extent limit the extent of their own reconfiguration.'[22] The point is rather that particular sayings, signs and deeds could be added to the tradition provided they were broadly consonant with what was already there and could be fitted into the existing framework. Thus, for example (though this is not Thatcher's example), a story about Jesus healing a man blind from birth and the controversy ensuing from it could quite comfortably be added to the tradition if it fitted the sort of thing Jesus was believed to have done, and if the ensuing controversy story aligned both with the community's understanding of Jesus and its perception of its own situation (in conflict with a form of Judaism that wished to exclude it from membership of the synagogue, say).

At least some of the content of collective memory is relatively stable, and in this connection Thatcher refers to Halbwachs's concept of *landmarks*, which are particularly salient events, people and times around which the memory of the past is organized. But while these landmarks may acquire a certain stability, they can have a distorting effect on everything else, since they tend to attract (and absorb) other figures, times and events. This schematization into a few salient landmarks aids collective memory by simplifying matters into more easily manageable patterns, but at the cost of blurring the distinctiveness of particular people

---

[21] Thatcher, *Why John WROTE*, 108–11.
[22] Thatcher, *Why John WROTE*, 123.

and events (for example, Jesus' disputes with a number of different figures might become blended into a few paradigmatic discourses aimed at a generalized group of Pharisees). Thatcher goes on to suggest, however, that the landmarks in John's Jesus tradition were not so fixed that his opponents could not reconfigure them to support their own view. Such an opportunity would arise in part because the further the founding figure, Jesus, receded into the community's past, the greater would become the need to adjust the community's understanding of him to meet current needs. While John adopted a conservative, 'dogmatic' approach to this adjustment that insisted that the Spirit's role was to remind the community of what they had known all along, his opponents apparently adopted a more 'mystical' mode, appealing to what Christ was saying now through the Spirit, and thereby setting up a 'countermemory'. Since John and his opponents shared the same theory of Spirit-guided memory, John was particularly vulnerable to this kind of attack, and his response was to write a book that fixed both the boundaries of what content was essential to the memory of Jesus and the frameworks through which that content was to be viewed.[23]

We have already suggested (in Chapter 2) that certain aspects of this reconstruction may be problematic. In particular, it is unclear what the Antichrists' countermemory was meant to look like. One might suppose from 1 John 2.22 that they denied that Jesus was the Christ (but surely that would put them outside the bounds of the community altogether) or from 1 John 4.1–3 that the Antichrists were incipiently docetic (that is, that they claimed that Jesus was not really human, but only appeared to be so), but while John's Gospel is clearly concerned to affirm that Jesus is indeed the Messiah, there is little apart perhaps from John 1.14 and 19.33–35 that appears aimed at countering Docetism. Rather, as noted in Chapter 2, John's Gospel seems exercised less by internal tensions within his own group than by pressure from outside, in particular from unbelieving 'Jews' and an unbelieving 'world'. These pressures may well have been tempting some members of John's community to defect, or at least to retreat from some of the high Christological claims that John regards as being the correct way to remember Jesus (e.g. John 6.66). Part of John's strategy was then to insist that the currently experienced opposition was what Jesus predicted all along, and was thus no reason to depart from the one true way to eternal life (e.g. John 15.18—16.4). Fixing such predictions in writing would then help to preserve them in the community's collective memory against the threat of external pressures that might otherwise squeeze them out should conformity to the world come to appear a more attractive way to adapt.

If Thatcher is right that John's stance is basically conservative (to preserve his community's collective memory against some form of threat), then clearly that

---

[23] Thatcher, *Why John WROTE*, 99–102, 118–24.

collective memory is both a constraint and a resource for John: a constraint because he has to remain with the bounds of what he wants to conserve, and a resource because the community's collective memory would provide both content and frameworks of interpretation John could put to good use in his composition. But John's situation may have been more complex than that; in particular his written Gospel may have been at least in part innovative, however conservative his intent may have been. The process of reflecting on the tradition to render it as a narrative text suited to meet current needs is unlikely to have left it entirely unchanged. At this point collective memory might provide a more subtle constraint, providing not simply the bounds within which John consciously wanted to remain, but also the frameworks with which he would have to conform if his Gospel was to be accepted as a valid expression of the community's tradition. Yet such constraints need not have been at all rigid; the frameworks, interpretations and memories could all have been more or less subtly reshaped in the process of being rendered in writing. John's Gospel was never simply a static repository of its community's collective memory of Jesus at some point in time, but rather a dynamic response within that collective memory that would in turn help shape the Church's collective memory of Jesus from then on.

The construction of reputation

A large part of the collective memory of any salient figure is constituted by his or her reputation. The Evangelists would have had to reckon with the reputation of Jesus both as it came to them and as they wished to promote or adapt it. Yet while scholars frequently refer to Jesus' reputation, Rafael Rodriguez has complained that few have paused to analyse the concept.[24] Drawing on the work of scholars such as Barry Schwartz and Gary Alan Fine, Rodriguez suggests that a reputation is a socially constructed image that is employed in social interaction. A person's reputation depends not simply on what they said and did, but on the social context in which they are remembered and on the efforts of reputational entrepreneurs, who are people with the means, motive and opportunity to promote someone's (good or evil) reputation. A reputational entrepreneur is someone who conceives it to be in his or her own interests to promote the reputation in question, who is well placed institutionally or socially to be credible, and who has the ability to construct a narrative that resonates with a wider audience.[25]

---

[24] Rafael Rodriguez, *Structuring Early Christian Memory: Jesus in Tradition, Performance and Text* (LNTS, 407; ed. M. Goodacre; London: T. & T. Clark, 2010), 64.

[25] Rodriguez, *Structuring*, 65–7; Gary Alan Fine, 'Reputational Entrepreneurs and the Memory of Incompetence: Melting Supporters, Partisan Warriors and Images of President Harding', *AJS* 105 (1996), 1159–93 (1162–3, 1186).

Thus, for example, Fine argues that given the historical facts, there are a number of ways in which the reputation of Warren Harding (US President 1920–3) could have been constructed. The reason that he is remembered as a failure is largely because the vast majority of people who were in a position to defend his reputation did not see it as being in their interests to do so in the wake of the scandals that came to light shortly after his death. Republicans wished to distance themselves from the taint of scandal while Democrats, along with liberal-inclined journalists and academics, wanted to discredit his conservative agenda.[26]

The effect of context on reputation is further illustrated by Barry Schwartz's work. In an article discussing the persons and events commemorated in the United States Capitol building, Schwartz found that prior to the Civil War such commemoration was almost entirely restricted to the War of Independence and the period of colonization, since these were the only periods upon which a nation at risk of tearing itself apart could agree as providing symbols of common identity.[27]

In another study Schwartz found a substantial decline in Abraham Lincoln's reputation from the 1960s on. This had little to do with the facts of Lincoln's life being challenged, or with anyone actively trying to tarnish his reputation. Rather, Schwartz argued, the chief cause seems to have been the postmodern turn in post-war American society, in which metanarratives lost much of their credibility and society became more sceptical of heroes in general and politicians in particular. The decline in Lincoln's prestige (as measured in opinion polls and quantitative literature surveys) was thus part of a wider decline of the prestige of once-popular presidents (although Schwartz also argued that the postmodernist case was overstated by some theorists, since there appeared to be a limit to the decline in reputation because many people still need meaningful links with the past).[28] In contrast, Lincoln's reputation rose in the first half of the twentieth century, and his heroic image was frequently invoked in the USA during the Second World War both to help legitimate that nation's entry into the conflict and to provide orientation. In the language of keying, the Second World War was *keyed* to the American Civil War so that it was seen as a continuation of the war against slavery, but also as an endeavour requiring endurance, effort and sacrifice.[29]

The example of Lincoln is a reminder that societies need their heroes, not simply to provide stirring examples, but as symbols embodying the society's

[26] Fine, 'Reputational Entrepreneurs', 1163–4, 1167–85.
[27] Barry Schwartz, 'The Social Context of Commemoration: A Study in Collective Memory', *SF* 61 (1982), 374–402.
[28] Barry Schwartz, 'Postmodernity and Historical Reputation: Abraham Lincoln in Late Twentieth-Century American Memory', *SF* 77 (1998), 63–103.
[29] Schwartz, 'Memory as a Cultural System', 911–25.

beliefs and values. Societies also need their villains, since their evil reputations as transgressors of social values also serve as reminders of what those values are. Moral outrage against a notorious villain can help build social solidarity as effectively as public celebration of a great hero.[30] According to Ducharme and Fine, '[c]ommunities solidify the reputations of their villains in collective memory' through the processes of demonization and transformation into nonpersonhood. Demonization refers to the removal of all moral ambiguities, so that the villain's character becomes seen as wholly and essentially evil, while nonpersonhood means 'the denial of the virtuous aspect of self in the villain's commemoration.'[31] In other words, even if, as may be likely, the villain was previously known for virtuous acts earlier in life, the memory of these virtuous acts is erased, or else reinterpreted so that the person's motivation is seen as questionable or as providing a sharp contrast with the fall that followed, in a way that serves to magnify his or her depravity. Unlike heroes, villains are generally remembered only for one act, the deed that defines their villainy (although there are surely exceptions to this: the most notorious villain of the twentieth century, Adolf Hitler, is remembered for a multitude of misdeeds, although he fits other aspects of the model well enough).

The example Ducharme and Fine go on to analyse is that of Benedict Arnold, an American general who gained a heroic reputation in the War of Independence but who is now remembered principally for his defection to the British. The model Ducharme and Fine apply to Arnold would apply equally well to Richard III (who, in Shakespeare's words, was 'determinèd to prove a villain'). Richard III's defining act of villainy is often taken to be his (alleged) murder of his nephews, although Alison Hanham regards it as having been (in the eyes of his contemporaries) his denying his nephews their inheritance on grounds widely felt to be inadequate.[32] In popular collective memory these alleged misdeeds are probably so closely linked as to constitute two aspects of the same villainous action (though Tudor writers were hardly slow to attribute a number of other wicked actions to Richard).

A villainous reputation is thus supposedly constructed differently from a heroic one. 'While heroes may have their virtues magnified and their flaws overlooked, the transformation of a sinner into a demon, and the erasure of all personal virtue, may be a more significant transformation.'[33] Or, more fully:

---

[30] Lori J. Ducharme and Gary Alan Fine, 'The Construction of Nonpersonhood and Demonization: Commemorating the Traitorous Reputation of Benedict Arnold', *SF* 73 (1995), 1309–31 (1309–10).

[31] Ducharme and Fine, 'Construction', 1310–12.

[32] Alison Hanham, *Richard III and His Early Historians 1483–1535* (London: Oxford University Press, 1975), 196.

[33] Ducharme and Fine, 'Construction', 1311.

A collective memory cannot permit a highly differentiated view of events and persons; complexity must be reduced for collective meaning. While the faults of heroes can be explained away as proof of their 'humanity,' virtuous elements in the biographies of villains cannot be so neatly explained. Such actors must be made totally evil, and all hints of virtue must be excised.[34]

The reputation of Jesus of Nazareth may be a slightly odd case. Of course, for some people he was a villain; at least if passages such as the Beelzebul Controversy (Mark 3.22–30) are anything to go by, Jesus' opponents were all too willing to demonize him. But for the Gospels Jesus was not a hero whose 'faults' were 'explained away as a proof of [his] humanity', since, unlike the heroes Ducharme and Fine have in mind, by the time the Evangelists write about him, Jesus is a hero who could do no wrong and one well on the way to divinization. In some respects, then, Jesus' reputation mirrors (in the sense of inverts) the demonization of a villain more closely than might that of a more conventional hero.

While reputations are social constructs, this should not be taken to mean that they are constructed out of nothing, or that the raw material from which they are constructed is infinitely malleable, as if Jesus' reputation could have been constructed as that of a great warrior or Richard's as an itinerant prophet. In discussing Harding's reputation, Fine notes the 'objective view' that reputations reflect reality, and allows not only that most people 'feel comfortable with at least a partially objective view', but also that such a view has at least some role to play in a middle-ground 'weak' constructionist view: 'The weak view suggests that objective features of events affect reputations but that objective features are mediated through political strategies and discursive practices.'[35]

To be sure, Fine is discussing the reputation of a US president and regards 'reputational entrepreneurship' as particularly relevant to a politically combative democracy such as the USA. One may thus wonder how far any general conclusions he draws can be applied to the very different situation of the primitive Church. For one thing, the relationship between reputation and 'objective' historical fact is likely to be rather different in ancient and modern situations, given the very different media situation. That is to say, even if 'objective' is taken to mean little more than 'generally agreed upon', what counts as 'objective historical fact' is likely to be rather different in a culture that has to rely mainly on oral tradition from one that can consult official archives, contemporary news reports and photographic records, and in which collective memory has been shaped by mass media.

That said, the point remains that reputations are not purely arbitrary, even if the retrievable facts allow them to be constructed in more than one way (as is

---

[34] Ducharme and Fine, 'Construction', 1327.
[35] Fine, 'Reputational Entrepreneurs', 1165–7.

surely the case with both Jesus of Nazareth and Richard III). As Rodriguez (following Schwartz) points out, it is not enough to discuss *how* a reputation was shaped; one also has to enquire *why* it was shaped in this way, and in particular, why one individual rather than another should be singled out as a model.[36] The reception of reputations is another important factor; a reputation is unlikely to take root unless it makes sense to and is acceptable to the group of people who are meant to give it credence.[37]

To give an example that is a little closer in kind to Jesus than a US president or an English monarch, we may consider the case of the Mexican-American folk healer (or *curandero*) Pedrito Jaramillo who operated in south Texas in the late nineteenth and early twentieth centuries. There were many folk healers around at the time, but unlike most of his contemporaries, Pedrito achieved a kind of folk sainthood, and his shrine was still being visited 50 years after his death. After considering a number of factors that may have contributed to Pedrito's extraordinary reputation, Octavio Romano concludes that what made him stand out from his peers was his 'performing his role in relatively strict accordance with the fundamental and generic definition of healer role as provided by tradition.'[38] He put into practice a dormant ideal of the totally selfless healer, and thereby 'singularly reasserted tradition by making the pre-existent "ideal" into a tangible and recognizable entity.'[39]

Expressed in other terms, Romano's proposal is that Pedrito gained an elevated reputation through conformity to a pre-existing cultural script. It is this that made his stories resonate with a segment of the population; the accounts of his activities were especially well attuned to the cultural logic of his situation. This then raises the question of the relation between the cultural script employed to interpret his actions and what he actually did: was it Pedrito's actions that conformed to cultural scripts or only the subsequent stories about those actions? The answer is probably a bit of both. If there was nothing about the deeds that suggested particular conformity to cultural scripts, then it is hard to see why Pedrito should have been selected as the bearer of the reputation he was accorded. On the other hand, once his deeds began to be seen in the light of these cultural scripts it would

---

[36] Rodriguez, *Structuring*, 69; Barry Schwartz, *Abraham Lincoln and the Forge of National Memory* (Chicago: The University of Chicago Press, 2000), 253–5.

[37] Rodriguez, *Structuring*, 70–4.

[38] Octavio I. Romano, 'Charismatic Medicine, Folk-Healing, and Folk-Sainthood', *American Anthropologist* 67 (1965), 1151–73 (1170).

[39] Romano, 'Charismatic Medicine', 1170; see also Eric Eve, *The Jewish Context of Jesus' Miracles* (JSNTSup, 231; Sheffield: Sheffield Academic Press, 2002), 357–60; Eric Eve, *The Healer from Nazareth: Jesus' Miracles in Historical Context* (London: SPCK, 2009), 58–61; for accounts of Pedrito Jaramillo see Ruth Dodson, 'Don Pedro Jaramillo: The Curandero of Los Olmos' in Wilson M. Hudson (ed.), *The Healer of Los Olmos and Other Mexican Lore* (Dallas: South Methodist University Press, 1951), 9–70.

be extraordinary if the scripts failed to exercise any influence over the way the stories continued to be told. Furthermore, it is by no means impossible that if Pedrito began gaining his reputation during his ministry, this will have influenced what he chose to do. He could easily have (consciously or unconsciously) felt under pressure to conform to the expectations he had generated, leading to the kind of positive feedback loop that Romano sees as propelling Pedrito up the 'healing hierarchy'. Once someone starts to gain a reputation, it may constrain the way he or she acts. The model applied here to Pedrito Jaramillo could well prove illuminating for Jesus of Nazareth.

To summarize: a person's reputation is not simply a matter of what people happen to remember about him or her; it is a social construct that is in some way founded on the facts of that person's life, but which consists of a particular way of interpreting those facts to serve the interests of a society or group. These interests need not necessarily be immediate material interests; they may be more a matter of using a past figure as a symbol of shared values (and hence shared identity), either through a hero who embodies certain virtues or through a villain whose wickedness can be generally abhorred. For a reputation to take hold, a number of conditions must hold. First, it must seem plausible in relation to what is already known or believed about its subject. Second, it must be promoted by one or more reputational entrepreneurs who have the motivation (or perceived self-interest) to promote it along with the right sort of social or institutional location (to be taken seriously) and the ability to tell a story that resonates with the cultural logic of their target audience. This leads to the third condition, namely the willingness of others to receive and give credence to the reputation that is being proposed. This does not, however, mean that a successful reputational entrepreneur can never challenge previously established reputations or existing cultural logic (indeed, changes in social and political circumstances may make it easy or even necessary to do so).

From reputation to written text

It should by now be apparent that collective memory is not primarily a matter of what facts people in general happen to remember about the past; it is rather about how a group of people interpret and evaluate a particular view of the past and how that view shapes their values and their sense of identity. While collective memory may indeed assert certain facts about the past, such as that Richard III died in battle, or that Jesus died on a cross, it is not purely or even primarily about such facts. It is as much about shared symbols, commemorative rituals and artefacts, accepted values and ways of behaving. One obvious example of this in relation to the Jesus tradition would be the celebration of the Lord's Supper in Paul's churches. Paul's complaint at 1 Corinthians 11.17–34 is not that the

Corinthians have got their facts wrong, but that their conduct of the Lord's Supper subverts the very values it is meant to instantiate. By having everyone go ahead with their own meal so that some go hungry while others are inebriated, the Corinthians have turned what was meant to be a sacrament of unity into a demonstration of divisiveness, in which the wealthier members of the church humiliate the poorer ones by their inappropriate show of conspicuous consumption.

The Gospels, however, are not commemorative rituals (even if they came to be read in ritual settings) or purely symbols (whatever symbolic value they subsequently came to acquire); they are first and foremost texts that narrate events that supposedly occurred in the past. They are nevertheless heavily invested in collective memory, both as they are shaped by it and as they go on to shape it in turn. Rather than understanding the Gospels as records of 'facts' drawn from some 'pool' of collective memory, we could think of the Evangelists as reputational entrepreneurs. This means that the Evangelists will have perceived themselves as having some interest in promoting a particular image of Jesus, that they will have occupied a social location that enabled them to do so, that they had the ability to construct narratives that resonated with the cultural logic they set out to address, and that what they wrote was appropriate to their particular social or political situation.

Here the example of Richard III may once again be suggestive. Although Shakespeare presumably did not set out to be a reputational entrepreneur, it would seem that in the four centuries or so since it was first performed, his *Richard III* has made a huge impact on popular perception (and hence collective memory) of the last Plantagenet king. To be sure, there has been a spate of books published down the years offering alternative views of Richard, but the very fact that more than half a millennium after his death people are still keen to defend or damn his reputation is at least in part a tribute to the effect of Shakespeare's play. One suspects that Richard III would not seem half so fascinating, even to his most ardent modern defenders, were it not for the image of the scheming hunchback conjured up by Shakespeare's drama.

To say that Shakespeare was a dramatic genius may be true, but it hardly suffices as an explanation for the enduring success of his portrayal of King Richard. Schwyzer suggests that the reason Shakespeare's Richard became so influential is that he is made to embody so much of the previous tradition associated with Richard III into the one character. Shakespeare's Richard is witty, clever, charismatic and engaging, not least when he takes the audience into his confidence. At the same time he is the quintessential embodiment of an evil schemer, loyal only to himself, concerned solely with his own ambition for the crown, as warped morally as he is bodily. These various elements had all existed in one form or another in the earlier traditions about Richard III, but they had tended to be distributed among a number of different characters. It is Shakespeare who brought them together in the person of his larger-than-life anti-hero.[40] One might then say that Shakespeare was supremely successful in tapping into the cultural logic of his tradition, and so producing a strongly resonant tale. Perhaps one reason it continues to resonate so strongly is that the world is by no means rid of people who are ruthlessly ambitious for power, even if its resonance at the time probably owed much to the dominant Tudor view of the last Plantagenet king and to anxieties over a contemporary succession crisis (the issue of who would follow the childless Queen Elizabeth onto the English throne).

This raises the question whether the Gospels that found a ready reception in Christian circles did so, at least in part, because they presented a Jesus who crystallized the traditions about him in a particularly apt form while confirming the Church's nascent sense of identity and speaking to its concerns. The Gospels might then have succeeded in both embodying and creatively enhancing the Jesus traditions as well as Shakespeare did the Ricardian ones.

We can only speculate how this might have come about, since we can only speculate about the particular circumstances in which each Gospel was written, even if our speculations are guided by clues in the text. For example, we might locate the writing of John's Gospel in the reign of Domitian and see the hostility of the world of which it speaks as a reflection of the Church's refusal to participate in the emperor cult. Presumably, as followers of an ancient religion which the Roman authorities felt obliged to respect, Jews would have been exempt from the obligation to sacrifice to the emperor. Being expelled from the synagogue (John 9.22) might then leave Christians particularly vulnerable to execution if they refused to participate in the emperor cult (John 16.2). Johannine references to the 'ruler of this world' (John 12.31; 14.30; 16.11) would then be double-edged, alluding both to the Roman emperor and to Satan (or to the emperor seen as satanic on account of his pretensions to divinity). Bitter experience of this kind of persecution from 'the world', aided and abetted by Jewish opponents, might then account for the sharply dualistic language that characterizes the Fourth Gospel, not least the sense of being hated by the world (John 15.18–20; 17.14). That the 'ruler of the world' is to be associated with Rome may be further suggested by the similarity of language about the ruler of the world and Pilate both lacking power over Jesus (14.30 and 19.11); that Rome and the Jewish authorities were seen as colluding in the persecution of the Church may be suggested by 19.15. This in turn may be part of what drives the accusation that the Jews are murderous children of the devil (John 8.44). It may also be part of what drives John's high Christology, or, to put in other terms, the supremely enhanced reputation accorded to Jesus in the Fourth Gospel, a Jesus who is made explicitly divine in order to compete with the claims of 'the ruler of this world'. The function of such an

---

[40] Schwyzer, *Remains*, 204–5.

enhanced reputation would in part be to strengthen the Christian communities to which the Fourth Gospel was initially addressed, and in particular to nerve them against the temptation to lapse back into a more conventional form of Judaism in order to escape persecution (John 6.66–69; 9.22; 12.42). Indeed, Jesus' reputation is so enhanced in the Fourth Gospel that he becomes the *only* way to the Father and the *only* valid source (or conduit) of true life (John 1.4; 3.15–16, 36; 5.21, 25–26, 39–40; 6.35, 40, 48–57, 68; 10.9; 11.25; 14.6). At the same time, even more than Shakespeare's Richard, John's Jesus is a figure who is fully in control of events, even those surrounding his death. He is fully a hero who lays down his life voluntarily, and thus a figure to be emulated and admired, while also being the guarantor of the Church's ultimate vindication.

To say all this is not to reduce John's theology to his social situation; John's proven fertility for subsequent Christian theological reflection would make such a reduction self-evidently absurd. Neither is it to claim that we *know* it to be the case that John's Gospel was written in response to a particular experience of persecution; we quite clearly *know* no such thing. Rather the scenario sketched above has been offered as an example of how the model of reputational entrepreneurship might work in relation to one Gospel. The constraints of space prohibit the attempt to carry out similar exercises on Matthew, Mark and Luke, although we might suppose that in each case Jesus' reputation would need to have been configured to embody the identity and ethos of the target audience.

Collective memory and socially embedded authorship

Chapter 4 examined a number of models of composition, just as Chapter 2 proposed a number of reasons for writing a Gospel. Neither discussion suggested a picture of a detached author penning a purely personal account of the ministry of Jesus for purely disinterested reasons. We should thus guard against picturing an isolated individual somehow engaging with an abstraction called 'collective memory' as he wields his pen, rather than a socially embedded author continually interacting with others in the course of composition. However keen they may have been to shape the communities for whom they wrote, the Evangelists would almost certainly have first been shaped by them. In speaking of collective memory, we should not think of it as either a constraint or a resource that was external to the people who wrote. If collective memory provided the social frameworks which guided the way people spoke about Jesus, it also provided the frameworks that shaped the way the Evangelists thought about him. Collective memory was not something the Evangelists would have observed in some kind of detached way as they listened to oral tradition or observed Christian rituals; it was something they would have internalized as part of their own ethos, sense of identity and way of relating to the past.

To be sure, it may also have presented itself as external resource and constraint; other people might well have been able to supply the Evangelists with traditions they lacked, or interpretations that had not occurred to them, and there would no doubt have been powerful pressures to conform to group norms, particularly in a society where personal identity was so tied up with group identity. Feelings of loyalty and attachment to other members of the group will also have played a part. Moreover, the many aspects of collaborative authorship discussed in Chapter 4 will have provided constant reminders of how other members of the group thought and felt about the matters being written about. Collective memory would have been experienced as both internal and external, like the air the Evangelists breathed, or the stream of tradition in which they were immersed. Collective memory is something distinct from individual memories, but it thoroughly penetrates them through socially shared frameworks, the irreducibly social dimension of all individual acts of remembering and the shared experience of living in a believing community.

Conclusions

This chapter looked at a number of ways in which collective memory might bear on the writing of the Gospels. The topic is far from straightforward, since the idea of collective memory is hard to pin down. Far more could (and probably should) have been said on it, but hopefully enough has been said here to illustrate what collective memory can contribute to our understanding of Gospel authorship. In particular, although there can hardly be a complete divorce between collective memory and what goes inside individual people's heads, the collective memory of Jesus available to the Evangelists should not be seen as simply as the sum of the individual memories they were in contact with. Nor should it be seen as a body of shared factual knowledge about Jesus. The Church's collective memory of Jesus will not have been totally devoid of some facts (or supposed facts) about his career, such as his death by crucifixion, and his reputation no doubt included the fact that he taught, healed people and came into conflict with the Jewish authorities; but it will also have embodied a certain kind of ethos, so that the collective memory of Jesus will also have been manifested in the way Christian groups behaved, or thought they should behave, in the light of his teaching. This need not have been so much memory of specific teachings of Jesus, though this too will have played a part, as an embodiment of their general tenor. One would not have needed to recall a specific saying of Jesus to know, for example, that it was more in the spirit of his teaching to help people in need than to trample over the poor for one's own advantage.

'Collective memory' is thus not primarily the name of a pool of tradition on which the Evangelists could draw to provide material for their Gospels, although it will have included that. Rather, collective memory would have intimately concerned the way a Christian group used the past to construct and maintain its present identity. This will have provided a constraint on the Evangelists since there would be limits on the extent to which any group anxious to maintain its identity would tolerate challenges to its collective memory, but it would also provide opportunities, whether to shift the group's understanding of its identity or to exploit it by providing a new account of Jesus that resonated with the group's existing cultural logic. Moreover, changes in circumstances would probably have brought changes in the way collective memory needed to be configured, changes which the Gospels may themselves have been in part written to address.

None of this is meant to suggest that the Evangelists were merely passive conduits of some mysterious force called 'collective memory'; a constraint is not a straitjacket and in any case the Evangelists clearly had their own perspectives to contribute. Neither is it meant to suggest that the categories of social memory and reputational entrepreneurship can explain everything that can usefully be said about the composition of the Gospels. The point is rather that social memory contributes an important perspective on the writing of the Gospels, and that it suggests another way in which the compositional activities of the Evangelists may have differed from that of the Graeco-Roman literary elites, not because the latter were free of the resources and constraints of collective memory (far from it) but because their different social location would have resulted in their experiencing these factors rather differently; in particular they would not have shared the Evangelists' concern to shape and define their community's identity in relation to a recent founding figure.

Once written and disseminated, the Gospels would themselves contribute to the collective memory of the Church. One consequence of this is that the later Gospels may have to have reckoned with one or more of the earlier ones as part of the collective memory with which they had to do. The use of earlier Gospels by later ones will form the subject of the next chapter.

7

Gospel relations

Any account of the writing of the Gospels has to reckon with the likelihood that the later Evangelists employed the work of one or more of their predecessors. This raises the issue of the literary relationships between the Gospels, and in particular the Synoptic Problem, which is concerned with the relationship between the three Synoptic Gospels: Matthew, Mark and Luke. It will hardly be possible to solve the Synoptic Problem in the course of a single chapter (let alone to resolve the question of the relation between John and the Synoptic Gospels) but we should explore how our discussion of composition and memory might bear on it. But before we can discuss *how* the Evangelists may have used earlier Gospels as sources, we need to consider *whether* they did so, an assumption that has been challenged by advocates of orality and performance.

Is there a literary relationship between the Gospels?

The Gospels of Matthew, Mark and Luke contain a great deal in common. About 90 per cent of the content of Mark is found in Matthew, and slightly more than 50 per cent in Luke. Material common to all three Synoptic Gospels is often referred to as the *triple tradition*. In addition Matthew and Luke share a substantial body of material, mostly sayings of Jesus, which Mark lacks; this is often called the *double tradition*. In places the distinction between double and triple tradition becomes blurred, mainly in pericopae such as the Temptation Story or the Beelzebul Controversy where Matthew and Luke both have versions of a Markan story expanded with similar material not found in Mark. Moreover, there is a considerable amount of material common to Matthew and Mark that is not found in Luke (notably most of that contained in Mark 6.16–29; 6.45—8.21), which is sometimes thought of as belonging to the triple tradition even though it only appears in two Gospels. Finally, each of these three Gospels has material not found in any of the others, although the amount peculiar to Mark is small.

The order of the triple-tradition material is similar (though not identical) in all three Synoptic Gospels. Where there is disagreement in order, Mark generally agrees in order with either Matthew or with Luke. There is also considerable (though slightly less impressive) agreement in order in the double-tradition material in Matthew and Luke. In addition to agreements in order there are often (though by no means always) substantial agreements in wording between two or three of the Synoptic Gospels, although the extent of this agreement differs markedly, especially in the double tradition where at one extreme (e.g. the preaching of John the Baptist at Matthew 3.12 || Luke 3.17) there is near-verbatim agreement over a substantial number of words, while at the other (e.g. the Parable of the Pounds/Talents – Matthew 25.14–30 || Luke 19.12–27) there are hardly any words in common at all.[1]

These facts have led the majority of New Testament scholars to suppose that there must be a literary relationship between the Gospels of Matthew, Mark and Luke to explain both the degree of common order and the extent of common wording. Since around the middle of the nineteenth century the dominant theory of synoptic relations has been the Two Document Hypothesis (2DH), which holds that Mark wrote first, and that Matthew and Luke independently used Mark and a second (no longer extant) document conventionally referred to as Q (from the German *Quelle*, meaning 'source').[2] Earlier in the nineteenth century the dominant theory had been the Griesbach Hypothesis, which held that Mark had used both Matthew and Luke. Attempts to revive this have been made from around the middle of the twentieth century, in the shape of the neo-Griesbach or Two Gospel Hypothesis (2GH) which holds that Matthew came first, Luke used Matthew, and Mark used Matthew and Luke.[3] The other main challenger to the Two Document Hypothesis is the Farrer Hypothesis (FH, sometimes referred to as the Farrer–Goulder Hypothesis or Mark without Q). This agrees with the 2DH that Mark wrote first and was used by Matthew and Luke, but dispenses with the need for Q by postulating that Luke derived his double-tradition material from Matthew.[4]

---

[1] Mark Goodacre, 'Too Good to Be Q: High Verbatim Agreement in the Double Tradition' in John C. Poirier and Jeffrey Peterson (eds), *Marcan Priority without Q: Explorations in the Farrer Hypothesis* (LNTS, 455; London: Bloomsbury T. & T. Clark, 2015), 82–100.

[2] For a classic formulation of this position, see Burnett Hillman Streeter, *The Four Gospels: A Study of Origins Treating of the Manuscript Tradition, Sources, Authorship, and Dates* (London: Macmillan and Co., 1926). For more recent defences see, e.g., Christopher M. Tuckett, *Q and the History of Early Christianity* (Edinburgh: T. & T. Clark, 1997), 1–39; John S. Kloppenborg Verbin, *Excavating Q: The History and Setting of the Sayings Gospel* (Edinburgh: T. & T. Clark, 2000), 11–54.

[3] For the classic formulation see William R. Farmer, *The Synoptic Problem: A Critical Analysis* (Macon, GA: Mercer University Press, 1976). See also David L. Dungan, 'Mark – The Abridgement of Matthew and Luke' in David G. Buttrick and John M. Bald (eds), *Jesus and Man's Hope*, vol. 1 (Pittsburgh, PA: Pittsburgh Theological Seminary, 1970), 51–97; and Allan J. McNicol, David L. Dungan and David B. Peabody, *Beyond the Q Impasse: Luke's Use of Matthew* (Valley Forge: Trinity Press International, 1996); for a critique see Christopher M. Tuckett, *The Revival of the Griesbach Hypothesis: An Analysis and Appraisal* (SNTSMS, 44; Cambridge: Cambridge University Press, 1983).

[4] For the classic formulation see A. M. Farrer, 'On Dispensing with Q' in D. E. Nineham (ed.), *Studies in the Gospels: Essays in Memory of R. H. Lightfoot* (Oxford: Basil Blackwell, 1955), 55–88; for more recent defences see M. D. Goulder, *Midrash and Lection in Matthew* (London: SPCK, 1974); M. D. Goulder, *Luke: A New Paradigm* (JSNTSup, 20; Sheffield: Sheffield Academic Press, 1989); Mark Goodacre, *The Case against Q: Studies in Markan Priority and the Synoptic Problem* (Harrisburg, PA: Trinity Press International, 2002); Francis Watson, *Gospel Writing: A Canonical Perspective* (Grand Rapids, MI and Cambridge: Eerdmans, 2013), 117–285.

These three theories do not exhaust the possibilities that have been proposed, but they will suffice for the purposes of the present chapter.[5]

While the majority of New Testament scholars continue to hold that there must be some sort of literary relationship between the Synoptic Gospels, this near consensus has occasionally been challenged. One of the founding figures of twentieth-century orality studies, Albert Lord, proposed that the Gospels were a form of oral-traditional literature, so that the differences and similarities between them should be seen more in terms of oral-performance variations than literary copying and editing. His argument was challenged by Charles Talbert, but Talbert's critique has in turn been criticized by Pieter Botha.[6] Botha's own position is not entirely clear, however. In one place he states that he wants 'to argue for the relative independence of the Gospels, against theories of literary dependence', apparently on the grounds that in the light of his discussion of memory, performance and reading practices 'the *linear, literary* connections seen as a solution to the so-called synoptic problem become highly problematic'.[7] The concept of 'relative independence' is left undeveloped, however. In his critique of Talbert, Botha questions the claim that the degree of verbal agreement between the Synoptic Gospels necessitates a literary relationship, but his questioning amounts to little more than a dismissal of the claim, without any real attempt to engage with the evidence.[8]

Botha may be correct to challenge some of Talbert's arguably more typographic assumptions, and he is no doubt correct to suggest that the Synoptic Problem needs rethinking in the light of research into ancient media, but his own

---

[5] For the theory that Matthew used Luke, see Ronald V. Huggins, 'Matthean Posteriority: A Preliminary Proposal', *NovT* 34 (1992), 1–22; and Martin Hengel, *The Four Gospels and the One Gospel of Jesus Christ: An Investigation of the Collection and Origin of the Canonical Gospels* (tr. John Bowden; London: SCM Press, 2000), 169–207; for the so-called 'Augustinian' hypothesis (Matthew then Mark then Luke), see John Chapman, *Matthew, Mark and Luke: A Study in the Order and Interrelation of the Synoptic Gospels* (London; New York; Toronto: Longmans, Green and Co., 1937); B. C. Butler, *The Originality of St Matthew: A Critique of the Two-Document Hypothesis* (Cambridge: Cambridge University Press, 1951); and John Wenham, *Redating Matthew, Mark and Luke: A Fresh Assault on the Synoptic Problem* (London: Hodder & Stoughton, 1991). For surveys and assessments of various theories see E. P. Sanders and Margaret Davies, *Studying the Synoptic Gospels* (London/Philadelphia: SCM Press/Trinity Press International, 1989), 51–119; Christopher M. Tuckett, 'The Current State of the Synoptic Problem' in Paul Foster, Andrew Gregory, John S. Kloppenborg and J. Verheyden (eds), *New Studies in the Synoptic Problem* (BETL, 139; Leuven: Leuven University Press, 2011), 9–50 and Eric Eve, 'The Synoptic Problem without Q?' in Foster et al. (eds), *New Studies*, 551–70.

[6] See Albert B. Lord, 'The Gospels as Oral Traditional Literature' in William O. Walker (ed.), *The Relationships among the Gospels: An Interdisciplinary Dialogue* (Trinity University Monograph Series in Religion, 5; San Antonio: Trinity University Press, 1978), 33–91; Charles H. Talbert, 'Oral and Independent or Literary and Interdependent? A Response to Albert B. Lord' in Walker (ed.), *Relationships*, 93–102; Pieter J. J. Botha, *Orality and Literacy in Early Christianity* (BPC, 5; ed. H. E. Hearon and P. Ruge-Jones; Eugene, OR: Cascade, 2012), 176–8.

[7] Botha, *Orality and Literacy*, 110–11 (emphasis original).

[8] Botha, *Orality and Literacy*, 177.

position appears to rest on drawing a sharp distinction between 'orality' and modern print culture and then ruling in favour of the former as the more reliable guide to Gospel relations. This both oversimplifies the ancient media situation and fails to allow for a compositional paradigm that is different both from pure 'orality' and from modern print.

A similar problem afflicts James Dunn's treatment of the issue, although Dunn does at least engage with the data in some detail. He sets out a number of synoptic parallels from both the double and triple traditions, pointing out that whereas the degree of verbal agreement is often so high that some theory of literary copying seems to be required, this is not always the case; often the degree of verbal agreement between synoptic parallels is quite low, so low, in fact, that according to Dunn a theory of direct literary copying is not the best way to explain the evidence. In Dunn's view the different versions of common material in these Gospel parallels look not so much like literary redactions of one another as oral retellings, either of a common oral tradition, or of one Evangelist's recollection of another Evangelist's account. In support of the former possibility Dunn urges that it is unlikely that none of the material in Mark or Q was familiar to Matthew and Luke until they found it in Mark, so that the later Evangelists would almost certainly have been familiar with oral traditions parallel to the material they found in their written sources.[9]

Dunn does have a point: the variation in the degree of verbal agreement in synoptic parallels is quite striking, and where agreement is low the classical model of 'redaction', that is, of one Evangelist editing the work of another which he has in front of him, may not be the best way to describe the Evangelists' method of working. But Dunn has suggested two rather different alternatives, either that the later Evangelists were reliant on oral tradition for their different accounts or that they were reliant on their memory of an earlier Evangelist. He has then rushed to espouse the former of these two possibilities with no further ado. This seems to have arisen from a desire to counter an anachronistic 'print paradigm' with a so-called 'oral paradigm', without stopping to consider that these may not be the only two possibilities. In particular Dunn is too quick to equate 'literary paradigm' with 'print paradigm', as if there were not also an ancient 'literary paradigm' based on manuscripts, memory and scribal techniques.[10]

---

[9] James D. G. Dunn, 'Altering the Default Setting: Re-envisaging the Early Transmission of the Jesus Tradition', *NTS* 49 (2003), 139–75; James D. G. Dunn, *Jesus Remembered* (Christianity in the Making, 1; Grand Rapids and Cambridge: Eerdmans, 2003), 212–38.

[10] So also Robert A. Derrenbacker, 'The "External and Psychological Conditions under Which the Synoptic Gospels Were Written": Ancient Compositional Practices and the Synoptic Problem' in Paul Foster, Andrew Gregory, John S. Kloppenborg and J. Verheyden (eds), *New Studies in the Synoptic Problem* (BETL, 139; Leuven: Leuven University Press, 2011), 435–57 (453–4); and Alan Kirk, 'Memory, Scribal Media, and the Synoptic Problem' in Foster et al. (eds), *New Studies*, 459–82 (469).

John Kloppenborg is thus able to counter Dunn's argument by pointing out that the variations between synoptic parallels to which he appeals are well within the bounds of the way in which other ancient writers used their sources. As Kloppenborg goes on to point out, what is odd about the synoptic parallels in relation to ancient literary practice is not the degree to which they differ but the extent to which they agree.[11]

Since Dunn accepts that literary copying is the best explanation for some synoptic parallels, and indeed, since he continues to espouse the Two Document Hypothesis, he presumably thinks that Matthew and Luke were both familiar with Mark. Moreover, since either or both of the two later Evangelists nearly always agree with Mark's order, they must (on the basis of the 2DH which Dunn accepts) have been aware of Mark's version of the material they share with him even when their wording substantially departs from his. This leaves oral tradition little role left to play. It leaves it even less of a role to play when, again on the basis of Dunn's own assumptions, one takes oral tradition to be highly malleable; in other words, oral tradition would not provide an alternative fixed text for Matthew and Luke to follow in preference to what they found in Mark, and in any case oral tradition would only have been present to the Evangelists in the form of their memory of oral performances or their general knowledge of the collective memory of their communities. This memory of oral tradition might then just as well be memory of another text (as Dunn also acknowledges). Thus, insofar as Dunn's arguments have any force, rather than undermining a theory of literary dependence, they qualify it in favour of literary dependence through one Evangelist's memory of another Evangelist's work.

Relying on one's memory of a written source presupposes that one has a written source to remember, and in particular that one has previously read it and either deliberately committed it to memory, or reread (or heard) it a sufficient number of times to become conversant with its contents. The kind of verbal agreement in different versions of oral tradition to which Botha appeals occurs, for example, in different performances of an epic poem by the same performer (often relying on a stock of set phrases), or in songs and poems in which rhythm, metre, alliteration, assonance, rhyme and melody all act as aids to memory and so tend to stabilize wording.[12] These are very different situations from the occurrence of extensive similarities of wording found in prose texts by different authors. Verbatim memory of this kind of material, apart from short poems or aphorisms, rarely occurs in purely oral cultures, while in cultures such as that of the first-century Roman Empire where oral transmission occurs alongside written texts, there is always liable to be cross-fertilization between the two.

---

[11] John S. Kloppenborg, 'Variation and Reproduction of the Double Tradition and an Oral Q?', *ETL* 83 (2007), 53–80.

[12] Botha, *Orality and Literacy*, 177.

None of this is intended to deny the possibility, or even the likelihood, that the Evangelists made use of non-written sources, such as their memory of oral traditions. Neither is it meant to rule out the possibility that the Evangelists were influenced by their recollection of oral traditions in some instances where they were writing an account paralleled by material in another Gospel. It is, however, to suggest that there is no general need of the latter hypothesis, even if we may sometimes wish to invoke it in particular cases; in other words, there is nothing to prevent us from using the hypothesis of literary dependence as our basic starting point, or from treating it as more likely than not.[13] That said, as pointed out in Chapter 3, literary dependence need not be direct and unmediated, in the sense of the Evangelists constantly having their written sources in front of them as they composed their own Gospels. Here we shall be exploring the hypothesis that the Evangelists' primary method of working with their predecessor Gospels was through memory. But before doing so we should first revisit a related question, namely why someone in possession of an existing Gospel should have gone about rewriting it in the first place.

Why rewrite a Gospel?

In the course of discussing why someone might write a Gospel Chapter 2 considered reasons why someone might write another Gospel in response to an existing one. To recapitulate briefly, the point was made that, on the assumption of Markan priority, Matthew and Luke do not simply augment Mark with additional information, as if their motives were primarily archival; rather they absorb Mark into narratives of their own design in order to promote their own understanding of Jesus' significance. In the language of Chapter 6, Matthew and Luke act as reputational entrepreneurs who effectively silence Mark's version of Jesus by incorporating it into their own while reconfiguring it to present a Jesus who is both like and unlike Mark's. For the later Evangelists, Mark is both constraint and resource. It would have been a constraint insofar as Christian communities already familiar with Mark may have come to regard his account of Jesus as definitive, so that Matthew and Luke would have to reckon with it in promoting their own versions. It would have been both constraint and resource insofar as Mark's narrative provided part of the cultural logic with which any subsequent attempt to write a Gospel would need to resonate if it were to gain traction. Moreover, Matthew's need to rewrite Mark (say) would have been constrained by his own particular social and historical situation. That is to say, we should not imagine

---

[13] So also Andrew Gregory, 'What Is Literary Dependence?' in Paul Foster, Andrew Gregory, John S. Kloppenborg and J. Verheyden (eds), *New Studies in the Synoptic Problem* (BETL, 139; Leuven: Leuven University Press, 2011), 87–114 (103–7).

Matthew writing a Gospel simply because he thought he could improve on Mark; we should rather think of Matthew being faced with a situation where he felt he needed to 'improve' on Mark by transmuting Mark's Gospel into something that more directly addressed the needs and circumstances of his own target audience.

The reason for emphasizing these rather obvious points is to guard against the misleading implications of terms like 'literary copying' that crop up in discussions of the Synoptic Problem. Such language is no doubt suggested by parallel passages in the Synoptic Gospels where the wording is very close, which make it appear that one Evangelist simply copied the work of another. The term 'copying' is misleading, however, if used to describe how one Evangelist treated the work of another in general. The later Evangelists clearly did not set out to copy the work of their predecessors, but to write new Gospels of their own. Questions of the sort 'If Y was using X why didn't he copy what X did at A and B?' may thus be fundamentally misconceived. If Y simply copied everything X had done, Y would be a copyist, not an Evangelist. Moreover, the Evangelists were not modern scholars faithfully quoting their sources in the interests of academic accuracy.

This is particularly important to bear in mind when using the compositional techniques of contemporary Graeco-Roman authors as a control on those of the Evangelists. With suitable caveats this is a reasonable thing to do (as was explored in Chapter 4), but one of those caveats is that the elite authors we know about were more concerned to employ their sources than to displace them. For example, in rewriting much of the Old Testament for his *Antiquities*, Josephus had no intention of replacing or competing with the Septuagint; his aim was simply to suit the material to a different audience (while slanting it in accordance with his own tendencies). Likewise we need not suppose that in composing his parallel Lives Plutarch was actively seeking to silence any sources on which he drew. With Matthew and Luke it may well have been otherwise, which could well have led them to take a more aggressive stance towards reworking their sources than was typical of Josephus, Plutarch or any other elite authors used as a comparison.

As has been mentioned, given ancient compositional techniques the puzzle is not why the later Evangelists changed their sources to the extent they did, but why they preserved so much of their wording. Given that the norm in antiquity was for authors to rework their sources quite thoroughly, the degree of verbal agreement between the Synoptic Gospels in some parallel passages is surprising.[14] This could be taken as suggesting that after all the Evangelists must have been closely attending to their written sources by eye in order to reproduce so much of their wording. But it might alternatively suggest that the Evangelists were

---

[14] See F. Gerald Downing, 'Writers' Use or Abuse of Written Sources' in Paul Foster, Andrew Gregory, John S. Kloppenborg and J. Verheyden (eds), *New Studies in the Synoptic Problem* (BETL, 139; Leuven: Leuven University Press, 2011), 523–48 (531–6); Kloppenborg, 'Variation and Reproduction', 63–74.

working with texts they had memorized and internalized to such an extent that the wording of these texts spilled naturally over into their own compositions (in line with the 'scribal' model of Chapter 4). A further possibility is that the later Evangelists were deliberately trying to borrow or supplant the authority of their predecessors by reproducing wording that would have a familiar ring to their target audiences. But whatever the explanation, and despite this apparent evidence of some copying in the strict sense, we should think of the later Gospels not as revised and expanded versions of their predecessors, but as fresh compositions in their own right, which, as was argued in Chapter 4, may have drawn on other modes of composition besides those typically employed by elite authors.

Memory and the Synoptic Problem

Ancient writers' use of their memory of written sources was extensively discussed in Chapter 5, where it was argued that it was common for writers to rely on their memory of written sources at least up to the end of the Middle Ages. This is hardly a fresh insight, and its potential application to the Synoptic Problem has already been discussed by a number of scholars, including Andrew Gregory, Robert Derrenbacker and Alan Kirk.[15]

For Gregory, memory features primarily as one possible mode of literary dependence. If, he suggests, Luke had Mark open in front of him and at the same time possessed memory command of Matthew, he could have worked backwards and forwards through Matthew's text rather as Michael Goulder proposes for the FH but without the mechanical difficulty of having to wind backwards and forwards through an unwieldy scroll. Conversely, if the 2DH Matthew and Luke each had memory command of Q, then they would have been able to draw on Q passages out of sequence while following their main source, Mark, open in front of them. Thus, for Gregory, the Evangelists' possible use of memory of their sources does not strongly select between the FH and the 2DH, although Gregory suspects 'that it may be less helpful for the 2GH'.[16]

Derrenbacker points out that all three of the 2DH, FH and 2GH require at least one of the Evangelists to have conflated two of his sources, contrary to the normal practice of ancient authors. On the 2GH Mark would have to have closely conflated Matthew and Luke; on the FH Luke would have conflated Matthew and Mark; while on the 2DH there are sections where Matthew would have been conflating Mark and Q. According to Derrenbacker, it is the 2DH Matthew who would have to perform the least conflation, and so the 2DH is to

[15] Gregory, 'Literary Dependence', 95–107; Derrenbacker, 'External and Psychological Conditions', 445–53; Kirk, 'Memory'.
[16] Gregory, 'Literary Dependence', 102.

be preferred as being the least problematic of the three in this respect. It then remains to be explained how the 2DH Matthew achieved the conflation of Mark and Q that he would nevertheless still have to have performed. It is in this connection that Derrenbacker invokes Matthew's memory of Q, suggesting that there is an analogy between Matthew's use of Q from memory and Paul's use of the Jewish Scriptures in that both authors seem able to cluster material drawn from scattered sources. Derrenbacker finally suggests that the composition of Matthean passages such as the Sermon on the Mount is far easier to understand if we envisage Matthew using Q from memory when he cites it out of order. In support of this Derrenbacker points out that Matthew tends to deviate more from the wording of Q when he departs from the order of Q (assuming that the order of Q is represented by that of the double-tradition material in Luke), which would seem to indicate Matthew's greater reliance on memory when using Q material out of Q's sequence.

As an account of how a 2DH Matthew may have worked, this seems fair enough, but the statement that Matthew tends to vary from the wording of Q more when he departs from the order of Q presupposes the 2DH. The wording of Q is reconstructed by comparing the double tradition in Matthew and Luke. The empirical basis for asserting that Matthew departs from the wording of Q in certain passages can only be that Matthew and Luke disagree in wording in those passages. Likewise, the empirical basis for asserting that Matthew departs from Q's order in certain passages is simply that Matthew and Luke differ in their ordering of the two passages. Thus, the evidential basis for Derrenbacker's claim could only be that in the double tradition, Matthew and Luke tended to differ more in wording in passages where they also differed in order (to the extent that this is actually the case). This could just as well be described on the FH as Luke tending to depart from Matthew's wording more when he uses Matthew's material out of Matthew's order, which in turn could be an indication of Luke's use of memory in these passages. The Evangelists' employment of memory thus does not select between the 2DH and the FH on this argument.

Derrenbacker's claim that an FH Luke would have to have performed more conflation than a 2DH Matthew also stands in need of further justification, since on the face of it Luke's alleged 'conflation' of Matthew and Mark might better be described as his principally working from Matthew in certain passages in which he occasionally betrays recollections of Mark. Given that the 2DH Luke is thought to have used Mark and Q in separate blocks of material, while the 2DH Matthew seems readier to combine Mark and Q more closely, it would be the 2DH Matthew who would have carried out the greater amount of conflation.

Alan Kirk lays an even heavier emphasis on the use of memory than the previous two writers, and provides a detailed discussion of how this might bear on the three principal theories of synoptic relations considered here. In Chapter 5 we questioned his view about the minimum size of cognitive units that could be accessed in memory, while allowing that his point is probably valid if it is really about what can readily be *processed* in memory. We also questioned what appeared to be his implication that an author using a written source from memory would tend to be constrained to follow the order of that source. To be fair, though, Kirk's main point is about the mnemonic efficiency of cueing. His point is that the narrative arrangement of a text, or its arrangement into sequences of conventional moral *topoi*, would aid memory by providing a network of cues. Other things being equal it would probably be easier for someone working from memory to follow the cues provided by the structure of the memorized texts than to retrieve items from the text in some other order. Kirk does not deny that someone working from memory *could* on occasion retrieve items out of order (indeed, as he acknowledges, on any theory of synoptic relations involving substantial use of memory, at least one Evangelist must have done so). Moreover, it is one thing to cite a few items from memory in random sequence, and quite another to use a large number of items from memory out of sequence while at the same time keeping track of what one has or has not used.

Yet, it is possible that other things may not always be equal; it may be, for example, that an Evangelist had some other cueing system at his disposal to facilitate memory access to his source text (for example by keyword or topical association, as Kirk proposes for Matthew's use of Q), or that he had various external aids to memory, as we shall discuss below. Kirk's emphasis on the role of memory in the composition of the Gospels is welcome, but it should not be taken to the extreme of envisaging the Evangelists as working entirely from their own unsupported individual memories.

Kirk disposes of the 2GH fairly briskly, by suggesting that the close comparison and word-by-word conflation of Matthew and Luke that would be required by the 2GH Mark is something that can really only be envisaged in a print culture. It would be extremely difficult to perform by eye, given the need to scroll back and forth through unwieldy manuscripts, and no easier to carry out in memory (as indicated in Chapter 4 above). He considers the defence that such conflation was nevertheless carried out by Tatian in his *Diatesseron* (a combination of all four Gospels into a single account), but counters that in Tatian's time the Gospel texts had reached 'greater fixation and external objectification' than they had at the time Mark wrote.[17] This counter is in some tension with the additional objection that Mark's supposed conflation of Matthew and Luke is the product of a print-culture imagination, since Tatian's project was clearly not conceived in a print culture. The point may stand, however, that Tatian was working with texts that had acquired near-canonical status while the 2GH Mark was probably not.

---

[17] Kirk, 'Memory', 479–82.

It is also unclear why the 2GH Mark should go to all the effort he would need to have done to produce the text he did (which looks far from being either a successful or a mere harmony of Matthew and Luke), whereas Tatian's motive seems easier to conceive. But in any case, since no complete Greek text of Tatian's work survives, it is unclear precisely what Tatian achieved or how he went about it.[18]

Kirk also finds some difficulties with the 2DH, at least as traditionally conceived, complaining that, not least, it has failed to account adequately for the variations in the degree of verbal agreement found across synoptic parallels. As Kirk rightly points out, it will not do (as Dunn suggests) to assign close verbal agreement to literary copying and verbal variation to oral tradition.[19] In Kirk's view 'Dunn lacks a model for coordinating the written/oral dynamics he postulates for oral composition', while Kloppenborg is similarly in want of 'a model for a strong interface of scribal tradition with oral-traditional dynamics', which takes account of the fact that 'the synoptics embody immanent scribal reenactments of the constitutive base tradition itself, enactments which at the same time function to *transmit* the base tradition'.[20] The point is not simply that the Evangelists are competent performers of the tradition in which they are steeped, like Ben Sira on the scribal-memorial model outlined in Chapter 4, but that they stand much closer to their foundational tradition, and it is this (in Kirk's view) that gives rise to the distinctive range of agreements and disagreements we find across the Synoptic Gospels.

Kirk then proposes that the 2DH might be more in accord with ancient compositional practices if memory is given a more prominent role, and in particular if Matthew and Luke are assumed to have had memory command of Mark and Q. The fact that Mark and Q were both nonetheless texts with an intelligible order inscribed in writing would account for the degree of common order found in Matthew and Luke despite their independent use of these two sources (Matthew and Luke would have been working from their memory of these fixed *texts*, whose order would have helped make them intelligible in oral performance). Luke's use of Q is then relatively unproblematic, since (according to the 2DH) Luke more or less uses Q material in Q's original order, and alternates blocks of Q and Markan material much in the manner of other ancient authors who make use of more than one source. More problematic is Matthew's use of Q, which departs from Q's (supposed) order and tends to be more closely intermingled with material taken from Mark. Kirk proposes that Matthew had memory control of Q, and was able to access it out of order by following cued sequences forward

[18] Christopher M. Tuckett, *The Revival of the Griesbach Hypothesis: An Analysis and Appraisal* (SNTSMS, 44; Cambridge: Cambridge University Press, 1983), 42–3.
[19] So also Eric Eve, *Behind the Gospels: Understanding the Oral Tradition* (London: SPCK, 2013), 111.
[20] Kirk, 'Memory', 469–70 (emphasis original).

from various textual locations. In part following Vincent Taylor, Kirk suggests that although Matthew indeed often uses Q sequences out of order, in general he moves forward both through Q as a whole and through the shorter sequences of sayings he employs from Q.[21]

Kirk finds problems with the FH's account of Luke's method of working as it has been propounded both by Michael Goulder and by Mark Goodacre, not least criticizing both writers' occasional appeals to memory as ancillary and *ad hoc*. Kirk argues that Goulder's model of Luke scrolling around (and often backwards) through his copy of Matthew to find particular passages seems implausible in the light of ancient media realities, but Kirk then allows that in principle Goulder's proposal may be more realistic if one envisages Luke as having memory control of Matthew rather than attempting to manipulate a physical scroll.[22] Kirk nevertheless objects to this on the grounds that Luke's use of Matthew would have required too many backward movements through Matthew's text (especially in his travel narrative), contrary to Luke's presumed 'memory competence in Matthew as an intelligibly performed script'. In Kirk's view this compares unfavourably with the predominantly forward movement the 2DH Matthew would have made through Q. Kirk also draws attention to the difficulty the FH Luke would have had in assembling the *topoi* sequences in his travel narrative from material embedded in Matthean narrative contexts compared with the relative ease with which the 2DH Matthew could have followed the *topoi* sequences in Q (assuming the use of memory in both cases).[23]

A further problem Kirk finds with the FH is Luke's clean separation of Matthean from Markan material passages where there are major agreements of Matthew and Luke against Mark (so that Matthew has either expanded Mark with his own material or combined it with material taken from elsewhere). This would have been difficult enough to achieve by eye through comparing manuscripts of Matthew and Mark, and even more difficult to have achieved through memory of the two texts. Given 'the standard FH explanation of the Minor Agreements as memory interference from Matthew when Luke is following Mark' (to which we shall return below), it becomes even harder to explain the apparent absence of Markan influence on Luke's treatment of major agreement passages.[24]

Kirk's discussion substantially advances the proposal that the Evangelists should be understood as working primarily (though not necessarily exclusively) from

---

[21] Kirk, 'Memory', 471–3.

[22] But see John C. Poirier, 'The Roll, the Codex, the Wax Tablet and the Synoptic Problem', *JSNT* 35 (2012), 3–30 (3–14) for a defence of the theoretical possibility of the procedure proposed by Goulder together with the rejoinder in Robert A. Derrenbacker, 'Texts, Tables and Tablets: A Response to John C. Poirier', *JSNT* 35 (2013), 380–7 (381–2) and the discussion in Chapter 3 above.

[23] Kirk, 'Memory', 473–7.

[24] Kirk, 'Memory', 476, 478.

memory of their sources rather than through eye contact with manuscripts and agrees with the position being explored here. It is another matter, however, whether it selects between the 2DH and FH quite as strongly as he supposes.

To start with, in support of his contention that Luke jumps around the Matthean material too much in his travel narrative, Kirk estimates that these nine chapters of Luke contain roughly 'seventeen backward and twenty-three forward movements' through Matthew. On my rough count, the Sermon on the Mount (Matthew 5—7) contains some nine backward and eight forward movements through Q (although since there may be more than one way of reckoning forward and backward movements we may not be exactly comparing like with like). Luke's 17 backward movements over nine chapters works out at 1.89 backward movements per chapter; it is not immediately clear why this should be regarded as excessive in relation to the 2DH Matthew's 3.00 backward movements per chapter in the Sermon on the Mount, even if it be argued that such statistics do not tell the full story. Jeffrey Peterson, for example, suggests that Edwin Lummis's proposal of three forward scans through Matthew by the FH Luke compares favourably with Vincent Taylor's 15 scans through Q by the 2DH Matthew, though such proposals clearly need to be examined in more detail than space allows here.[25]

On the face of it Kirk has an interesting point about mnemonic sequencing, namely that it would be easier for the 2DH Matthew to access the pure *topoi* sequences in Q to extract material to rearrange from memory than it would be for the FH Luke to access Matthean sayings material embedded in narrative contexts in order to separate them out and redeploy them in a *topos* sequence of his own devising (notably in his travel narrative). But on close examination it is unclear how much Lukan material this actually applies to, since the great majority of the double-tradition material the FH Luke would have redeployed from Matthew comes in blocks of discourse material in Matthew. Presumably Kirk has in mind such passages as Luke 10.23–24; 12.54–56 and possibly 17.22–37 (although the last of these is discourse rather than narrative), but they are very much in the minority of the double-tradition material that the FH Luke would have taken from Matthew, and it is far from clear that such very occasional lifting of sayings material from Matthean narratives would have been all that difficult for the FH Luke.

Moreover, a Luke working from memory could be using memory cues in part supplied by his own design, and not just that of his source material, so that, for example, a saying embedded in a Matthean narrative context but nevertheless well known to Luke might be cued by the topic Luke had in mind at the time (in other words Luke's memory access might be via cues supplied by his own schema

---

[25] Jeffrey Peterson, 'Order in the Double Tradition and the Existence of Q' in Mark Goodacre and Nicholas Perrin (eds), *Questioning Q* (London: SPCK, 2004), 28–42 (32).

rather than Matthew's). While there may be no clear overall structure to his travel section, there is a tendency for material to cluster around topics such as discipleship, prayer, riches, criticism of the Pharisees, judgement and the eschaton, and it may have been these topics which provided Luke with his mnemonic cues.[26] A full analysis of the Lukan travel narrative cannot be conducted here, but if there is anywhere where an FH Luke would have to be conceived of as working from memory it is surely in this section.[27]

A further question is whether Luke's alleged unpicking of Markan material from the major agreements accurately describes the data. Ken Olson has argued otherwise.[28] Kirk is aware of Olson's argument but objects to it on the grounds that 'Authors selecting material alternatively from two or more closely related sources is no true analogy', but even if this is a valid objection (and since Kirk does not elaborate on it this is hard to tell), it seems to refer only to a subsidiary point in Olson's argument and completely sidesteps Olson's detailed demonstration that the FH Luke did *not* unpick Mark from Matthew in the four passages Olson examines.[29]

Perhaps a bigger question for the FH is why, if Luke knew and used Matthew from memory, he should have bothered with Mark at all. Since virtually the whole substance of Mark was contained in Matthew, it would surely have been easier for Luke to have worked from the one source (Matthew) than to try to combine two sources that were often very similar.

To be sure, there may be places where Luke does not use Mark as his main source even when there is a Markan parallel to what he writes. In some sections of his Gospel (e.g. Luke 3.1—4.13 and 11.14–32) it might make better sense of the data to suggest that Luke was primarily following Matthew. This may even be so for sections of the Gospel where Luke is commonly supposed to be following Mark, such as parts of the Passion narrative where he appears to have slightly more agreements with Matthew (although here Matthew and Mark are often so similar that it can be hard to distinguish the signal of minor agreements from

---

[26] Cf. Mark A. Matson, 'Luke's Rewriting of the Sermon on the Mount' in Mark Goodacre and Nicholas Perrin (eds), *Questioning Q* (London: SPCK, 2004), 43–70 (54–62).

[27] For some suggestions on what the FH Luke may have been doing in his travel section, see John Drury, *Tradition and Design in Luke's Gospel: A Study in Early Christian Historiography* (London: Darton, Longman and Todd, 1976), 138–71; Eric Franklin, *Luke: Interpreter of Paul, Critic of Matthew* (JSNTSup, 92; Sheffield: JSOT Press, 1994), 328–52; Jeffrey Peterson, 'Order in the Double Tradition and the Existence of Q' in Mark Goodacre and Nicholas Perrin (eds), *Questioning Q* (London: SPCK, 2004), 28–42 (38–40); Watson, *Gospel Writing*, 178–216.

[28] Ken Olson, 'Unpicking on the Farrer Theory' in Mark Goodacre and Nicholas Perrin (eds), *Questioning Q* (London: SPCK, 2004), 127–50; cf. Eric Eve, 'The Devil in the Detail: Exorcising Q from the Beelzebul Controversy' in John C. Poirier and Jeffrey Peterson (eds), *Marcan Priority without Q: Explorations in the Farrer Hypothesis* (LNTS, 455; London: Bloomsbury T. & T. Clark, 2015), 16–43.

[29] Kirk, 'Memory', 476 n. 92; Olson, 'Unpicking', 138–46.

the noise of textual variants). Moreover, Luke omits Mark 6.45—8.26 altogether, and makes sparing use of Mark during his long travel section. It is thus an over-simplification to regard the FH Luke as simply following Mark and using Matthew to supplement it. The question still remains, however, why Luke should make any use of Mark.

One answer proposed by Mark Goodacre is that Luke was already thoroughly familiar with Mark before he came across Matthew, and it certainly seems reasonable to suppose that such thorough familiarity would be reflected in Luke's composition.[30] Francis Watson suggests that in setting out an 'orderly account' (Luke 1.3) Luke was trying to mediate between discrepancies in the Markan and Matthean orders.[31] Again this seems reasonably plausible provided Luke had sufficient motive to combine both sources. Despite the fact that Luke departs from the Markan order only when Matthew retains it, a case could be made for his trying to reconcile the narrative order of both his sources (at least for Luke 3.1—9.50) while introducing a small number of variations on his own initiative at critical points near the start of Jesus' ministry, particularly in passages he substantially recasts (notably Luke 4.16–30; 5.1–11) and omitting the substance of Mark 6.18–29; 6.45—8.26 together with some Markan passages (e.g. Mark 3.22–30; 4.30–32) that had Matthean parallels he employed later. It is at least conceivable that Luke recognized Mark as Matthew's primary source and valued it accordingly (although the lack of any patristic recognition of this relationship militates against this proposal). Luke may in any case have wanted to use Mark for some of the more vivid narrative touches missing from Matthew. Or, to combine these various suggestions in slightly different terms, there could well have been places where, after reading or recalling both versions, Luke chose to follow Mark rather than Matthew both for the content and for the order where it better suited his own narrative design. A final possibility is that in aiming to displace both Gospels for a widespread audience, some of whom may have been more familiar with Mark and others more familiar with Matthew, Luke was anxious to compose an account that would appeal to both constituencies by retaining elements that would resonate with each.

Memory and minor agreements

The term 'minor agreements' refers to relatively small (hence 'minor') agreements of Matthew and Luke against Mark in the triple tradition. These may be as minor as changing a verb in the present tense to the aorist or using *de* for *kai* to express 'and', or they may comprise a run of several words common to Matthew and Luke

---

[30] Goodacre, *Case against Q*, 88–90; cf. Franklin, *Luke*, 313–15.
[31] Cf. Watson, *Gospel Writing*, 124–31.

but not found in the Markan parallel, such as the common addition in both Matthew and Luke of the words *tis estin ho paisas se* ('Who is it that struck you?') at Matthew 26.68 || Mark 14.65 || Luke 22.64 and of *exelthōn exō eklausen pikrōs* ('he went out and wept bitterly') at Matthew 26.75 || Mark 14.72 || Luke 22.62. Such 'minor agreements' are often distinguished from 'major agreements' where Matthew and Luke share a substantial amount of material not found in Mark in passages where they are otherwise parallel to Mark (such as the Temptation Story and the Beelzebul Controversy), although Mark Goodacre has complained that this distinction is artificial, and that one should instead see a continuum in the degree of agreement of Matthew and Luke against Mark.[32]

If, as on the 2DH, Matthew and Luke were independently using Mark and Q, then they ought not to agree with each other against Mark at all frequently. Some (such as Michael Goulder) have seen this as the Achilles' heel of the 2DH, but the issue is not that simple. At least some minor agreements could be explained as coincidence, for example where Matthew and Luke independently hit on the same way of improving Mark's text as they recast it into slightly more literary Greek. Others could perhaps be explained by textual contamination of one Gospel from another in the course of the manuscript tradition. A scribe copying Luke, for example, might inadvertently reproduce some of the wording of Matthew, particularly if he were more familiar with that Gospel. This might then create the appearance of a minor agreement between Matthew and Luke although none had existed originally. In any case the copies of Mark known to Matthew and Luke were certainly not identical with any modern printed Greek text of Mark, so some apparent minor agreements may be due to their having been familiar with a different text of Mark.

The question is whether all the minor agreements can be explained like this. It is, for example, highly uncertain that all the minor agreements can be explained by textual corruption.[33] This then prompts the question how many minor agreements are too many to be explained as coincidence. Richard Vinson has argued that there are far too many minor agreements to be explained in this way.[34] But against Vinson it could be argued both that the experiment on which he relies for his conclusion does not adequately reproduce the compositional methods of antiquity, and that, in any case, there is no objective way of enumerating how many minor agreements there actually are (although this does not necessarily

---

[32] Goodacre, *Case against Q*, 163–5.

[33] See Peter M. Head, 'Textual Criticism and the Synoptic Problem' in Paul Foster, Andrew Gregory, John S. Kloppenborg and J. Verheyden (eds), *New Studies in the Synoptic Problem* (BETL, 139; Leuven: Leuven University Press, 2011), 115–56 (149–51).

[34] Richard Vinson, 'How Minor? Assessing the Significance of the Minor Agreements as an Argument against the Two-Source Hypothesis' in Mark Goodacre and Nicholas Perrin (eds), *Questioning Q* (London: SPCK, 2004), 151–64.

invalidate his conclusion).[35] It may be more productive to look for patterns or clusters of minor agreements, such as occur in the Healing of the Paralytic (Mark 2.1–12 || Matthew 9.1–8 || Luke 5.17–26), since these seem harder to explain as coincidence than individual minor agreements taken in isolation may be.[36]

If the existence of minor agreements does not furnish a knock-down proof for Luke's use of Matthew (or vice versa), it nevertheless presents the 2DH with a difficulty that needs to be explained. On the face of it such minor agreements would tend to favour the FH (or 2GH), since if Luke used Matthew there would seem to be no problem with explaining why they sometimes agree with each other against Mark. But matters are not quite so simple since, as Christopher Tuckett has pointed out, the problem with the minor agreements is that many of them are *so* minor.[37] If Luke were following Mark as his main source, it seems hard to explain why he should bother to introduce such minor details into his text from Matthew, and indeed as a deliberate redactional procedure based on the assumption of Luke using copies of Matthew and Mark open in front of him it would make very little sense. If, on the other hand, Luke had memory command of Matthew and Mark (or of one of them while accessing the other as a written source), then it is easy to see how memory of one Gospel might 'contaminate', or at least influence, Luke's composition on the basis of the other. This would apply even more if Luke were employing both sources from memory, in which case the conflation of two similar and parallel accounts might occur quite naturally without any conscious intent on Luke's part.

This is what Kirk refers to as 'the standard FH explanation of the Minor Agreements'. While he allows that 'In principle this resembles the memory phenomenon of "proactive interference"', he nevertheless raises two objections to it as an explanation of the minor agreements on the FH. The first is that if Luke's use of Mark had been coloured by memory interference from Matthew, 'one would then expect (the memory factor being a constant) a more consistent pattern of these small-scale, involuntary harmonizations to Matthew'. The second is that on Goodacre's thesis of 'Luke's decidedly stronger memory familiarity with Mark' it is hard to see why memory interference from Matthew should occur.[38]

Neither of these objections is persuasive. The phrase 'the memory factor being a constant' is presumably meant to suggest that since the same explanation (proactive interference) is operative throughout, one should expect a uniform distribution of minor agreements (assuming this is what Kirk means by 'consistent pattern'),

---

[35] M. Eugene Boring, 'The "Minor Agreements" and Their Bearing on the Synoptic Problem' in Paul Foster, Andrew Gregory, John S. Kloppenborg and J. Verheyden (eds), *New Studies in the Synoptic Problem* (BETL, 139; Leuven: Leuven University Press, 2011), 227–51.

[36] For a discussion of this particular cluster, see Sanders and Davies, *Studying*, 68–73.

[37] Tuckett, *Q and the History of Early Christianity*, 28.

[38] Kirk, 'Memory', 475–8.

but this is far from obviously the case. For one thing, memory interference might be only one factor among a number of others that could also include textual corruption and coincidental agreement in making obvious improvements to Mark's Greek. For another, Kirk offers no experimental evidence or theoretical demonstration that memory interference should result in a uniform distribution of agreements rather than, say, a randomly varying one.

Indeed, there are a number of reasons why one might expect the distribution of agreements not to be uniform. As we saw in Chapter 5 many factors can cue recall, and what might cue recall of wording that constitutes interference in any particular case is surely unpredictable, since far more would be going on in the minds of the Evangelists than we could ever know. In particular, we can never know what particular associations were most salient in Luke's mind as he wrote. Moreover, if Luke may be allowed to occasionally refresh his memory from eye contact with either of his sources, this may also affect the phenomenon of interference. Also, depending on how good Luke's memory of the wording of particular passages in his sources was, there may be some occasions when a minor agreement resulted from deliberate choice rather than accidental interference, or at least where the interference was partly, if unconsciously, driven by what Luke wanted to say and how he preferred to say it (for example, by polishing Mark's rough Greek). There will also have been other random factors such as what someone had just said to him or what train of thought he had been following when composing a particular passage, which are also quite unknowable.

Finally, in the absence of any objective means of counting minor agreements it would be hard to demonstrate that their observed distribution differed from the expected one (whatever that should be) in a statistically significant way. At the very least, then, a rather more robust demonstration of oddity needs to be made before Kirk's first objection can be allowed much weight. In any case Kirk's concern about the non-uniform distribution of minor agreements would surely apply to any other explanation that might be offered if such an explanation is taken to be a 'constant factor' in generating minor agreements.

The second objection only applies if we assume that Luke was thoroughly familiar with Mark but scarcely knew Matthew at all, but has rather less force if Luke had memory command of both sources (which would have made it far easier for him to access Matthew out of sequence). In any case interference can be retroactive as well as proactive; in other words, more recent and less recent memories can each interfere with the other.[39] Finally, whereas the 'standard FH explanation' is able to give some kind of explanation for the minor agreements, Kirk ends up giving none at all.

---

[39] Alan Baddeley, Michael W. Eysenck and Michael C. Anderson, *Memory* (Hove and New York: Psychology Press, 2009), 201–5.

Other factors

Derrenbacker has quite rightly called attention to other factors besides memory that entered into ancient compositional practice, such as 'note taking, excerpting, epitomizing, dictation, etc.'[40] Strangely, however, these other factors tend to drop out of sight when the discussion moves on to the implications of ancient compositional practices for particular theories of synoptic relations. The foregoing discussion of memory has also tended to proceed as if (on the 2DH) Matthew produced his Gospel directly from Mark and Q without any intermediate steps or (on the FH) Luke similarly produced his directly from Matthew and Mark in one go. It is as if the Evangelists were conceived as data-processing devices producing an output (their Gospels) directly from their input (their sources) in a single-stage process. This is a somewhat implausible model, however, given that, as we have already seen, ancient composition tended to be both a collaborative and a multi-stage process. Thus, while it is valuable to consider how an Evangelist might have gone about employing his sources from memory, this cannot be taken as the whole story.

Given both inherent plausibility and what we know of how other ancient authors worked, it is most unlikely that the composition of any of the Gospels was a single-step process. Neither the 2DH Matthew nor the FH Luke would have been obliged to reorder and combine their sources either by unaided memory alone or by working through their source documents (in memory or by eye) in a single pass. Although it is impossible to state with any certainty just how the Evangelists would have worked, it would not be unreasonable to allow them something like the following six stages: (1) reading through the source documents they intended to use to refresh their memories, and discussing the projected work with friends and colleagues; (2) excerpting passages and/or making notes of some of the material they intended to use; (3) dictating a rough draft to an assistant; (4) polishing up the rough draft (possibly with reference to notes and memory, and occasional visual checking of sources); (5) trying out the polished draft on a circle of friends or fellow church-members; (6) revising the polished draft in the light of the feedback obtained. It may be, of course, that the Evangelists' actual procedure did not fall quite so neatly into six such distinct stages, but as a rough working model this allows either the 2DH Matthew or the FH Luke plenty of scope for reworking some parts of their sources more thoroughly than might be readily achieved in a single hit.

In this connection John Poirier has recently proposed that the compositional task of the FH Luke may have been eased by the use of wax tablets at an intermediate stage. Poirier argues that Luke composed his Gospel in three segments

---

[40] Derrenbacker, 'External and Psychological Conditions', 454.

(corresponding in length to the number of wax tablets he had at his disposal) and that he would readily have been able to reorder the tablets containing the material for his central, travel narrative, section, thus enabling his rearrangement of material taken from Matthew.[41]

While cautiously welcoming Poirier's recognition of media apart from the scroll that might have been used in composition, Derrenbacker counters first, that some of the evidence Poirier adduces for the use of wax tablets could refer to other media such as papyrus or parchment notebooks, and second that while it may have been technically possible for Luke to reorder his stack of tablets, Poirier neither offers any explanation for why he may have wished to do so nor proposes any ancient literary parallel to such a procedure.[42] F. Gerald Downing estimates that Poirier's Luke would need a stack of around 180–200 tablets to contain each third of his Gospel, and while allowing that this is imaginable suggests that it might nevertheless have been exceptional. Downing further objects that Poirier's Luke would have been taking rather more detailed notes than would have been the ancient norm.[43] A further question that might be raised is whether it would have been mechanically feasible to shuffle a stack of 180 tablets (or more) to produce a new literary arrangement. Both Catherine Hezser and Jocelyn Small point out that wax tablets (and other ancient note-taking media such as ostraca or papyrus scraps) could not be readily stacked, sorted or otherwise organized like modern note-cards, so that ancient authors were far more likely to have relied on their memory.[44] While the point concerns notes rather than complete drafts, the mechanical difficulty would remain.

A modified suggestion that avoids these difficulties might involve two distinct uses of wax tablets (or other proto-codex type media): first taking *brief* notes that might function as aides-memoire for the process of composition (in the case of the FH Luke, brief notes of sayings in Matthew; in that of the 2DH Matthew, brief notes of passages in Q), and second as an intermediate stage in composition to hold a first rough draft for subsequent correction and transcription onto a scroll, at which point further minor changes might be made, although an author who had an ample supply of papyrus (as a Luke supported by a patron may have done) may well have used a papyrus scroll or codex (notebook) for the rough draft. The main work of composition and reordering would have been performed in memory (albeit with the various types of support mentioned above).

---

[41] Poirier, 'Roll', 19–24.

[42] Derrenbacker, 'Texts, Tables and Tablets', 384–5.

[43] F. Gerald Downing, 'Waxing Careless: Poirier, Derrenbacker and Downing', *JSNT* 35 (2013), 388–93 (391).

[44] Catherine Hezser, *Jewish Literacy in Roman Palestine* (Texts and Studies in Ancient Judaism, 81; Tübingen: Mohr Siebeck, 2001), 422–3; Jocelyn Penny Small, *Wax Tablets of the Mind: Cognitive Studies of Memory and Literacy in Classical Antiquity* (Abingdon: Routledge, 1997), 188.

For example, in working through Matthew's Sermon on the Mount in steps (1) and (2) the FH Luke could have noted (on wax tablets, say) passages that he proposed omitting from his Sermon on the Plain but thought he might use later. A Luke with good memory command of Matthew might need only to note a few words (such as 'placate your accuser') to act as a prompt for his memory of a passage (Matthew 5.25–26) he thought he might use later (in this case, at Luke 12.57–59), albeit in adapted form as recomposed by Luke on the basis of the prompt his note provided. This sort of process would make it far easier for Luke to use Matthean passages out of order than would the use of unaided memory alone. Luke's memory in any case may have been aided by his having thought about and discussed the overall plan of his Gospel before he began to compose in earnest. When he came to dictate his first draft (if he was not his own scribe), his secretary may also have provided further assistance (assuming he or she also had some knowledge of Matthew and/or Mark) by prompting Luke's memory and pointing out inadvertent slips. On reviewing this first draft Luke would then have had some opportunity for correcting any glaring errors that struck him (such as unintentional use of the same Matthean passage more than once) as well as, perhaps, inserting material he had either forgotten to use first time round or had not immediately found a place for (Quintilian's advice at *Inst.* 10.3.33 to leave blank space in a first draft suggests both how something of the sort could be done and that some people did it). The feedback from his trial audience might then have prompted further such changes before Luke arrived at the 'final' version of his Gospel.

This is not to say that the FH Luke (or, *mutatis mutandis*, the 2DH Matthew) must have taken the opportunity to make such changes at each stage, but only that it would have been possible to do so. Thus, while in all probability Matthew and Luke would have had a fairly good idea of the overall plan of their Gospels in their minds before they began to dictate their respective first drafts, it would be odd if nothing in the finished versions of their Gospels reflected second thoughts. The plausibility of any source hypothesis should thus not be made to rest solely on what an author working largely from his unaided memory might be able to achieve in a single step, but what such an author working from memory alongside 'note taking, excerpting, epitomizing, dictation, etc.' might be able to achieve in several steps with assistance from collaborators.

Conclusions

This chapter has not attempted to solve the Synoptic Problem. Such an attempt would require at least a book-length treatment and would need to examine the evidence in far more depth than has been possible here. That said, a few tentative conclusions may be drawn. First, it is both feasible and probable that memory played a major role in the composition of the Gospels, and in the Evangelists' use of sources, including any earlier Gospels they may have employed. Second, this does not, however, mean that the composition of the Gospels should be seen as a single-stage process involving nothing but the unaided memory of the individual Evangelists. Other factors (such as multi-stage collaborative composition, the use of notes and at least the occasional checking of sources by eye) also need to be considered in any complete picture of the most probable model of the way the Evangelists worked, as should the role that earlier traditions and written Gospels played in the collective memory of the Evangelists' communities. Third, a more detailed examination of synoptic parallels could well suggest a mixed mode of working, that is, in some sections (e.g. Luke 3.2b—4.13) it may be most plausible to envisage an Evangelist (in this example, the FH Luke) working from a written source open in front of him while in others (e.g. Luke 6.20—7.35; 9.51—17.37) the use of memory may provide a better explanation. Fourth, while the considerations discussed in this chapter, particularly the use of memory, do seem to pose potential problems for the 2GH, they do not (at this level of generality) select strongly between the 2DH and the FH, though clearly more detailed work is needed in this area.

In any case, nothing said in this chapter leaves the 2DH and the FH as the only possible contenders. It might be equally feasible to suppose, for example, that while Luke did indeed make use of both Matthew and Mark, he may also have employed one or more other sources, one or more of which may have overlapped or have been common to Matthew and Luke. Whether it is necessary to postulate such additional sources can only be argued in the context of a detailed examination of the evidence, but partly depends on whether one is trying to reconstruct what actually happened (which may well be impossible) or to construct the most economical model that can account for the data (economical, that is, both in terms of minimizing the need for hypothetical sources and in terms of the plausibility of the compositional methods demanded of the Evangelists). Finally, space does not allow any attempt here to settle the question of John's use or otherwise of the Synoptics, although it would certainly seem plausible that John could have made use of one or more of the Synoptic Gospels from memory along with his own special material to come up with a much freer reworking of his sources than the Synoptic Evangelists produced.

8

Conclusion

This book has set out to accomplish four things: to explore how the Evangelists went about writing their Gospels, to argue that memory played a central role in that task, to consider the implications of the centrality of memory for Gospel writing and finally, in the course of doing all these, to chart a middle course between lapsing into anachronistic print-culture assumptions on the one hand, and into overstatements of the oral functioning of ancient society on the other. The culture in which the New Testament was written was neither a modern print culture nor a preliterate one; both modern use of printed material and pure primary orality are equally likely to prove misleading guides to first-century manuscript production. What is needed is not some crude binary opposition between literate and oral modes of text production, but a model of ancient scribal practices that takes account of the continuous interface between writing, speech and memory, and which strives to keep a balance between the individual and communal dimensions of composition.

It is, of course, impossible to reconstruct exactly how the Evangelists went about writing their Gospels. We know too little either about them as individuals or about their precise social locations, so we only have analogy, inference and plausible guesswork to go on. We also struggle to arrive at an adequate (but for us counterintuitive) understanding of compositional methods that may have felt intuitively obvious to the ancient writers we are seeking to describe. What this book gives, therefore, is not some neatly packaged model of Gospel composition that can be summarized in a couple of sentences, but a series of attempts to view the issue from different perspectives (reasons for writing, materials employed, models of composition, and the role of both individual and collective memory).

That said, some kind of picture does emerge. While it has been argued that the Gospels were not oral-traditional compositions, neither were they the products of the literary elite, so that while employing what is known of the techniques of elite authors as a control on the likely working practices of the Evangelists is helpful, it is unlikely to give the full picture. The Evangelists' compositional techniques may well have shared a number of features with those of their elite contemporaries including the use of dictation, heavy reliance on memory, use of notes, some form of collaboration, multiple stages and the following of no more than one principal source at a time. But there will also have been significant

147

differences due to both social location and aim. Much of an elite Roman author's assistance will have come from his slaves, whereas the Evangelists were most likely collaborating with people whom they more or less regarded as equals, which would have affected the dynamics of their interaction. The Evangelists would have had a far greater investment in collective memory, not least as it affected the identity of the community of which both they and their helpers were a part. Their aim was not primarily to record history for posterity or hold up their subject for admiration, but to promote a particular reputation of their founding figure in the interests of community identity. Collective memory is often contested memory, and the Gospels aimed at participating in that contest.

In particular the later Evangelists were most likely responding to the efforts of their predecessors by absorption and transformation in order to create fresh accounts they considered more suitable for the needs of the Church. In the process they would be both transmitting and transmuting the collective memory of which those earlier Gospels were a part. This suggests a rather different relation to their sources than that of an elite historian or biographer who was simply employing earlier texts as sources of information to be selected and adapted into a freshly worded account. In contrast the Evangelists were both more conservative and more radical: more conservative in retaining some wording, particular in that of sayings material believed to have come from the Master, which may in any case have been concurrently cultivated orally in the church (or 'school') tradition in which the Evangelists were immersed; more radical in the willingness to rework tradition to meet new challenges and new situations and in their preparedness to employ something like the scribal-memorial model to compose new material on the basis of the tradition. While they may have lacked their elite contemporaries' advanced rhetorical training, they shared their ambition to persuade, and in the service of the gospel that ambition could sometimes have led them to a more substantial reshaping of existing material in the interest of community identity and religious conviction than would commonly be envisaged in an elite historian's employment of documentary sources.

Implications for Gospel criticism

The implications of this study for *source criticism* were summarized at the end of the previous chapter, but may be briefly restated as follows: where a later Evangelist made use of the work of an earlier one (or of some other written source such the hypothetical Q), our default assumption should be that this would have been largely (though not exclusively) through memory. Even if this overstates the case, such an overstatement may be valuable as a means of preventing our lapsing into naive print-culture assumptions about how Matthew or Luke would have used written sources. The substantial use of memory turns out to be problematic for the Two Gospel Hypothesis, but does not obviously select between the Two Document Hypothesis and the Farrer Hypothesis (or indeed between either of those and some compromise solution which sees Luke as using Matthew, Mark and some additional sources such as saying collections which could also have provided some of the material common to Matthew and Luke). This does not mean that the arguments advanced in this book have no bearing on the question of synoptic relations, but rather that they can only act as prolegomena to the far more detailed treatment of the Synoptic Problem that would be required to argue convincingly for one solution rather than another.

While nothing in this book undermines *redaction criticism*, it does qualify it, even to the extent of indicating that the name may be misleading (although it is probably pointless to propose alternatives to such well-established terminology). The notion that the Evangelists adapted what they found in their sources to their own theological (or ideological) purposes, and that these purposes will have been related to the circumstances of their communities (in the loosest sense of that term), remains sound. What needs to be re-envisaged is how this works out in detail. In particular the use of one Evangelist (or of any other source) by another should be conceived as a process not so much of literary editing (as we might copy-edit a printed text on our desk, or an electronic text on our personal computer) as of composing a fresh version that makes selective use of what went before. Many redaction-critical observations about large-scale tendencies of one Evangelist in relation to another may well remain broadly valid in such a re-envisaging; what will be called into question is the identification of small-scale differences between the wording of one Evangelist and another as if these generally represent conscious editorial decisions on the part of the later Evangelist. Such an assumption becomes unlikely if a later Evangelist is reworking his source from memory.

This in turn would seem to favour methods such as *composition criticism* and *narrative criticism*, which consider the texts of the Gospels as a whole. The considerations advanced in this book should, however, serve to guard against treating the Gospel narratives as if they were modern novels, or as if it were a responsible method of Gospel criticism to treat the Gospel accounts as self-contained narratives independent of the context of their production and reception; in reality they will have been thoroughly entangled with the collective memory of the communities in which they were produced and subsequently used. This in turn would seem to provide a continuing justification, not only for traditional historical criticism, but for a kind of *social scientific criticism* that focuses particularly on social memory theory. Finally, one area of study that has scarcely been touched on here, though it could also contribute to the discussion, is *rhetorical criticism*, since there are clearly likely to be connections between the uses of memory in rhetoric (particularly written rhetoric) and text production, and between the ways in which orators and Evangelists attempt to persuade their respective target audiences.

Implications for historical Jesus research

The implications for historical Jesus study of the present book differ little from those of my previous one on oral tradition.[1] The emphases are a little different, however, for while the former study focused on the traditions that may have been available to the Evangelists, the present one has focused on the compositional techniques of the Evangelists. Here again it is necessary to navigate between two extremes. On the one hand there is little justification for supposing that the Evangelists had no concern with the past or that they did not intend to refer to what had actually happened in the past. On the other, that of itself is no guarantee of their concern for what we should regard as factual accuracy. The Gospels were not concerned with providing historical records of the past for its own sake, but with employing the past to create formative and normative accounts that could serve to solidify particular configurations of collective memory. For such purposes the Gospel accounts had to appear reasonably plausible, but they did not need to be factually accurate in every particular.

In any case the problem facing the historical Jesus scholar is not merely one of trying to discern which of the deeds and sayings reported in the Gospels have the best claim to go back to the man Jesus of Nazareth, for what is of more interest is the overall picture that emerges (however important particularly salient events may be to forming that picture). The Gospels are not ragbag databases of potential facts, but rhetorically shaped portraits that already configure the tradition to promote particular views of Jesus' reputation as a particular kind of hero, and the historian has to reckon with these overall portraits every bit as much as with the elements that go into their making or else risk being bewitched by the Evangelists' rhetoric.

Imagine for the moment the plight of scholars endeavouring to reconstruct the historical Richard III from the plays of Shakespeare together with some general picture of fifteenth-century England. A criterion of general plausibility will help detect certain elements in Shakespeare's plays that must be unhistorical, such as the account in Act 5, Scene 2 of *Henry VI Part II* of Richard's active participation in the First Battle of St Albans (which took place in 1455 when Richard was less than three years old), but it will not settle the matter of Richard's reputation. What is contentious in modern debates about Richard III is not the bare factual outline (even assuming our hypothetical historical Richard scholars could obtain such a thing from Shakespeare) but the construction put upon those facts (which

---

[1] Eric Eve, *Behind the Gospels: Understanding the Oral Tradition* (London: SPCK, 2013), 181–3.

in turn then guides the assessment of other historical events such as the fate of the princes in the Tower). Gary Fine argues in the case of Warren Harding that there are a number of ways in which the known facts would allow Harding's reputation to have been constructed; similarly the broadly agreed events of Richard's career (derived from sources rather closer to those events than Shakespeare) still leave room for his reputation to be constructed in quite different ways by his supporters and detractors. It is primarily this reputational issue that is at stake in modern debates over Richard III; even more will it have been reputational issues at stake in the Evangelists' depiction of Jesus, although with the difference that the issue would not have been whether Jesus was a good man or a bad one, but over how what he said and did provide legitimation and guidance for Christian faith and practice in the present.

In sum, the Gospels are not the kind of literature that will yield many significant fresh insights about the historical Jesus simply by close critical dissection of individual pericopae (one is almost tempted to imagine an Historical Richard III Seminar attempting to apply criteria of authenticity to Shakespeare). To be sure, in some instances there will be particular events, such as those surrounding Jesus' execution, that are of sufficient salience in any overall portrait of the man that they will need to be critically assessed and that are also reasonably susceptible to considerations of historical plausibility. Moreover, there are clearly gains to be made by correlating the Gospels' account of Jesus with whatever we can glean from other sources about the nature of his social, political, economic and geographical environment, provided we maintain vigilance against mistaking verisimilitude for factual accuracy. We can also assume that Jesus must have been the sort of person who could plausibly give rise to the particular reputations the Gospels afford him, from which we might cautiously but reasonably conclude that the overall picture they paint bears some relation to reality, allowing that there is more than one way in which the facts could have been construed; although one might alternatively attempt to devise a plausible account of how the Gospels came to systematically mislead. But if (for all the difference in their aims) the Evangelists were no more interested in objective history than was Shakespeare, many questions may remain as open for Jesus as they do for Richard III (for whom the range of sources is far more abundant).

Implications for Christian faith and theology

Some believers may feel threatened by the conclusion that the Gospels cannot be relied upon to give factually accurate accounts of Jesus, although to say this is hardly to say anything new. Neither is it to say anything new to point out that the Evangelists' concern for truth was probably rather different from the modern concern for factual accuracy. Here Tom Thatcher's account of John's theory of charismatic memory (discussed in Chapter 6 above) may be helpful. While the Evangelists were indeed concerned with a real past, what was of primary importance was arriving at an interpretation of that past proper to Christian identity, faith and practice. For such a purpose it matters not at all to establish the precise words Jesus uttered to Pilate or which side of Jericho he happened to be on when he healed a blind beggar; neither does it matter all that much to reconstruct a full inventory of his healings and sayings (even assuming such a task were possible). It does matter for Christian faith and theology that Jesus of Nazareth was both a real person and more or less the kind of person the Gospels make him out to be; it does not matter in the slightest if the Gospels are not accurate in every detail, and it matters very little if the Evangelists have taken some liberties with the facts in order to clarify Jesus' significance. In any case, establishing a catalogue of verified facts would not of itself help anyone to understand Jesus' significance, since such a (possibly quite meagre) catalogue would be patient of more than one interpretation, as is often the case with any historical figure.

As has been pointed out many times before, what matters for Christian faith and Christian theology is not the historical Jesus (a modern scholarly construct – or rather a whole range of modern scholarly constructs) but the Jesus of the Gospels, which remain among the most important foundational documents of the Church. In reality, of course, the Church has always known this. Christian theology may like to be assured that the Gospels are not simply fantasy, but beyond that its task is not so much to do with the historical Jesus as with how far the Evangelists' construal of Jesus can remain authoritative in the very different circumstances of the modern world. If the writing of the Gospels was intimately tied up with the collective memory of the earliest Jesus movement, and that collective memory was in turn intimately concerned with issues of community identity in the face of the particular historical, social and political circumstances of the first-century Roman Empire, then some might question whether the Gospels' interpretations of Jesus can remain relevant to the very different circumstances of the modern world. Yet the Gospels clearly continue to speak powerfully and effectively to millions of people today. What matters most about the writing of the Gospels is whether in interpreting Jesus of Nazareth as they did, the Evangelists managed to lay secure foundations for future developments in Christian faith and practice. It seems they did so most effectively, for all the challenges that poses to us in applying their compositions today.

Bibliography

Achtemeier, Paul J., 'Omne verbum sonat: The New Testament and the Oral Environment of Late Western Antiquity', *JBL* 109 (1990), 3–37.

Achtemeier, Paul J., 'Toward the Isolation of Pre-Markan Miracle Catenae', *JBL* 89 (1970), 265–91. Alexander, Loveday, 'Luke's Preface in the Context of Greek Preface-Writing', *NovT* 28 (1986), 48–74.

Alexander, Loveday, 'Luke's Preface in the Context of Greek Preface-Writing', *NovT* 28 (1986), 48–74.

Alexander, Loveday, 'Memory and Tradition in the Hellenistic Schools' in Werner H. Kelber and Samuel Byrskog (eds), *Jesus in Memory: Traditions in Oral and Scribal Perspectives* (Waco: Baylor University Press, 2009), 113–53.

Alexander, Loveday, *The Preface to Luke's Gospel: Literary Convention and Social Context in Luke 1.1–4 and Acts 1.1* (paperback 2005 edn; SNTSMS, 78; ed. Margaret E. Thrall; Cambridge: Cambridge University Press, 1993).

Alexander, Philip S., 'Midrash and the Gospels' in Christopher M. Tuckett (ed.), *Synoptic Studies: The Ampleforth Conferences of 1982 and 1983* (JSNTSup, 7; Sheffield: JSOT Press, 1984), 1–18.

Allison, Dale C., *The New Moses: A Matthean Typology* (Edinburgh: T. & T. Clark, 1993).

Arnal, William E., *Jesus and the Village Scribes: Galilean Conflicts and the Setting of Q* (Minneapolis: Fortress Press, 2001).

Assmann, Jan, 'Communicative and Cultural Memory' in Astrid Erll and Ansgar Nünning (eds), *A Companion to Cultural Memory Studies* (Berlin: De Gruyter, 2010), 109–18.

Assmann, Jan, *Cultural Memory and Early Civilization: Writing, Remembrance, and Political Imagination* (tr. David Henry Wilson; Cambridge: Cambridge University Press, 2011).

Assmann, Jan, *Religion and Cultural Memory* (tr. Rodney Livingstone; Stanford, CA: Stanford University Press, 2006).

Aune, D. E., 'Luke 1:1–4: Historical or Scientific *Prooimion?*' in A. Christopherson, C. Claussen, J. Frey and B. Longenecker (eds), *Paul, Luke and the Graeco-Roman World: Essays in Honour of Alexander J. M. Wedderburn* (JSNTSup, 217; Sheffield: Sheffield Academic Press, 2002).

Aune, David E., *The New Testament in Its Literary Environment* (Cambridge: James Clarke, 1988).

Baddeley, Alan, Eysenck, Michael W. and Anderson, Michael C., *Memory* (Hove and New York: Psychology Press, 2009).

Bartlett, F. C., *Remembering: A Study in Experimental and Social Psychology* (Cambridge: Cambridge University Press, 1995 [1932]).

Bauckham, Richard, 'For Whom Were Gospels Written?' in Richard Bauckham (ed.), *The Gospels for All Christians: Rethinking the Gospel Audiences* (Edinburgh: T. & T. Clark, 1998), 9–48.

Bauckham, Richard, *Jesus and the Eyewitnesses: The Gospels as Eyewitness Testimony* (Grand Rapids and Cambridge: Eerdmans, 2006).

Bibliography

Bauckham, Richard, 'John for Readers of Mark' in Richard Bauckham (ed.), *The Gospels for All Christians: Rethinking the Gospel Audiences* (Edinburgh: T. & T. Clark, 1998), 147–71.

Beaton, Richard C., 'How Matthew Writes' in Markus Bockmuehl and Donald A. Hagner (eds), *The Written Gospel* (Cambridge: Cambridge University Press, 2005), 116–34.

Boring, M. Eugene, 'The "Minor Agreements" and Their Bearing on the Synoptic Problem' in Paul Foster, Andrew Gregory, John S. Kloppenborg and J. Verheyden (eds), *New Studies in the Synoptic Problem* (BETL, 139; Leuven: Leuven University Press, 2011), 227–51.

Botha, Pieter J. J., 'Mark's Story as Oral Traditional Literature: Rethinking the Transmission of Some Traditions about Jesus', *HTS* 47 (1991), 304–31.

Botha, Pieter J. J., *Orality and Literacy in Early Christianity* (BPC, 5; ed. Holly E. Hearon and Philip Ruge-Jones; Eugene, OR: Cascade, 2012).

Bryan, Christopher, *A Preface to Mark: Notes on the Gospel in Its Literary and Cultural Settings* (Oxford: Oxford University Press, 1993).

Burridge, Richard A., *What Are the Gospels? A Comparison with Graeco-Roman Biography* (paperback edn; SNTSMS, 70; Cambridge: Cambridge University Press, 1995).

Butler, B. C., *The Originality of St Matthew: A Critique of the Two-Document Hypothesis* (Cambridge: Cambridge University Press, 1951).

Byrskog, Samuel, *Story as History – History as Story: The Gospel Tradition in the Context of Ancient Oral History* (Leiden and Boston: Brill, 2002).

Carr, David M., *Writing on the Tablet of the Heart: Origins of Scripture and Literature* (Oxford: Oxford University Press, 2005).

Carruthers, Mary, *The Book of Memory: A Study of Memory in Medieval Culture* (2nd edn; Cambridge Studies in Medieval Literature; Cambridge: Cambridge University Press, 2008).

Carson, Annette, *Richard III: The Maligned King* (updated edn; Stroud: History Press, 2013).

Catchpole, David R., 'On Proving Too Much: Critical Hesitations about Richard Bauckham's *Jesus and the Eyewitnesses*', *JSHJ* 6 (2008), 169–81.

Chapman, John, *Matthew, Mark and Luke: A Study in the Order and Interrelation of the Synoptic Gospels* (London; New York; Toronto: Longmans, Green and Co., 1937).

Coleman, Janet, *Ancient and Medieval Memories* (Cambridge: Cambridge University Press, 1992).

Connerton, Paul, *How Societies Remember* (Themes in the Social Sciences; ed. John Dunn, Jack Goody, Eugene A. Hammel and Geoffrey Hawthorn; Cambridge: Cambridge University Press, 1989).

Cubitt, Geoffrey, *History and Memory* (Historical Approaches; ed. Geoffrey Cubitt; Manchester and New York: Manchester University Press, 2007).

Derrenbacker, R. A., *Ancient Compositional Practices and the Synoptic Problem* (BETL, 186; Leuven: Peeters-Leuven, 2005).

Derrenbacker, Robert A., 'The "External and Psychological Conditions under Which the Synoptic Gospels Were Written": Ancient Compositional Practices and the Synoptic Problem' in Paul Foster, Andrew Gregory, John S. Kloppenborg and J. Verheyden (eds), *New Studies in the Synoptic Problem* (BETL, 139; Leuven: Leuven University Press, 2011), 435–57.

Derrenbacker, Robert A., 'Texts, Tables and Tablets: A Response to John C. Poirier', *JSNT* 35 (2013), 380–7.

Dewey, Joanna, 'The Gospel of Mark as Oral Hermeneutic' in Tom Thatcher (ed.), *Jesus, the Voice and the Text: Beyond the Oral and the Written Gospel* (Waco: Baylor University Press, 2008), 71–87.

Dewey, Joanna, 'The Survival of Mark's Gospel: A Good Story?', *JBL* 123 (2004), 495–507.

Dodson, Ruth, 'Don Pedrito Jaramillo: The Curandero of Los Olmos' in Wilson M. Hudson (ed.), *The Healer of Los Olmos and Other Mexican Lore* (Dallas: South Methodist University Press, 1951), 9–70.

Donahue, John R. and Harrington, Daniel J., *The Gospel of Mark* (Sacra Pagina, 2; Collegeville, MN: Michael Glazier, 2002).

Downing, F. Gerald, 'Compositional Conventions and the Synoptic Problem', *JBL* 107 (1988), 69–85.

Downing, F. Gerald, *Doing Things with Words in the First Christian Century* (JSNTSup, 200; Sheffield: Sheffield Academic Press, 2000).

Downing, F. Gerald, 'Waxing Careless: Poirier, Derrenbacker and Downing', *JSNT* 35 (2013), 388–93.

Downing, F. Gerald, 'Writers' Use or Abuse of Written Sources' in Paul Foster, Andrew Gregory, John S. Kloppenborg and J. Verheyden (eds), *New Studies in the Synoptic Problem* (BETL, 139; Leuven: Leuven University Press, 2011), 523–48.

Drury, John, *Tradition and Design in Luke's Gospel: A Study in Early Christian Historiography* (London: Darton, Longman and Todd, 1976).

Ducharme, Lori J. and Fine, Gary Alan, 'The Construction of Nonpersonhood and Demonization: Commemorating the Traitorous Reputation of Benedict Arnold', *SF* 73 (1995), 1309–31.

Dundes, Alan, *Holy Writ as Oral Lit: The Bible as Folklore* (Lanham, MD and Oxford: Rowman & Littlefield, 1999).

Dungan, David L., 'Mark – The Abridgement of Matthew and Luke' in David G. Buttrick and John M. Bald (eds), *Jesus and Man's Hope*, vol. 1 (Pittsburgh, PA: Pittsburgh Theological Seminary, 1970), 51–97.

Dunn, James D. G., 'Altering the Default Setting: Re-envisaging the Early Transmission of the Jesus Tradition', *NTS* 49 (2003), 139–75.

Dunn, James D. G., *Jesus Remembered* (Christianity in the Making, 1; Grand Rapids and Cambridge: Eerdmans, 2003).

Dunn, James D. G., *Romans 1—8* (Word Biblical Commentary, 38A; Milton Keynes: Word Books, 1988).

Eisenstein, Elizabeth, *The Printing Press as an Agent of Change: Communications and Cultural Transformations in Early-Modern Europe* (Cambridge: Cambridge University Press, 1980).

Evans, Craig A., 'How Mark Writes' in Markus Bockmuehl and David A. Hagner (eds), *The Written Gospel* (Cambridge: Cambridge University Press, 2005), 135–48.

Eve, Eric, *Behind the Gospels: Understanding the Oral Tradition* (London: SPCK, 2013).

Eve, Eric, 'The Devil in the Detail: Exorcising Q from the Beelzebul Controversy' in John C. Poirier and Jeffrey Peterson (eds), *Marcan Priority without Q: Explorations in the Farrer Hypothesis* (LNTS, 455; London: Bloomsbury T. & T. Clark, 2015), 16–43.

Eve, Eric, 'The Growth of the Nature Miracles' in Graham Twelftree (ed.), *The Nature Miracles of Jesus: Historical and Theological Perspectives* (Eugene, OR: Wipf & Stock, forthcoming).

Eve, Eric, *The Healer from Nazareth: Jesus' Miracles in Historical Context* (London: SPCK, 2009).

Eve, Eric, *The Jewish Context of Jesus' Miracles* (JSNTSup, 231; Sheffield: Sheffield Academic Press, 2002).

Eve, Eric, 'Spit in Your Eye: The Blind Man of Bethsaida and the Blind Man of Alexandria', *NTS* 54 (2008), 1–17.

Eve, Eric, 'The Synoptic Problem without Q?' in Paul Foster, Andrew Gregory, John S. Kloppenborg and J. Verheyden (eds), *New Studies in the Synoptic Problem* (BETL, 139; Leuven: Leuven University Press, 2011), 551–70.

Farmer, William R., *The Synoptic Problem: A Critical Analysis* (Macon, GA: Mercer University Press, 1976).

Farrer, A. M., 'On Dispensing with Q' in D. E. Nineham (ed.), *Studies in the Gospels: Essays in Memory of R. H. Lightfoot* (Oxford: Basil Blackwell, 1955), 55–88.

Fayol, Michel, 'From On-line Management Problems to Strategies in Written Composition' in Mark Torrance and Gaynor Jeffery (eds), *The Cognitive Demands of Writing* (Amsterdam: Amsterdam University Press, 1999), 13–23.

Fentress, James L. and Wickham, Chris, *Social Memory* (New Perspectives on the Past; Oxford and Cambridge, MA: Basil Blackwell, 1992).

Fine, Gary Alan, 'Reputational Entrepreneurs and the Memory of Incompetence: Melting Supporters, Partisan Warriors and Images of President Harding', *American Journal of Sociology* 105 (1996), 1159–93.

Finnegan, Ruth, *Communicating: The Multiple Modes of Human Interconnection* (London: Routledge, 2002).

Finnegan, Ruth, *Literacy and Orality* (Oxford: Basil Blackwell, 1988).

Finnegan, Ruth, *The Oral and Beyond: Doing Things with Words in Africa* (Oxford: James Currey, 2007).

Finnegan, Ruth, *Oral Poetry: Its Nature, Significance and Social Context* (Bloomington and Indianapolis: Indiana University Press, 1992).

Foley, John Miles, *The Singer of Tales in Performance* (Voices in Performance and Text; ed. John Miles Foley; Bloomington and Indianapolis: Indiana University Press, 1995).

Foley, John Miles, *The Theory of Oral Composition: History and Methodology* (Bloomington and Indianapolis: Indiana University Press, 1988).

Franklin, Eric, *Luke: Interpreter of Paul, Critic of Matthew* (JSNTSup, 92; Sheffield: JSOT Press, 1994).

Gamble, Harry Y., *Books and Readers in the Early Church: A History of Early Christian Texts* (New Haven and London: Yale University Press, 1995).

Gavrilov, A. K., 'Techniques of Reading in Classical Antiquity', *Classical Quarterly* 47 n.s. (1997), 56–73.

Gilliard, Frank D., 'More Silent Reading in Antiquity: Non Omne Verbum Sonabat', *JBL* 112 (1993), 689–94.

Goodacre, Mark, *The Case against Q: Studies in Markan Priority and the Synoptic Problem* (Harrisburg, PA: Trinity Press International, 2002).

Goodacre, Mark, 'Fatigue in the Synoptics', *NTS* 44 (1998), 45–58.

Goodacre, Mark, 'Scripturalization in Mark's Crucifixion Narrative' in Geert van Oyen and Tom Shepherd (eds), *The Trial and Death of Jesus: Essays on the Passion Narrative in Mark* (Leuven: Peeters, 2006), 33–47.

Goodacre, Mark, 'Too Good to Be Q: High Verbatim Agreement in the Double Tradition' in John C. Poirier and Jeffrey Peterson (eds), *Marcan Priority without Q: Explorations in the Farrer Hypothesis* (LNTS, 455; London: Bloomsbury T. & T. Clark, 2015), 82–100.

Gorman, Heather M., 'Crank or Creative Genius? How Ancient Rhetoric Makes Sense of Luke's Order' in John C. Poirier and Jeffrey Peterson (eds), *Marcan Priority without Q: Explorations in the Farrer Hypothesis* (LNTS, 455; London: Bloomsbury T. & T. Clark, 2015), 62–81.

Goulder, M. D., *Luke: A New Paradigm* (JSNTSup 20; Sheffield: Sheffield Academic Press, 1989).

Goulder, M. D., *Midrash and Lection in Matthew* (London: SPCK, 1974).

Graham, William A., *Beyond the Written Word: Oral Aspects of Scripture in the History of Religion* (Cambridge: Cambridge University Press, 1987).

Green, H. Benedict, *Matthew, Poet of the Beatitudes* (JSNTSup, 203; Sheffield: Sheffield Academic Press, 2001).

Gregory, Andrew, 'What Is Literary Dependence?' in Paul Foster, Andrew Gregory, John S. Kloppenborg and J. Verheyden (eds), *New Studies in the Synoptic Problem* (BETL, 139; Leuven: Leuven University Press, 2011), 87–114.

Güttgemanns, Erhardt, *Candid Questions Concerning Gospel Form Criticism: A Methodological Sketch of the Fundamental Problematics of Form and Redaction Criticism* (Pittsburgh Theological Monograph Series, 26; ed. Dikran Y. Hadidian; tr. William G. Doty; Pittsburgh, PA: Pickwick Press, 1979).

Halbwachs, Maurice, *On Collective Memory* (The Heritage of Sociology; ed. Donald N. Levine; tr. Lewis A. Coser; Chicago and London: University of Chicago Press, 1992).

Hanham, Alison, *Richard III and His Early Historians 1483–1535* (London: Oxford University Press, 1975).

Harris, William V., *Ancient Literacy* (Cambridge, MA; London: Harvard University Press, 1989).

Head, Peter M., 'Textual Criticism and the Synoptic Problem' in Paul Foster, Andrew Gregory, John S. Kloppenborg and J. Verheyden (eds) *New Studies in the Synoptic Problem* (BETL, 139; Leuven: Leuven University Press, 2011), 115–56.

Hengel, Martin, *The Four Gospels and the One Gospel of Jesus Christ: An Investigation of the Collection and Origin of the Canonical Gospels* (tr. John Bowden; London: SCM Press, 2000).

Hezser, Catherine, *Jewish Literacy in Roman Palestine* (Texts and Studies in Ancient Judaism, 81; Tübingen: Mohr Siebeck, 2001).

Hooker, Morna D., 'Beginnings and Endings' in Markus Bockmuehl and David A. Hagner (eds), *The Written Gospel* (Cambridge: Cambridge University Press, 2005), 184–202.

Horsley, Richard A., *Hearing the Whole Story: The Politics of Plot in Mark's Gospel* (Louisville, KY: Westminster John Knox Press, 2001).

Horsley, Richard A., *Jesus in Context: Power, People, and Performance* (Minneapolis: Fortress Press, 2008).

Horsley, Richard A., 'Prominent Patterns in the Social Memory of Jesus and Friends' in Alan Kirk and Tom Thatcher (eds), *Memory, Tradition, and Text: Uses of the Past in Early Christianity* (SBL Semeia Studies, 52; ed. G. A. Yee; Leiden and Boston: Brill, 2005), 57–78.

Horsley, Richard A., *Scribes, Visionaries and the Politics of Second Temple Judea* (Louisville, KY and London: Westminster John Knox Press, 2007).

Horsley, Richard A., *Text and Tradition in Performance and Writing* (BPC, 9; ed. D. Rhoads; Eugene, OR: Cascade, 2013).

Horsley, Richard A. and Draper, Jonathan, *Whoever Hears You Hears Me: Prophets, Performance and Tradition in Q* (Harrisburg, PA: Trinity Press International, 1999).

Huggins, Ronald V., 'Matthean Posteriority: A Preliminary Proposal', *NovT* 34 (1992), 1–22.

Hurtado, Larry W., 'Oral Fixation and New Testament Studies? "Orality", "Performance" and Reading Texts in Early Christianity', *NTS* 60 (2014), 321–40.

Irwin-Zarecka, Iwona, *Frames of Reference: The Dynamics of Collective Memory* (New Brunswick and London: Transaction, 2009).

Johnson, William A., *Readers and Reading Culture in the High Roman Empire: A Study of Elite Communities* (New York: Oxford University Press, 2010).

Johnson, William A., 'Toward a Sociology of Reading in Classical Antiquity', *The American Journal of Philology* 121 (2000), 593–627.

Keith, Chris, *Jesus' Literacy: Scribal Culture and the Teacher from Galilee* (LNTS, 413; ed. M. Goodacre; New York and London: T. & T. Clark, 2011).

Keith, Chris, 'Prolegomena on the Textualization of Mark's Gospel: Manuscript Culture, the Extended Situation, and the Emergence of the Written Gospel' in Tom Thatcher (ed.), *Memory and Identity in Ancient Judaism and Early Christianity: A Conversation with Barry Schwartz* (Semeia Studies, 78; ed. G. O. West; Atlanta: SBL, 2014), 161–86.

Keith, Chris, 'Social Memory Theory and Gospels Research: The First Decade (Part One)' in *EC* 6 (2015), 354–76.

Kelber, Werner H., *Imprints, Voiceprints and Footprints of Memory: Collected Essays of Werner Kelber* (Resources for Biblical Study, 74; Atlanta: SBL, 2013).

Kelber, Werner H., *The Oral and the Written Gospel: The Hermeneutics of Speaking and Writing in the Synoptic Tradition, Mark, Paul and Q* (Voices in Performance and Text; Bloomington and Indianapolis: Indiana University Press, 1997).

Kelber, Werner H., 'The Works of Memory: Christian Origins as MnemoHistory – A Response' in Alan Kirk and Tom Thatcher (eds), *Memory, Tradition, and Text: Uses of the Past in Early Christianity* (SBL Semeia Studies, 52; ed. G. A. Yee; Leiden and Boston: Brill, 2005), 221–48.

Kellogg, Ronald T., 'Components of Working Memory in Text Production' in Mark Torrance and Gaynor Jeffery (eds), *The Cognitive Demands of Writing* (Amsterdam: Amsterdam University Press, 1999), 43–61.

Kennedy, George A., *Progymnasmata: Greek Textbooks of Prose Composition and Rhetoric* (tr. George A. Kennedy; Atlanta: SBL, 2003).

Kirk, Alan, 'Memory, Scribal Media, and the Synoptic Problem' in Paul Foster, Andrew Gregory, John S. Kloppenborg and J. Verheyden (eds), *New Studies in the Synoptic Problem* (BETL, 139; Leuven: Leuven University Press, 2011), 459–82.

Kirk, Alan, 'Social and Cultural Memory' in Alan Kirk and Tom Thatcher (eds), *Memory, Tradition, and Text: Uses of the Past in Early Christianity* (SBL Semeia Studies, 52; ed. G. A. Yee; Leiden and Boston: Brill, 2005), 1–24.

Kloppenborg, John S., 'Variation and Reproduction of the Double Tradition and an Oral Q?', *ETL* 83 (2007), 53–80.

Kloppenborg Verbin, John S., *Excavating Q: The History and Setting of the Sayings Gospel* (Edinburgh: T. & T. Clark, 2000).

Last, Richard, 'The Social Relationships of Gospel Writers: New Insights from Inscriptions Commending Greek Historiographers', *JSNT* 37 (2015), 223–52.

Lord, Albert B., 'The Gospels as Oral Traditional Literature' in William O. Walker (ed.), *The Relationships among the Gospels: An Interdisciplinary Dialogue* (Trinity University Monograph Series in Religion, 5; San Antonio: Trinity University Press, 1978), 33–91.

Lord, Albert B., *The Singer of Tales* (2nd edn; Harvard Studies in Comparative Literature, 24; Cambridge, MA; London: Harvard University Press, 1960).

McIver, Robert K., *Memory, Jesus and the Synoptic Gospels* (Atlanta: SBL, 2011).

Mack, Burton L., *A Myth of Innocence: Mark and Christian Origins* (Philadelphia: Fortress Press, 1988).

McNicol, Allan J., Dungan, David L. and Peabody, David B., *Beyond the Q Impasse: Luke's Use of Matthew* (Valley Forge: Trinity Press International, 1996).

Manier, David and Hirst, William, 'A Cognitive Taxonomy of Collective Memories' in Astrid Erll and Ansgar Nünning (eds), *A Companion to Cultural Memory Studies* (Berlin: De Gruyter, 2010), 253–62.

Marcus, Joel, *The Way of the Lord: Christological Exegesis of the Old Testament in the Gospel of Mark* (Studies of the New Testament and Its World; ed. John Riches; Edinburgh: T. & T. Clark, 1993).

Martin, Michael W., 'Progymnastic Topic Lists: A Compositional Template for Luke and Other Bioi?', *NTS* 54 (2008), 18–41.

Mason, Steve, *Josephus and the New Testament* (Peabody, MA: Hendricksen, 1992).

Matson, Mark A., 'Luke's Rewriting of the Sermon on the Mount' in Mark Goodacre and Nicholas Perrin (eds), *Questioning Q* (London: SPCK, 2004), 43–70.

Millard, Alan, *Reading and Writing in the Time of Jesus* (The Biblical Seminar, 69; Sheffield: Sheffield Academic Press, 2000).

Misztal, Barbara A., *Theories of Social Remembering* (Theorizing Society; ed. Larry Ray; Maidenhead and Philadelphia: Open University Press, 2003).

Moles, John, 'Luke's Preface: The Greek Decree, Classical Historiography and Christian Redefinitions', *NTS* 57 (2011), 461–82.

Morgan, Teresa, *Literate Education in the Hellenistic and Roman Worlds* (Cambridge Classical Studies; Cambridge: Cambridge University Press, 2007).

Niditch, Susan, *Oral World and Written Word: Orality and Literacy in Ancient Israel* (Library of Ancient Israel; ed. Douglas A. Knight; London: SPCK, 1997).

Nolland, John, *The Gospel of Matthew* (NIGTC; Grand Rapids, MI/Bletchley: Eerdmans/ Paternoster, 2005).

Noonan Sabin, Marie, *Reopening the Word: Reading Mark as Theology in the Context of Early Judaism* (Oxford and New York: Oxford University Press, 2002).

Olick, Jeffrey K., 'Products, Processes, and Practices: A Non-Reificatory Approach to Collective Memory', *BTB* 36 (2006), 5–14.

Olson, Ken, 'Unpicking on the Farrer Theory' in Mark Goodacre and Nicholas Perrin (eds), *Questioning Q* (London: SPCK, 2004), 127–50.

Ong, Walter J., *Orality and Literacy: The Technologizing of the Word* (New Accents; London and New York: Routledge, 2002).

Parker, David C., *The Living Text of the Gospels* (Cambridge: Cambridge University Press, 1997).

Parker, Holt N., 'Books and Reading Latin Poetry' in William A. Johnson and Holt N. Parker (eds), *Ancient Literacies: The Culture of Reading in Greece and Rome* (New York: Oxford University Press, 2009), 186–229.

Patterson, Stephen J., 'Can You Trust a Gospel? A Review of Richard Bauckham's *Jesus and the Eyewitnesses*', *JSHJ* 6 (2008), 194–210.

Pelling, C. B. R., 'Plutarch's Adaptation of His Source-Material', *JHS* 100 (1980), 127–40.

Pelling, C. B. R., 'Plutarch's Method of Work in the Roman Lives', *JHS* 99 (1979), 74–96.

Peterson, Jeffrey, 'Order in the Double Tradition and the Existence of Q' in Mark Goodacre and Nicholas Perrin (eds), *Questioning Q* (London: SPCK, 2004), 28–42.

Poirier, John C., 'Delbert Burkett's Defence of Q' in John C. Poirier and Jeffrey Peterson (eds), *Marcan Priority without Q: Explorations in the Farrer Hypothesis* (LNTS, 455; London: Bloomsbury T. & T. Clark, 2015), 191–225.

Poirier, John C., 'The Roll, the Codex, the Wax Tablet and the Synoptic Problem', *JSNT* 35 (2012), 3–30.

Rigney, Ann, 'The Dynamics of Remembrance: Texts between Monumentality and Morphing' in Astrid Erll and Ansgar Nünning (eds), *A Companion to Cultural Memory Studies* (Berlin: De Gruyter, 2010), 345–53.

Rodriguez, Rafael, *Oral Tradition and the New Testament: A Guide for the Perplexed* (London and New York: Bloomsbury T. & T. Clark, 2014).

Rodriguez, Rafael, *Structuring Early Christian Memory: Jesus in Tradition, Performance and Text* (LNTS, 407; ed. Mark Goodacre; London: T. & T. Clark, 2010).

Rohrbaugh, Richard L., 'The Social Location of the Marcan Audience', *BTB* 23 (1993), 114–27.

Romano, Octavio I., 'Charismatic Medicine, Folk-Healing, and Folk-Sainthood', *American Anthropologist* 67 (1965), 1151–73.

Ross, Charles, *Richard III* (new edn; Yale English Monarchs; New Haven and London: Yale University Press, 1999).

Rubin, David C., 'Introduction' in David C. Rubin (ed.), *Remembering Our Past: Studies in Autobiographical Memory* (Cambridge: Cambridge University Press, 1995), 1–15.

Rubin, David C., *Memory in Oral Traditions: The Cognitive Psychology of Epic, Ballads, and Counting-out Rhymes* (Oxford and New York: Oxford University Press, 1995).

Bibliography

Bibliography

Saldarini, Anthony J., *Pharisees, Scribes and Sadducees in Palestinian Society* (Grand Rapids/Cambridge/Livonia, MI: Eerdmans/Dove, 2001).

Sanday, William, 'The Conditions under Which the Gospels Were Written, in Their Bearing upon Some Difficulties of the Synoptic Problem' in William Sanday (ed.), *Oxford Studies in the Synoptic Problem* (Oxford: Clarendon Press, 1911), 3–26.

Sanders, E. P. and Davies, Margaret, *Studying the Synoptic Gospels* (London/Philadelphia: SCM Press/Trinity Press International, 1989).

Schacter, Daniel L., *Searching for Memory: The Brain, the Mind, and the Past* (New York: Basic Books, 1996).

Schams, Christine, *Jewish Scribes in the Second-Temple Period* (JSOTSup, 291; ed. David A. Clines and Philip R. Davies; Sheffield: Sheffield Academic Press, 1998).

Schnelle, Udo, *The History and Theology of the New Testament Writings* (tr. M. Eugene Boring; London: SCM Press, 1998).

Schudson, Michael, *Watergate in American Memory: How We Remember, Forget and Reconstruct the Past* (New York: Basic Books, 1992).

Schwartz, Barry, *Abraham Lincoln and the Forge of National Memory* (Chicago: The University of Chicago Press, 2000).

Schwartz, Barry, 'Christian Origins: Historical Truth and Social Memory' in Alan Kirk and Tom Thatcher (eds), *Memory, Tradition, and Text: Uses of the Past in Early Christianity* (SBL Semeia Studies, 52; ed. G. A. Yee; Atlanta: SBL, 2005), 43–56.

Schwartz, Barry, 'Jesus in First Century Memory – A Response' in Alan Kirk and Tom Thatcher (eds), *Memory, Tradition, and Text: Uses of the Past in Early Christianity* (SBL Semeia Studies, 52; ed. G. A. Yee; Atlanta: SBL, 2005), 249–61.

Schwartz, Barry, 'Memory as a Cultural System: Abraham Lincoln in World War II', *American Sociological Review* 61 (1996), 908–27.

Schwartz, Barry, 'Postmodernity and Historical Reputation: Abraham Lincoln in Late Twentieth-Century American Memory', *SF* 77 (1998), 63–103.

Schwartz, Barry, 'The Social Context of Commemoration: A Study in Collective Memory', *SF* 61 (1982), 374–402.

Schwartz, Barry, 'Where There's Smoke, There's Fire: Memory and History' in Tom Thatcher (ed.), *Memory and Identity in Ancient Judaism and Early Christianity: A Conversation with Barry Schwartz* (SBL Semeia Studies, 78; ed. G. O. West; Atlanta: SBL, 2014), 7–37.

Schwyzer, Philip, *Shakespeare and the Remains of Richard III* (Oxford: Oxford University Press, 2013).

Shiner, Whitney, 'Memory Technology and the Composition of Mark' in Richard A. Horsley, Jonathan A. Draper and John Miles Foley (eds), *Performing the Gospel: Orality, Memory and Mark* (Minneapolis: Fortress Press, 2006), 147–65.

Sim, David C., 'Matthew's Use of Mark: Did Matthew Intend to Supplement or to Replace His Primary Source?', *NTS* 57 (2011), 176–92.

Small, Jocelyn Penny, *Wax Tablets of the Mind: Cognitive Studies of Memory and Literacy in Classical Antiquity* (Abingdon: Routledge, 1997).

Streeter, Burnett Hillman, *The Four Gospels: A Study of Origins Treating of the Manuscript Tradition, Sources, Authorship, and Dates* (London: Macmillan and Co, 1926).

Talbert, Charles H., 'Oral and Independent or Literary and Interdependent? A Response to Albert B. Lord' in William O. Walker (ed.), *The Relationships among the Gospels: An Interdisciplinary Dialogue* (Trinity University Monograph Series in Religion, 5; San Antonio: Trinity University Press, 1978), 93–102.

Thatcher, Tom, *Why John WROTE a Gospel: Jesus – Memory – History* (Louisville, KY: Westminster John Knox Press, 2006).

Thomas, Rosalind, *Literacy and Orality in Ancient Greece* (Key Themes in Ancient History; ed. P. A. Cartledge and P. D. A. Garnsey; Cambridge: Cambridge University Press, 1992).

Tolbert, Mary Ann, *Sowing the Gospel: Mark's World in Literary-Historical Perspective* (Minneapolis: Fortress Press, 1989).

Tonkin, Elizabeth, *Narrating Our Pasts: The Social Construction of Oral History* (Cambridge Studies in Oral and Literate Culture, 22; ed. Peter Burke and Ruth Finnegan; Cambridge: Cambridge University Press, 1995).

Torrance, Mark and Jeffery, Gaynor, 'Writing Processes and Cognitive Demands' in Mark Torrance and Gaynor Jeffery (eds), *The Cognitive Demands of Writing* (Amsterdam: Amsterdam University Press, 1999), 1–11.

Tuckett, Christopher M., 'The Current State of the Synoptic Problem' in Paul Foster, Andrew Gregory, John S. Kloppenborg and J. Verheyden (eds), *New Studies in the Synoptic Problem* (BETL, 139; Leuven: Leuven University Press, 2011), 9–50.

Tuckett, Christopher M., 'Form Criticism' in Werner H. Kelber and Samuel Byrskog (eds), *Jesus in Memory: Traditions in Oral and Scribal Perspectives* (Waco: Baylor University Press, 2009), 21–38.

Tuckett, Christopher M., *Q and the History of Early Christianity* (Edinburgh: T. & T. Clark, 1997).

Tuckett, Christopher M., *The Revival of the Griesbach Hypothesis: An Analysis and Appraisal* (SNTSMS, 44; Cambridge: Cambridge University Press, 1983).

Vinson, Richard, 'How Minor? Assessing the Significance of the Minor Agreements as an Argument against the Two-Source Hypothesis' in Mark Goodacre and Nicholas Perrin (eds), *Questioning Q* (London: SPCK, 2004), 151–64.

Watson, Francis, *Gospel Writing: A Canonical Perspective* (Grand Rapids, MI; Cambridge: Eerdmans, 2013).

Wenham, John, *Redating Matthew, Mark and Luke: A Fresh Assault on the Synoptic Problem* (London: Hodder & Stoughton, 1991).

Williams, Ritva, 'Social Memory', *BTB* 41 (2011), 189–200.

Wilson, Walter T., *Healing in the Gospel of Matthew: Reflections on Method and Ministry* (Minneapolis: Fortress Press, 2014).

Winsbury, Rex, *The Roman Book: Books, Publishing and Performance in Classical Rome* (London: Bristol Classical Press, 2009).

Wire, Antoinette Clark, *The Case for Mark Composed in Performance* (BPC, 3; ed. Holly E. Hearon and Philip Ruge-Jones; Eugene, OR: Cascade, 2011).

Yates, Frances A., *The Art of Memory* (London: Pimlico, 1992).

Ziesler, John, *Paul's Letter to the Romans* (TPI New Testament Commentaries; ed. Howard Clark Kee and Dennis Nineham; London/Valley Forge: SCM Press/Trinity Press International, 1989).

Index of ancient, mediaeval and biblical texts

Index of ancient, mediaeval and biblical texts

Index of modern authors

Note: Page numbers in **bold type** indicate a substantial discussion of a particular author.

Achtemeier, Paul 5 n. 10, 7 n. 18, 39 n. 1
Alexander, Loveday 35–7, 35 n. 36, 42, 43 n. 8, 71, 77 n. 78, **78–9**, 78 n. 79
Alexander, Philip 23 n. 10
Allison, Dale 47 n. 15
Anderson, Michael 89 n. 23, 142 n. 39
Arnal, William 18 n. 50
Assmann, Jan **26–8**, 27 nn. 20–1, 28 n. 23, 37, 73 n. 71, 75 n. 75, 77, 106, 107 n. 10
Aune, David 21 n. 3, 22 nn. 7–8, 23 n. 11, 35, 36 n. 39, 37 n. 42, n. 44

Baddeley, Alan 89 n. 23, 90 nn. 26–7, 91 nn. 29–31, n. 34, 95 n. 40, 142 n. 39
Bartlett, Frederick 87 n. 20, 88, 89 nn. 22–3
Bauckham, Richard 20 n. 1, 31 n. 29, 35 n. 38, 39 n. 39, 45 n. 11, 72 n. 69
Beaton, Richard 52 n. 3
Boring, M. Eugene 141 n. 35
Botha, Pieter 2 n. 2, 11 n. 28, 15 nn. 41–2, 58 n. 23, 60, **62–3**, 62 nn. 32–6, 63 n. 37, 69, 70, 72, 127 nn. 6–8, 129 n. 12
Bryan, Christopher 20 n. 2, 21 n. 3, 22 n. 8, 72 n. 70
Burridge, Richard 21 n.3
Butler, B. C. 127 n. 5
Byrskog, Samuel 15 n. 43, 35 n. 35, n. 37, 45 n. 10

Carr, David 73 n. 71, 81 n.1, 82 n. 5, 83 nn. 6–8, 84 n. 11
Carruthers, Mary 40 n. 5, 82 nn. 3–4, 83 n. 10, 84 nn. 12–15, 85 nn. 16–18, 86 n. 19, 97 nn. 44–5, 98 n. 46
Carson, Annette 105 n. 3

Catchpole, David 45 n. 12
Chapman, John 127 n. 5
Coleman, Janet 82 n. 3
Connerton, Paul 107 n. 11
Cubitt, Geoffrey 89 nn. 23–4, 106 n. 9, 109 n. 17

Davies, Margaret 127 n. 5, 141 n. 36
Derrenbacker, Robert xi n. 2, 23 n. 10, 40 n. 2, 41, 42 n. 7, 55 nn. 10–11, 128 n. 10, **132–3**, 132 n. 15, 136 n. 22, 143 n. 40, 144 n. 42
Dewey, Joanna 61, **65–7**, 65 nn. 51–2, 66 n. 54, n. 56, 67 n. 57, 69, **71**, 72, 80
Dodson, Ruth 118 n. 39
Donahue, John 96 n. 43
Downing, F. Gerald xi n. 2, 13 n. 34, 22 nn. 5–7, 28 n. 24, 54 n. 8, 55 n. 11, 76 n. 77, 77 n. 78, 131 n. 14, 144 n. 43
Draper, Jonathan xii n. 5, 3 n. 5
Drury, John 138 n. 27
Ducharme, Lori 116 nn. 30–1, n. 33, 117 n. 34
Dundes, Alan 60 n. 29
Dungan, David 126 n. 3
Dunn, James 63, 96 n. 42, **128–9**, 128 n. 9, 135

Eisenstein, Elizabeth xi n. 1, xii n. 3, 24 n. 14
Evans, Craig 39 n. 62, 69
Eve, Eric xiii n. 7, 25 n. 15, 28 n. 24, 44 n. 9, 45 n. 12, 48 n. 17, n. 19, 63 n. 41, 66 n. 55, 91 n. 34, 100 n. 52, 118 n. 39, 127 n. 5, 135 n. 19, 138 n. 28, 150 n. 1
Eysenck, Michael 89 n. 23, 142 n. 39

Index of subjects

Note: Page numbers in **bold type** indicate a substantial discussion of a particular topic.

Did you know that SPCK is a registered charity?

As well as publishing great books by leading Christian authors, we also . . .

. . . make assemblies meaningful and fun for over a million children by running www.assemblies.org.uk, a popular website that provides free assembly scripts for teachers. For many children, school assembly is the only contact they have with Christian faith and culture, and the only time in their week for spiritual reflection.

. . . help prisoners to become confident readers with our easy-to-read stories. Poor literacy is a huge barrier to re-habilitation. Prisoners identify with the believable heroes of our gritty fiction. At the same time, questions at the end of each chapter help them to examine their choices from a moral perspective and to build their reading confidence.

. . . support student ministers overseas in their training. We give them free, specially written theology books, the International Study Guides. These books really do make a difference, not just to students but to ministers and, through them, to a whole community.

Please support these great schemes: visit www.spck.org.uk/support-us to find out more.

24094316R00107

Made in the USA
Columbia, SC
18 August 2018